Writing with Scripture

Other Fortress Press Books
By Jacob Neusner

Foundations of Judaism
The Incarnation of God
The Character of Divinity in Formative Judaism
Judaism in the Beginning of Christianity
Judaism in the Matrix of Christianity
What is Midrash?
Guides to Biblical Scholarship Series

Edited by Jacob Neusner et al.

The Social World of Formative Christianity and Judaism
Essays in Tribute to Howard Clark Kee
Judaic Perspectives on Ancient Israel

Writing with Scripture

THE AUTHORITY AND USES
OF THE HEBREW BIBLE IN
THE TORAH OF FORMATIVE JUDAISM

by

Jacob Neusner

with

William Scott Green

FORTRESS PRESS   MINNEAPOLIS

BS
1186
.N48
1989

Writing with Scripture
The Authority and Uses of the Hebrew Bible in the Torah of Formative Judaism
Copyright © 1989 Augsburg Fortress

Cover design: Helen Melnis
Internal design: Polebridge Press

———————

Library of Congress Cataloging-in-Publication Data

Neusner, Jacob. 1932–
    Writing with scripture : the authority and uses of the Hebrew Bible in the Torah of formative Judaism / by Jacob Neusner with William Scott Green.
        p.   cm.
    Includes index.
    ISBN 0-8006-2330-4 (alk. paper)
    1. Bible. O.T.—Criticism, interpretation, etc., Jewish. 2. Halakic Midrashim. 3. Rabbinical literature—History and criticism. I. Green, William Scott. II. Title.
BS1186.N48   1989
222'.106—dc20   89-32976
                                                                      CIP

———————

The paper used in this publication meets the minimum requirements of American National Standard for Information Sciences—Permanence of Paper for Printed Library Materials. ANSI Z329.48–1984.   ∞™

Manufactured in the U.S.A.   1-2330

93   92   91   90   89   1   2   3   4   5   6   7   8   9   10

IN MEMORY OF

David Dornstein

Contents

Preface

This is a book about the authority and uses of scripture—called, variously, the written Torah, the Hebrew Bible, or "the Old Testament" —in the Torah, that is, the one whole Torah of Moses, our rabbi. "Torah" in Judaism is the word for Judaism. It is the Torah that defines what I mean by the Judaism of the dual Torah, oral and written. In these pages I propose to ask the question, How, in the formative age of the Judaism of the dual Torah, written and oral, did scripture, the written Torah, relate to, and serve within, the one whole Torah, oral and written, that constituted what we call "Judaism"? The basic proposition of this book is that "the Bible" for Christianity and "the Torah" for Judaism constituted single and seamless statements. Speaking principally within the framework of Judaism, I insist that scripture—the written Torah—formed only a component of the Torah. Other components of that same Torah, the oral ones, enjoyed a position and a place entirely coherent with the scripture, so that differentiating one part of the Torah from another part of that same Torah represented a (mere) exercise in internal exegesis, not a judgment as to the status and authority of a component of the larger canon.

Since that was the fact, the conception that authorships turned to the written Torah, or scripture, for proof texts proves monumentally beside the point, and in this book, I propose to persuade readers to abandon the category "proof texts" when they propose to understand the relationship of the New Testament to the Old or the oral Torah to the written one. The Old Testament in the New, the persistence of "as it is said" or "as it is written"—these constitute statements of a more profound proposition than the classification "proof texts" permits.

I express my thanks to Dr. Harold Rast for guiding this project from beginning to end. The conception "writing with scripture" comes from William Scott Green, whose contribution to this book, Chapter 2, is a partial reprinting, with permission, of his "Romancing the Tome: Rabbinic Hermeneutics and the Theory of Literature" (*Semeia* 40 [1987]: 147–68). The chapters in the shank of the book restate, for the present context, results of my analytical work.

As this book was going to press, word came of the death, in the sabotage of a Pan American Airlines flight over Scotland, on December 21, 1988, of David Dornstein, Brown University Class of 1985. I offer this book as a memorial and a modest tribute to a delightful student, and as an expression of my sorrow at his death. The immediately following pages present that memorial note.

DECEMBER 28, 1988

JACOB NEUSNER
Program in Judaic Studies
Brown University
Providence, Rhode Island

David Dornstein

IN MEMORY

The call came out of nowhere.

"Is this Professor Neusner?"

"Speaking."

"You don't know me, but he would have wanted me to tell you."

"Who would want you to tell me what?"

"David Dornstein. He was your student at Brown. You remember? He was on the Pan Am plane. He would have wanted you to know."

Silence.

I: "Yes, I remember. No one ever forgot David Dornstein. Thank you for telling me. You're right, I do want to know."

"Here is a number to call if you want more details."

"Thank you."

But I didn't know what other details I might want to know. What else is there to know when a young man dies? Then there no longer is a might-be. And who just now can bear the pain of might-have-beens?

David Dornstein graduated from Brown in the class of 1985. Later this year he would have been twenty-six years old, had he taken some other plane. Now the calls filter in from this one and that of his class: "He would have wanted you to know."

David was incandescent, a Roman candle, a sparkler burning bright in everybody's night. David could act, he could write, he could dream, he could charm. Oh, could he charm! Paper late—or never written? A smile would suffice. Appointment missed? A splendid question, elegantly framed, made up for it. What we hoped for David, all of us who knew him, knew no limit. The sky was the limit. Not that he was at the boundaries of his fate the day he died, not at all.

Where was he then in life? Last month, when he died, nowhere in particular. From Brown he went here and there. He took a job to support some other job, waited on tables while he looked for acting jobs, worked in a book store while he wrote. Everything was to sustain something else. He was never in any one place. He was here but going there.

He thought for a while of becoming a rabbi or a scholar of Judaism—or maybe he told me he was thinking about it to make me happy. That was David: He knew what you were dreaming, and he wanted to make it happen. That made him the actor, the ingenue, the writer, the aborning star of the firmament in whatever sky he chose to shine.

That was David, David of the burning eyes, David of the luminescent spirit, David of the vivid conversation, David of the vital argument, the one that mattered, that one you would remember. And that was the David who could write with fervor, but no discipline, who could dream of everything, but finish nothing. His was not a life that would ever get to finish anything. David floated through life with no clear direction in mind. Wherever he was, that is where he meant to be, and to be with all intensity: that minute, that place, nowhere else. Another minute—somewhere else.

I always thought David was destined for something special, something great, and I think he did too. So did everyone who ever knew him. Now comes no disappointment, for there remain no unkept promises, no unfulfilled hopes: The youth lies dead, along with everyone else who took the wrong plane that day. There are brutal truths in life.

Blazing star, sparkling light, in the gloom of a Scottish night the light gave way to the darkness. While he was among us, we already wondered what might be; we do not have now to ask what might have been. We know. How do you mourn the incandescent life, the star gone dark in the distant sky? Remembering the light from on high, I suppose. So David wept for Jonathan: "... glory ... lies slain on your heights."

1

Judaic and Christian Uses of Scripture

"AS IT IS SAID" OR "THE OLD TESTAMENT IN THE NEW"

Whereas the world at large treats Judaism as "the religion of the Old Testament," the fact is otherwise. Judaism inherits and makes the Hebrew scriptures its own, just as does Christianity. And just as Christianity rereads the entire heritage of ancient Israel in the light of "the resurrection of Jesus Christ," so Judaism understands the Hebrew scriptures as only one part, the written one, of "the one whole Torah of Moses, our rabbi." But what does that simple fact mean when we wish to understand the role of the scriptures of ancient Israel in Judaism and Christianity? This book proposes a fresh answer to that question as it addresses Judaism. Specifically, I wish to show that the writings of ancient Israel, which Judaism knows as "the written Torah," formed a principal component of the Torah, differentiated to be sure but an integral part of a single autonomous statement of a determinate logic and cogency.

To express that fact, I call this book "writing with scripture," by which I mean a simple thing. The received scriptures formed an instrumentality for the expression of a writing bearing its own integrity and cogency, appealing to its own conventions of intelligibility, and, above all, making its own points. Any notion, therefore, that the authorships of Judaism proposed a systematic exegesis of scripture conducted in terms of the original or historical program of scripture, or appealed to scripture for validation or vindication of doctrine or practice perceived as independent of scripture, distorts the character of the discourse of Judaism. Scripture formed part of the Torah. The authorships of Judaism, particularly in late antiquity, also participated in the discourse and

1

statement of the Torah. They did not write *about* scripture, they wrote *with* scripture, for scripture supplied the syntax and grammar of their thought, hence, "writing with scripture."

The Judaism of the dual Torah, oral and written, that people ordinarily mean when they speak of "Judaism," commonly makes its appearance as a "biblical religion." That is to say, people ordinarily take for granted that that Judaism (like all other Judaisms) appeals for validation to the Hebrew scriptures or Old Testament. Consequently, we tend to compare Judaism with Christianity, regarding both of them, each in its own way, as biblical: appealing to scripture, whether the written Torah (Judaism) or the Old Testament (Christianity). But when we adopt such a perspective about the two great religions of the European West, we treat as distinct and independent what for both religions forms part of an integrated whole. That is to say, we see scripture (written Torah, Old Testament) not as part of an integral revelation, in which each part illuminates all others (oral Torah, New Testament). Rather, we address one part on its own, ignoring the perspective of faith altogether. But if we read the written Torah/Old Testament distinct from the oral Torah/New Testament, what we do is deny the fundamental conviction of the faith of Judaism or Christianity.

We do just that when we describe as exegetical ("midrashic") the relationship of the oral to the written Torah or the New to the Old Testament. That is to say, we deem one document to be essentially autonomous of the other, then establish its relationship to the other through processes of rereading and reinterpretation. On that basis we develop the conception that the original scriptures (again: written Torah/Old Testament) enjoy an existence independent of the faith and the synagogue or church that preserve them. These original scriptures bear an autonomous meaning, determined by the criteria of initial context and historical circumstance, and that meaning stands in judgment, so to speak, upon the meanings imputed to these scriptures by the Judaism of the dual Torah or by the Christianity of the Bible, Old and New Testaments alike. Viewed historically, the collection of writings we know as the Hebrew scriptures or Old Testament obviously bears meaning determined by the original setting and intent of authors or authorships (individual, collective writers).

But that meaning never made a profound impact, prior to the nineteenth century, upon the reception and reading of the Israelite scriptures. What did make its mark was the uses of those scriptures for the makers of the Judaism of the dual Torah, on the one side, and the Christianity we now know as Orthodox—the Christianity of the Bible,

Old and New Testaments—on the other. And what mattered to those system builders concerned the revelation of God as they received it: the Torah of Moses, our rabbi, for the Judaism of the dual Torah; the person of Jesus Christ, God incarnate, for Christianity. To those protean conceptions, scripture served, as did all else, as testimony and testament. It formed part of a larger, wholly cogent statement. It served important purposes in the formation and expression of that statement. But it constituted a subordinated and merely instrumental entity, not the court of last appeal and final judgment, not the ultimate source of truth and validation, except—of course—after the fact. The fact found expression in the figure of the sage, in the model of Moses, our rabbi, or in the person, as the Church received him, of Christ Jesus.

People commonly suppose that when Judaic or Christian authorships turned to Israelite scripture, it was in search of proof texts. The relationship was exegetical or eisegetical. The representation of either religion as forming an essentially exegetical relationship to Israelite writings, however, vastly distorts the nature of that religion. When Judaic and Christian authorships proposed to compose their statements, they of course appealed to scripture. But it was an appeal to serve a purpose defined not by scripture but by the faith—the Judaic or Christian system—under construction and subject to articulation. Scripture formed a dictionary, providing a vast range of permissible usages of intelligible words. Scripture did not dictate the sentences that would be composed through the words found in that (limited) dictionary. Much as painters paint with a palette of colors, so authorships wrote with scripture. The paint is not the picture. Matthew's Gospel of Jesus is not (merely) a reprise of Isaiah. But the picture cannot be painted without the pigments on the palette, and Matthew's Gospel cannot have been created without the verses of Isaiah and other prophetic passages that provided Matthew's framework for the Gospel story of Jesus Christ. And when the Church in its first three centuries framed its scriptures—as everybody knows—it received the Israelite writings because of the Church's reading of those writings. It spoke through those writings. It appealed to their facts. It responded, in the formation of its imagination and metaphoric reality, to those writings. Its life and being were nourished by those writings. But the Church came first, then the scriptures, and, ultimately, the Bible, Old and New Testaments forming one complete and wholly harmonious, seamless statement and document. And so it was with the Judaism of the dual Torah, in its framework and within its inner logic and discipline.

What follows from these propositions is clear. If we wish to understand the place and power of the Israelite scriptures in the Judaism of the dual Torah and in the writings of nascent Christianity, we must begin by freeing ourselves of one conception and exploring the implications of another. The negative is this: We must abandon any notion of a perceived distinction between the oral and the written Torahs, or between the New and the Old Testaments. The positive is: We must see the two Torahs as the one whole Torah of Moses, our rabbi. We must see the two Testaments as "the Bible." The negative: We cannot take for granted that the appearance of a verse of the Israelite scriptures in a rabbinic composition or a New Testament writing serves a single, determinate purpose, e.g., as a "proof text," as a source of vindication or validation for a statement a later author wishes to prove. The positive: We have to undertake an inductive inquiry into the uses and authority of the received scriptures of ancient Israel, allowing diverse documents to provide, individually, its own indication of where and how the inherited, authoritative writings serve the purposes of an author or authorship.

Now to the book at hand. I aim to show how the founders of Judaism engaged in dialogue with the scriptures of ancient Israel. I define that relationship as one in which authors and authorships wrote with scripture, shaping a distinctive idiom of discourse in so doing. They turned to scripture not for proof texts, let alone for pretexts, to say whatever they wanted, anyhow, to say. They used scripture as an artist uses the colors on the palette, expressing ideas through and with scripture as the artist paints with those colors and no others. This reading of the ways in which the Judaic sages read scripture insists on two propositions.

First, the sages created within a limited and well-defined vocabulary of thought, contrary to the conception that these same sages engaged in an essentially indeterminate and unlimited process of thought. That is the argument of Chapter 2. Second, the sages appealed to scripture not merely for proof texts as part of an apologia but for a far more original and sustained mode of discourse. Verses of scripture served not merely to prove but to instruct. Israelite scripture constituted not merely a source of validation but a powerful instrument of profound inquiry.

Alongside that positive thesis, there is, second, a negative one. It concerns the category "proof texts" and aims to show that that classification does not correspond to the role and authority of scripture in the Torah. The contrary notion, which I wish to call into question, appeals to the conception of proof texts. That is to say, it is supposed people settled questions by discovering a verse to demonstrate what they wished to say, with the further implication, within Judaic and Christian apologetics of the present century, of an original and determinate meaning of a scripture, perceived as complete and autonomous, that validates, historically, the claim of the faith. That second premise, of course, imputes conceptions discovered only in modern times. We all recognize, of course, that ancient Israel no more testified to the oral Torah, now written down in the Mishnah and later rabbinic writings, than it did to Jesus as the Christ. In both cases, religious circles within Israel of later antiquity reread the entire past in the light of their own conscience and convictions. They took for granted that the Torah and the contents of their conscience and convictions coalesced. Hence, the conception that scripture formed a court of last appeal, an authoritative criterion established out of a completed past, contradicts the situation of intellect and faith in which the authorships of the Judaism at hand endured. True, the written Torah formed a distinct and always distinguished corpus of writing.

The distinction between the authority of scripture and the authority of scribes, for example, forms a commonplace. But that distinction did not bear the sense that has commonly been assigned to it, that the written Torah and the oral Torah constituted distinct entities, separated from one another by centuries. The Judaism of the dual Torah reached the firm conclusion that the two media in which the Torah was received accomplished the formulation and transmission of one whole Torah. Accordingly, the relationship between the Torah that derived from one medium, the written, and the Torah that derived from another medium, the oral, requires close analysis. That relationship cannot be imputed on the basis of a misunderstanding of the weight and implications of the distinction between the two media. In this book I begin what I anticipate will be a considerable exercise, lasting for some time, of inductive inquiry into a problem I regard as fresh in substance, hence in formulation: *the uses of scripture in the Torah.* I move from literary studies to exercises in the history-of-religions. What I seek to accomplish here is only to open fresh perspectives. I argue against one proposition, which is that the Judaic sages essentially accomplished a limited exegetical program, and in favor of another. *It is that these same sages wrote with scripture.*

It remains to set forth the plan of the book. It begins with a simple statement of what is at stake in the conception of writing with scripture, a brief survey of the rabbinic uses of scripture. This leads to a full theoretical account of the difference between writing without and writing with scripture. I then turn to four specific documents, three of them illustrative and probative of the thesis that sages wrote with scripture, one of them showing the opposite. In my account of Leviticus Rabbah I provide the simplest statement of what it means to write with scripture. When I come to Sifré to Deuteronomy, I dig deeper into the resort to scripture for the syntax and grammar of thought, not merely for proof texts or even for pretexts for sustained discourse. And that leads us, in the setting of the analysis of discourse in Sifra, to see how people not only write with scripture but argue through scripture, and that, once again, not merely through proof texts but at the deepest layers of intellect and reflection.

Finally, in the shank of the book, I turn to the null hypothesis. What would a document look like if its authorship simply did not write with scripture? Here, in Mekhilta Attributed to R. Ishmael, we see a piece of wiring in which the paramount forms are those of commentary, in which the logics are those of the fixed association that holds things together by appeal to a text that is commented upon, and in which there is no sustained proposition or argument, but rather, a sequence of episodic and ad hoc expositions. What we have then in Mekhilta Attributed to R. Ishmael is quite different from the other documents presented here. In place of systemic statements in sustained presentation and argument, we have brief essays that provide information. Instead of cogent discourse of an argumentative kind, we have a sequence of little expositions of information.

And, above all, in place of a flowing argument, one that says one thing in many ways, we have a display of points, in which many things are said in one way: the exegetical. We therefore see what it means to produce a document in which people are not writing with scripture, and that establishes the accuracy of our characterization of documents in which people are writing with scripture, for now I can show beyond doubt that people did make choices, and that these choices, affecting the rhetoric, logic, and topic of their documents, flowed from their fundamental theory of scripture: its authority, its uses, in their systemic compositions and constructions.

The concluding chapter draws from these facts the necessary consequences for the classification of Judaism: is the Judaism of the dual Torah a biblical religion, and is biblical theology therefore possible in that Judaism? I hold that the Judaism of the dual Torah is not a biblical religion, and that biblical theology bears no relevance for that Judaism, because the Judaism of the dual Torah writes with scripture. By that point in the unfolding of the argument of the book, this judgment takes on meaning and consequence.

2

Writing with Scripture

THE RABBINIC USES
OF THE HEBREW BIBLE

William Scott Green

It is commonplace to classify rabbinic Judaism as a "'religion of the Book,' religion in which practice and belief derive from the study and interpretation of Scripture" (Vermes: 60). The book-religion model depicts rabbinic Judaism as an interpretive supplement to a foundational text, an exegetical development out of scripture itself. It holds that "the Rabbis ... founded ... a religion of interpretation, a tradition of studying Scripture and putting it into practice that touched every member of the community and that elevated these activities to the very highest level" (Kugel: 72). The model makes reading and interpreting the Bible the quintessential rabbinic activities.

By assimilating religion to reading, the book-religion model effectively reduces rabbinic Judaism to a process of exegesis and thereby marks other rabbinic activities as secondary and derivative. The model's analytical focus on how rabbis read makes biblical exegesis into rabbinism's driving force, and, more abstractly, the interpretation of literature becomes the decisive variable for our understanding of rabbinic religion. Rabbinic piety not only appears epiphenomenal and ancillary but in principle and by definition it can be explained only as the consequence of rabbinic hermeneutical practice.

The book-religion model has dominated most of modern scholarship on ancient and rabbinic Judaism (Porton: 63–65), and its persistent appeal is understandable. The notion that for ancient rabbis "*midrash* ... was an all-consuming activity" (Kugel: 67), the claim that "Writing, the Holy Text, is the privileged term in Rabbinic thought" (Handelman: 168), the conception of *midrash* as a "life in ... scripture" (Hartman and

7

Budick: xi), and the idea that halakic observance was determined by Bible study (Vermes, Kugel) all impute to rabbinic religion a strong biblical orientation. Rabbinic Judaism emerges as Bible-centered—the Bible read, the Bible studied, the Bible interpreted, the Bible put "into practice"—and thus as a kind of religion easily recognizable and comprehensible in the modern West. Indeed, the picture of ancient rabbis as Bible readers expounding their religion out of scripture has a powerful intuitive plausibility in a culture in which religion is conceived largely in Protestant terms. Moreover, because in our world "Bible" is merely a species of the genus "text," it takes hardly any imagination at all to place these Bible-reading talmudic sages into the more general category of literary exegetes and to suppose that for them—just as for us—the interpretation of texts was a principal passion and preoccupation. The authority of the book-religion model, therefore, lies in its self-evidence.

The book-religion model fails because it works too well. It makes ancient rabbis so familiar and so tractable, and takes us back to the beginning so fast, that we meet no one new on the way. The model's self-evidence, which is its power, blocks our perception of the particularities of rabbinic culture and thereby diminishes the likelihood of analytically useful comparison. The model's framework categorizes ancient rabbis so much in our image and after our likeness that it begs more questions than it answers. Its narrow focus distorts both the rabbinic textual and historical records.

There is no doubt that the documents now variously called the "Old Testament," the "Hebrew Bible," or *"Tanakh"* had a fundamental importance in the different Judaisms that surrounded the ancient Mediterranean. Interest in scripture is evident across a wide spectrum of literatures: Qumran, the New Testament, Philo, Josephus, and the church fathers. Varied sources suggest that, particularly from the late first century, scripture was read as part of the liturgy in both native Palestinian and diaspora communities, and archaeological remains suggest that synagogues often were constructed to make the scroll of scripture the center of the worshipers' visual attention.

The Hebrew Bible had a fundamental place in rabbinic Judaism and constituted an important component of its conceptual background. No rabbinic document could have been written without knowledge of scripture. Nevertheless, the rabbis' interest in scripture was hardly comprehensive, and vast segments of it, including much of prophecy and the Deuteronomic History, escaped their interpretation. The Bible's role in rabbinic literature is more complex and fluid than the book-religion model suggests.

Scripture neither determined the agenda nor provided the ubiquitous focus of rabbinic literary activity and imagination. Rather, it was the major—but certainly not the only—source rabbis used to produce their literature. They also drew extensively on their own materials. Indeed, M. Hagigah 1:8 baldly asserts that substantial portions of rabbinic teaching —for example, on matters as basic and important as Sabbath observance —have scant scriptural support. A well-known saying, attributed to the tannaitic master Simeon b. Yohai, compares the study of scripture with that of rabbinic teachings as follows:

A. "He who occupies himself with Scripture [gains] merit (*mdh*) that is no merit.

B. He who occupies himself with Mishnah [gains] merit for which they receive a reward (*skr*).

C. He who occupies himself with Talmud—you have no merit greater than this."

(y. Shabbat 16:1 [15c]; b. Baba Mesi'a 33a)

To depict rabbinic Judaism as principally a religion of biblical exegesis, therefore, is to both oversimplify and overstate the evidence.

To account for the varied roles of scripture in rabbinic literature, it helps to remember that rabbinism's initial catalyst was neither the canonization of the Hebrew Bible nor readerly research of scripture but the demise of the Second Temple and its divinely ordained cult, the rites of which guaranteed God's presence in Israel's midst. The loss of the Holy of Holies—the principal locus of Israel's invisible and silent God— meant the absence of a stable cultural center and generated an acute religious crisis, primarily in the realm of behavior.

The commanding influence of the book-religion model on the study of early Judaism and Christianity has tended to deflect scholarly interest away from the kind of religion manifested by the Temple and advocated by its priestly personnel. Levitical religion, as it might be called, conceived of the life of Israel as a comprehensive and integrated system of disciplined engagement with God. That engagement largely took the form of prescribed and repeated behaviors, directed by a caste of priests, that revolved around and focused attention on a sacred center, a stable reference point, where access to God was certain to occur. Levitical religion mapped out a system of categories—usually binary opposites such as clean/unclean, fit/unfit, holy/profane—in which everything that mattered had its place. Its preferred literary form was the list—for instance, the genealogies and series of rules of the Pentateuch's P document—rather than the narrative. In its ritual and its writing, levitical religion promulgated a synchronic vision of a centered, structured, hierarchical, and orderly reality. Its practitioners celebrated precision, lineage, precedent, and concreteness and had an exceedingly low tolerance for uncertainty, confusion, and ambiguity.

To underestimate the pervasiveness or persistence of levitical religion in Judaic and Christian antiquity is a mistake. The pre-70 Palestinian Jewish religious groups about whom we know the most—Sadducees, Pharisees, the Dead Sea Sect—all operated within its sphere. Levitical religion was a primary negative, and therefore defining, focus of early Christian writing, and it remained so well after the Temple's destruction. Thus, Paul's early discarding of "the Law" sought to render levitical categories nugatory, and the evangelists could not tell of Jesus' death without recording that the curtain of the Holy of Holies "was torn in two, from top to bottom" (Mark 15:38; Matt. 27:51; cf. Luke 23:45). Other Christian writers, from the author of the *Epistle of Barnabas*, to Justin Martyr and Irenaeus, made the rejection of routine levitical rituals a central theme of their compositions.

In contrast to their patristic counterparts, the post-70 founders of rabbinism aimed to perpetuate a levitical system. The dictates and concerns of rabbinic literature show that living rabbinically consisted in a host of behaviors—food, purity, and kinship taboos, observance of Sabbaths, holy days, and festivals; prayer—that depended on and promulgated levitical categories. The rabbinic use of scripture was thus embedded in a complex of rabbinically ordained practices, many of which —including most of the rules for the treatment of scripture itself—do not derive from scripture at all. As Chapter 3 suggests, rabbinism's initial concern was the elaboration and refinement of its own system. Attaching the system to scripture was secondary.

It therefore is misleading to depict rabbinic Judaism primarily as the consequences of an exegetical process or the organic unfolding of scripture. Rather, rabbinism began as the work of a small, ambitious, and homogeneous group of pseudo-priests who professed to know how to maintain Israel's ongoing engagement with God—its life of sanctification—in the absence of a cult, and who, on that basis, aspired to lead the Jews. By the third century, the rabbis expressed their self-conception in the ideology of the "oral Torah," which held that a comprehensive body of teachings and practices (*halakot*) not included in scripture had been given by God and through Moses only to the rabbinic establishment. Thus, ancient rabbis advanced the proposition that even without a temple, Israel could still achieve holiness if the people's conduct conformed to rabbinic expertise and authority. Though rabbis articulated this claim in the language of the "oral Torah," they made it stick through their manipulation of the written one.

To achieve their goals, rabbis had to conquer a difficulty the pre-70 groups avoided: the absence of a sacred center. The community at Qumran at least had a real building in Jerusalem about whose recovery and control it could fantasize. But particularly after the Bar Kochba debacle in 132–35, rabbis must have known that the temple was gone for good. To compensate for that loss and to preserve the sacred center required by their piety, rabbinic Judaism developed a distinctive theory of the sanctity of scripture.[1]

In rabbinic Judaism scripture had a sacred status, and human dealings with it were hedged about with behavioral restrictions. M. Yadayim 3:5 declares that "all the holy writings render the hands unclean" (also see M. Kelim 15:6; Yadayim 3:2; 4:6). A scroll's sanctity was not limited to its text but extended to its blank margins (M. Yadayim 3:4; T. Yadayim 2:11) and its wrappings and containers (T. Yadayim 2:12). The sanctity of scripture outweighed even the Sabbath, and people were expected and permitted to violate Sabbath restrictions to save it and its wrappings from fire (M. Shabbat 16:1)—an exemption otherwise applied only to save a human life. Also, it was acceptable to make heave-offering unclean to rescue scripture from harm (T. Shabbat 13:2,6). A damaged, worn, or unfit scroll retained its sanctity and therefore was to be buried, by itself or in the coffin of a sage, but not burned or otherwise destroyed (b. Megillah 26b).

Although the category "holy writings" apparently could include works in Hebrew and in translation (M. Shabbat 16:1), rabbis gave the scroll of the Hebrew Pentateuch, the *sefer Torah*, pride of place. It was the scriptural paradigm and prototype. Every Jew was obliged to write or possess a *sefer Torah* (b. Sanhedrin 21b). According to M. Megillah 3:1, a Jewish community could do without a synagogue, an ark, scripture wrappings, or other books of scripture, but not a Torah scroll. The

1. This is not to claim that only rabbinic Judaism conceived the scroll of scripture as sacred but rather that the complex of restrictions discussed here is not present in other ancient Jewish writings. The Community Rule and Damascus Document, for instance, are silent on the question of the production and handling of scripture, and the common storage of what we regard as scripture together with writings produced by the sectaries themselves suggests that they may have given equal treatment to all writings they deemed valuable. Though the "Law of Moses" has authority in the Damascus Document, for instance, it is not clear that the sectarians' own writings did not have for them what we would identify as a scriptural authority.

Talmud's elaborate rules for the scroll's production and treatment decisively distinguish its content from ordinary writing. The *sefer Torah* was used in synagogue worship and was to be written without vocalization. It had to be transcribed on specially prepared parchment marked with lines (b. Megillah 19a),[2] in a particular script (b. Shabbat 104a; Sanhedrin 21b–22a; y. Megillah 1:11 [71b]), and with orthographic uniformity (b. ʿEruvin 13a; Megillah 18b; Yebamot 79a; Ketuvot 19b). In the scroll, seven Hebrew letters, each time they appeared, were to be drawn with *tagin*, three-stroke decorative crowns or titles at the top of the letter (b. Menahot 29b). A sheet that contained four errors was to be buried, not corrected (b. Megillah 29b), but scrolls produced by Jews deemed heretics or sectarians were to be burned (b. Gittin 45b). Worshipers were expected to rise in the presence of the Torah scroll (y. Megillah 4:1 [2a]; b. Makkot 22b; Qiddushin 33b), and no other type of scroll could be placed on top of it (t. Megillah 3:20). To touch the parchment of a Torah scroll with bare hands was judged an outrage (b. Shabbat 14a; Megillah 32a).

Rabbis used the Torah-writing for purposes other than reading. They wore it in phylacteries and affixed it to dwellings in *mezuzot*. On account of the segments of Torah-writing they contained, these items too had sacred status. Along with the bags and straps of phylacteries, sacks for holding scripture, and the mantle of the Torah scroll, they were labeled "instruments of holiness" (*tšmyšy qdwšh*) and had to be buried, but neither burned nor discarded, when worn out (b. Megillah 26b). M. Taʿanit 2:12 requires that prayers for rain be recited in front of the ark containing the Torah scrolls, which was to be brought to the public square, and M. Sanhedrin 2:4 imagines that the scroll itself would accompany the Israelite king in battle, when he judged, and when he ate.

Other passages illustrate the special position of the Torah scroll in rabbinic culture. Sifra (Behuqotai, Pereq 8:10) asserts that the possession of the "*sefer Torah* distinguished Israel from the peoples of the world" and is the reason for God's persisting loyalty. Finally, rabbis were expected to perform the mourning rite of *qeriʿah*, the ritual tearing of one's garment, at the sight of a burned Torah scroll (b. Megillah 25b), and on seeing a torn scroll, they were to perform *qeriʿah* twice, "once on

---

2. Faur's claim (106) that lines on the parchment "symbolize the invisible trace of the Holy Spirit" depends on his particular reading of y. Megillah 1:1 (70a) as a "folded pericope" (105). The passage itself offers no explicit warrant for the idea. Moreover, the drawing of lines, whose purpose is to keep the writing straight, was also practiced at Qumran. For a fuller account of the particularities of orthography and vocalization in the production and recitation of scripture, see Dothan.

account of the parchment and once on account of the writing" (b. Mo'ed Qatan 26a; also y. Mo'ed Qatan 3:7 [83b]).

These regulations suggest that rabbis regarded the Torah-writing itself as a sacred object. The idea that a missing or added letter in the Torah's transcription could "destroy the world" (b. 'Eruvin 13a) and the notion that one grieves for damaged writing as one does for a deceased human being imply that rabbis construed the very letters of the Torah-writing not as mere signs of an immaterial discourse but as sacred in themselves.

This possibility forces a reconsideration of the notion of the *sefer Torah* as text. Strictly speaking, the *sefer Torah* contains the two requisite components of text suggested by Scharlemann. It is a "written work in contrast to an oral performance" and is "a writing upon which commentaries can be written but which itself is not a commentary on another text" (Scharlemann: 7). But this definition can apply here only if we construe writing in a very minimal sense, to mean inscription or marking rather than discourse. For although a scroll required writing in order to be sacred, there are reasons to suppose that the writing did not have to constitute a discourse. Consider, for example, M. Yadayim 3:5:

A. A scroll (*spr*) that was erased and in which there remain eighty-five letters, like the section "And it came to pass when the ark set forward" (Num. 10:35–36), renders the hands unclean.

B. A sheet (*mglh*) [of a scroll] on which was written eighty-five letters, like the section "And it came to pass when the ark set forward" (Num. 10:35–36), renders the hands unclean.

Tosefta Yadayim 2:10 (ed. Zuckermandel, p. 683, lines 2–5) adds:

A scroll that wore out—if one can glean (*llqt*) from it eighty-five letters, like the section "And it came to pass when the ark set forward . . ." (Num. 10:35–36), it renders the hands unclean.[3]

On this issue, the late-third-century Babylonian masters Rav Huna and Rav Hisda are said to have agreed that if the eighty-five letters appeared as words, the scroll would make hands unclean if the words were randomly scattered, and Hisda declared the scroll sacred even if it contained eighty-five scattered letters (b. Shabbat 115b). Moreover, rabbis supposed it possible to deduce "mounds and mounds" of behavioral practices (*halakot*) from the *tagin* attached to the top of certain letters (b. Menahot 29b). Since these tittles were strictly ornamental markings,

---

3. See Neusner (1977: 142–43) and Lieberman (155) for Tosefta's ruling that a scroll, and not just a sheet, with 85 letters renders the hands unclean.

their interpretation did not require discerning a discourse. They were deemed meaningful nevertheless, and the Babylonian Talmud certifies their significant by imagining that they were affixed to the Torah-writing by God. Finally and most important, the "official" Torah-writing, that used in worship, contained, and could contain, no vowels. It thus did not and could not "fix" a discourse in writing and was not a text in Ricoeur's sense. Constituted solely of unvocalized consonants—only half a language—the writing in the *sefer Torah* was mute. Like the scroll and the *tagin*, it was envisioned as a material object. In rabbinic Judaism, therefore, the sanctity of scripture appears to have depended neither on what the writing said nor even on its being read, but rather on how and by whom it was produced. A scroll of heretics or sectarians, after all, was not inspected for accuracy but was simply condemned to burning on the a priori grounds that its producers were untrustworthy.

Whatever else it may have been, the writing we would call "scripture" was conceived by rabbinic culture as a holy object, a thing to be venerated. The Torah scroll was rabbinism's most revered and sacred artifact, and its sanctity was socially demonstrated, objectified, and certified by a network of rabbinic behavioral injunctions. Thus, the *sefer Torah*—both as scroll and as writing—constituted the ubiquitous material reference point of rabbinic religion. As an artifact, the Torah scroll, with its holy and allegedly unchanged and changeless writing, formed the requisite stable center for rabbinism's system of piety. In the absence of the temple and its Holy of Holies, the scroll and its writing became for ancient rabbis primary repositories and conveyers of social legitimacy, cultural authenticity, and religious meaning.

Since, in rabbinic Judaism, properly inscribed Torah-writing was sometimes—perhaps often—not a text (as with phylacteries and *mezuzot*) but was always a sacred object, its artifactual status dominated and defined its use as a text. Because it was a holy artifact, the Torah-writing by definition was heavy with significance; it was meaning-full. But because it had no vowels, and hence contained no discourse, in another way the Torah-writing was also meaning-less—evocative but profoundly inarticulate.[4]

4. The traits of the Torah scroll underscore the importance of Ricoeur's insistence, also shared by Scharlemann, that the minimum component of a text is the sentence, "the first and simplest unit of discourse" (Ricoeur: 148). By thus requiring that we distinguish discourse from writing, the *sefer Torah* challenges the deconstructionist use of "writing" as a dominant metaphor for complexity in communication. The Torah scroll was surely writing, certainly scripture, but it had neither textuality nor complexity until a discourse not in it was recited over it and attached to it. Moreover, the muteness of the Torah scroll explains why, despite its sanctity, it cannot satisfy Scharlemann's

The Torah scroll could not be read by itself because its writing was indeterminate script. To transform that script into a text, to make it readable, necessarily meant imposing a determinate discourse on it. For rabbis, in addition to supplying the absent vowels to make the letters into words, this transformation entailed the tradition of *qere'* ("what is read") and *ketiv* ("what is written"), in which some words were read differently from their written form, euphemisms were substituted for offensive written words (t. Megillah 3(4):39–40; b. Megillah 25b), and some written words and passages were not read at all. It also involved knowing how to divide lines of script into verses, when to introduce accents, stresses, and pauses (M. Megillah 4:4; b. Megillah 3a; Nedarim 37b; y. Megillah 4:1 [7d]; Genesis Rabbah 36), and the customary melody in which the scroll was chanted (b. Berakhot 62a; Megillah 32a). Since none of these, including the essential vowels, could ever be the property of the script, in rabbinic Judaism reading the *sefer Torah* was less a matter of deciphering an inscription than of reciting a previously known discourse and applying it to the writing.[5]

For rabbis, reading the *sefer Torah* could not be the consequence of ordinary literacy, although that surely was a prerequisite. Because the Torah-writing was both sacred and illegible, making it intelligible was a highly disciplined activity that demanded specialized knowledge. Since rabbis could neither recite what they wrote nor write what they recited, the determination of scripture's discourse had to reside almost entirely with them. Some sources suggest rabbinic awareness of this implication. For instance, b. Sanhedrin 3b–4b reports a lengthy dispute about whether authority is given to the vowels (*yš 'm lmqr'*) or to the consonants *yš 'm lmsrt*) in delineating scripture's discourse. Although the discussion favors the authority of vowels—and thereby confirms that scripture's discourse was not fixed by writing—the disagreement itself shows that rabbis appealed to both principles and outlawed neither. It thus depicts the sages, not the rules, as the final arbiters of discourse. More explicitly, an important saying, attributed to R. Isaac, a third-century Palestinian master, holds that

definition of text as "a writing in which there is a convergence between the meaning and the reality."

5. Faur (118–38) discusses this issue in terms of semiotics and semantics but bypasses both the question of the definition of text and Ricoeur's analysis of discourse as constitutive of text. Regrettably, the book's synchronic approach blurs all distinction between the classic rabbinic and the medieval (principally Sephardic) Jewish writings it examines and ignores nearly all modern scholarship—European, American, and Israeli—on rabbinic Judaism and literature. The lack of literary focus and historical precision weakens the force of its analyses.

A. The vocalization (*mqr'*) of the scribes, the [orthographic] omissions (*'ytwr*) of the scribes, and the [scripture words that are] read but not written and the [scripture passages that are] written but not read

B. [are] practice[s] (*hlkh*) [revealed] to Moses from Sinai.

(b. Nedarim 37b–38a)

The phrase that concludes the saying at B is a standard rabbinic expression that refers to the "oral Torah." The passage thus claims that not only *qere'* and *ketiv* but also the orthography and vocalization of scripture—its writing and its discourse—are not in scripture; rather they are the possession solely of rabbinic tradition. For rabbis, the credibility of scripture's discourse was guaranteed only by proper acculturation and training, in short, by rabbinic discipleship.

The rabbinic theory of scripture thus contained three complementary components that aimed to justify both the sages' vision of themselves and their claim to leadership over Israel. First, by declaring scripture sacred, rabbis endowed it with a unique and unassailable status. As a holy object, scripture possessed a givenness, a fixity, and a substantiality that made it seem independent of rabbis or their traditions. Second, rabbis reinforced the impression of scripture's autonomy and centrality by making ownership of a *sefer Torah* a religious obligation for every Jew. From a rabbinic perspective, scripture was not only the distinctive possession of all Israel; more important, it was the personal property of each individual Israelite. Finally, while they affirmed scripture as the heritage of all Jews, rabbis simultaneously claimed that its writing and its discourse were part of "oral Torah." They thereby asserted their singular mastery over—indeed, their exclusive right to manipulate—the sacred artifact they deemed the emblem of Israel's identity. In effect, rabbis proclaimed themselves coextensive with scripture and sought to acquire for themselves and their own discourse the same objectivity they attributed to it. The Palestinian Talmud (y. Mo'ed Qatan 3:7 [87b]) makes the identification explicit:

He who sees a disciple of a sage who has died is like one who sees a Torah scroll that has been burned.

In their theory and use of scripture, rabbis had it both ways. As much as scripture was the general legacy of all Israel, it also was intimately and inextricably bound to rabbinism's particular tradition. In the rabbinic view, in order to be "Israel," Jews had to invest themselves in scripture; but to do so they had equally to invest themselves in the sages' authority.

When we recall that all these components were realized in concrete and prescribed behaviors, the effect of the theory becomes clear. With their use of scripture, rabbis sought to develop and sustain a sociology of knowledge that made them indispensable.

The sanctity of scripture gave its writing an intrinsic efficacy, an almost totemic quality. The discourse attached to it had an unimpeachable authenticity and the power of authentication; it could make other discourses legitimate. Thus, in rabbinic Judaism the writing and discourse of scripture had to be inherently separable from, and could be neither merged nor confused with, the commentary upon them. To mix the two would have deprived rabbis of an artifact to control and violated the basic levitical distinction between the sacred and the profane. In rabbinic writing, therefore, passages and words of scripture are almost always identified as such by an introductory formula, such as "thus scripture says," "as it is written," "as it is said," or "a [scriptural] teaching says." The routine and nearly ubiquitous marking of scriptural passages undermines the claim that rabbinic interpretation of scripture is "intertextual"—at least in any revealing or distinctive sense—or that it is "allusive" in any sense at all. Indeed, in obvious contrast to the "inner biblical exegesis" described by Fishbane, in which later expansions and modifications are intricately embedded in earlier texts, and contrary to early Christian materials such as Luke's infancy narrative or the Book of Revelation, which subtly appropriate various Old Testament images, the rabbi's use of scripture is explicitly referential.

The rabbinic tendency to identify antecedent materials is not limited to scripture. The talmuds usually mark citations from tannaitic teachings with expressions such as "we have learned" (for the Mishnah) and "it was taught" or "our rabbis taught" (for *beraitot*, extra-Mishnaic teachings). The attributive formula "Said Rabbi X" and the little chains of tradition ("Said Rabbi X, said Rabbi Y"), typical of all rabbinic documents, served the same purpose. Rabbinic writing displays its sources.

But if the adjectives "allusive" and "intertextual" are analytically useless for a critical description of rabbinic hermeneutics, what about the correlative claim for "the endless multiple meanings which the Rabbinic tradition *ascribed* to each word and letter of the Torah" (Handelman: 131, italics supplied)? The following brief but representative passage helps to assess that judgment. It is from the Mekilta of Rabbi Ishmael, Tractate Shirta, Chapter 8 (ed. Horowitz-Rabin, p. 144, lines 14–22) and comments on the last two words of Exod. 15:11, "Who among the gods is like you, Lord? Who is like you, majestic in holiness, awesome in praises, *doing wonders*."

A. "Doing wonders"—

B. "Did (*'sh*) wonders" is not written here, but "doing (*'wsh* wonders"—in the Age to Come.

C. As it is said, "Therefore, says the Lord, the time is coming when men shall no longer swear, 'By the life of the Lord who brought the Israelites up from Egypt,' but, 'By the life of the Lord who brought the Israelites back from a northern land and from all the lands to which he had dispersed them'; and I will bring them back to the soil which I gave to their forefathers" (Jer. 16:14—15).

D. Another interpretation: "Doing wonders"—

E. He did wonders for us and he does wonders for us in each and every generation.

F. As it is said, "I will praise you, for I am filled with awe; you are wonderful and your works are wonderful; and you know my soul very well" (Ps. 139:14).

G. And it says, "You have done many things, Lord my God, your wonders and your thoughts towards us" (Ps. 40:6).

H. Another interpretation: "Doing wonders"—

I. He does wonders for the fathers, and in the future [he will] do [them] for the sons.

J. As it is said, "As in the days of his going forth from the land of Egypt, I will show him wonders" (Micah 7:15).

K. "I will show him"—what I did not show to the fathers.

L. For, look, the miracles and mighty acts that in the future [I will] do for the sons, they [will be] more than what I did for the fathers.

M. For thus scripture says, "To him who alone does great wonders, for his mercy endures forever" (Ps. 136:4).

N. And it says, "Blessed is the Lord God, God of Israel, who alone does wonders, and blessed be his glorious name forever, and may the whole earth be filled with his glory. Amen and Amen" (Ps. 72:18–19).

The passage begins at B by noting a difference between the orthography and the vocalization of scripture—its writing and its discourse. The word *'sh* can be vocalized—and these are not the only alternatives—as a verb in the *qal*, a third-person masculine singular perfect ("did," "has done"), or as a *qal* masculine singular present participle ("doing," "does"). Its defective spelling favors the former, but the discourse tradition, for good reason, affirms the latter. The passage exploits the discrepancy and, by the mere gloss with the rabbinic term "Age to Come," imputes an eschatological intention to the participle. The verses from Jeremiah, appended without comment at C, make "the Age to Come" refer to the return from exile.

The second interpretation (D–G), which focuses on the noun "wonders," consists of an assertion (E) that God's wonders for Israel are constant, which is then bolstered by two verses from Psalms. Considered apart from the statement at E, however, the verses discuss only God's wonderful qualities and actions, but neither Israel nor her generations. The third interpretation (H–N), also on the theme of God's wonders, asserts at I, with support from the verse from Micah at J, that Israel's past will be replicated in her future (*"As* in the days of his going forth . . ."). K–L makes this mean that God's acts for Israel's "sons" will be greater than those for the "fathers." The identifying formula at M ("For *thus* scripture says") suggests that the Psalm citations at M–N support this idea, but, as above, the verses simply praise God as the sole worker of wonders and make no reference to the future.

Although the interpretations in this passage are formally distinguished from one another at D and H by the disjunctive device *davar 'aher* ("another interpretation"), they operate within a limited conceptual sphere and a narrow thematic range. As is typical of most lists of *davar 'aher* comments in rabbinic literature, the three segments not only do not conflict but are mutually reinforcing. Taken together, B–C, D–G, and H–N claim that God's past wondrous acts in Israel's behalf will continue, and be even greater, in the future. Thus, rather than "endless multiple meanings," they in fact ascribe to the words "doing wonders" multiple variations of a single meaning.

The literary technique for presenting that meaning is worth noting. Instead of providing an actual exegesis of the words from Exod. 15:11, the passage strategically juxtaposes verses from prophecy and Psalms and preinterprets them with brief comments and glosses that are in no way integral to the verses themselves. The verses at C, F, G, M, and N stand alone, without elaboration. By gathering discrete verses from scripture's three divisions—the Pentateuch, the Prophets, and the Writings—the list form makes scripture itself seem naturally and ubiquitously to articulate a single message about God's persistent devotion to Israel. By providing multiple warrant for that message, the form effectively restricts the interpretive options. In this case, it excludes the possibility that God's miraculous acts for Israel have ceased.

If it is doubtful that rabbis ascribed "endless multiple meanings" to scripture, it is no less so that rabbinic hermeneutics encouraged and routinely tolerated the metonymical coexistence of different meanings of scripture that did not, and could not, annul one another. The evidence examined previously calls into question two proposals in particular: that rabbinic reading of scripture could entail the Heidiggerean practice of "crossing out", and that in rabbinic Bible interpretation "the literal is never cancelled" (Handelman: 55).[6] As to the first, since scripture's writing was only a facsimile of language, there was no written discourse to cross out. When rabbis recited "adonai" at the sight of the tetragrammaton, they probably did not encounter the text of God's proper name, which, by all accounts, they did not, and perhaps could not, pronounce anyway (Schiffman: 133–36).

The following passage suggests that the second proposal also does not do. Sifré to Numbers, Pisqa' 117 (ed. Horowitz, p. 134, lines 11–13), reads as follows:

A. "And the Lord spoke to Aaron" (Num. 18:8)—
B. I understand (*šm'*) [from this] that the speech was to Aaron.
C. A [scriptural] teaching says (*tlmwd lwmr*),
D. "It is a reminder to the children of Israel, so that an unqualified man [, not from Aaron's seed, should not approach to burn incense before the Lord, and should not be like Qorah and his company; (this was done) as the Lord instructed (*dbr*) him through (*byd*) Moses]" (Num. 17:5 [16:40]).
E. This teaches us that the speech was to Moses, who told [it] to Aaron.

C–E use Num. 17:5 to counter the obvious meaning of the discourse of Num. 18:8. The words recited there as "The Lord spoke to Aaron" are to be understood to mean that God did so "through Moses." Thus, the clear sense of the verse—as Loewe shows, the concept of "literal" meaning is an anachronism in a rabbinic context—is effaced, and a single contrary meaning, suggested by Num. 17:5, is assigned to replace it. The form of the passage presents that judgment not as an interpretation but as a fact of scripture.

The rhetorical pattern of this brief passage is typical of much rabbinic scriptural interpretation, especially of Sifra, Sifré to Numbers, and Sifré to Deuteronomy, and its effect should not be overlooked. The structure provided by B, C, and E ("I might think. . . . But scripture teaches. . . . Therefore . . .") limits rather than multiplies the possibilities of scripture's meaning and clearly is designed to reject what rabbis regarded as

6. Handelman writes, "Say the rabbis, 'No text ever loses its plain meaning' (*Shab.* 63a; *Yev.* 24a), even though every word of Scripture has many interpretations on many levels" (55). But as Raphael Loewe demonstrated nearly a quarter century ago, in a classic article not listed in Handelman's bibliography, the phrase *yn miqr' ywṣ' mydy pšwtw* means that a biblical passage "cannot be distorted from the meaning of its '*peshat*'" and was used to circumscribe the interpretation of a verse of scripture (164–67).

erroneous understandings. In this case, since rabbinic ideology held that God spoke directly only to Moses, Num. 18:8 had to mean something other than what its discourse plainly said. A different but very representative and forceful demonstration of the rabbinic limitation of scripture's meaning occurs in a famous passage at b. Bava' Qama' 83b–84a. There, rigorous talmudic argument that skillfully manipulates verses from Leviticus and Numbers shows that the famous *lex talionis* of Exod. 21:24 ("An eye for an eye, and a tooth for a tooth") does not mean what it says but refers instead to pecuniary compensation.

By juxtaposing discrete biblical verses in the form of a list, and by strategically placing them in established rhetorical patterns and propositional frameworks, rabbinic interpretation made scripture appear to speak by itself and for itself and also to restrict its own connotation. As we have seen, much rabbinic use of scripture was kaleidoscopic. Unlike Irenaeus's Rule of Faith, in which the theological value of the "Old Testament" requires the reader's acceptance of a fixed narrative line, rabbinic rules of interpretation (*middot*) provide instruction on how fragments of the holy writing can be mixed and matched to reveal patterns of signification. But the patterns can be meaningful only if they are constructed within a sealed sphere of reference. If the sphere is broken or corrupted, the pieces scatter randomly or fall into a heap. For rabbinism, scripture's sphere of reference was constituted of rabbinic practice, ideology, and discourse, but, most important, of the community of sages themselves.

Nothing in the materials considered previously supports the judgments that, in their use of scripture, rabbis confronted the "undecidability of textual meaning" (Hartman and Budick: xi) or that their mode of interpretation celebrated "endless multiple meanings." This result ought not to surprise us. As heirs and practitioners of a levitical piety, rabbis could afford little tolerance of ambiguity, uncertainty, or unclarity. The holy writing on the sacred scroll that was the stable center of their system could not appear to speak, as it were, with a forked or twisted tongue.

By controlling the scripture both as sacred artifact and as intelligible text, sages guaranteed that it would always refer to their concerns and interests, that it would always validate and justify—but never contradict—their *halakah* and the religious ideology that undergirded it. In their various literary compositions, rabbis did not so much write about or within scripture as they wrote with it, making it speak with their voice, in their idiom, and in their behalf. The rabbinic interpretation of scripture, therefore, was anything but indeterminate or equivocal. Rather, it was an exercise—and a remarkably successful one—in the dictation, limitation, and closure of what became a commanding Judaic discourse.[7]

7. My thanks go to Professors Jacob Neusner, Gary G. Porton, Jonathan Z. Smith, Beverly R. Gaventa, Ernest Frerichs, Fitz John Porter Poole, S. Dean McBride, Eugene D. Genovese, Howard Eilberg-Schwartz, and Mary Gerhart for invaluable corrections, essential clarifications, and stimulating criticism. Earlier versions were read at Arizona State University and the Pittsburgh Theological Seminary and were much improved by the responses of participants in both colloquia.

WORKS CONSULTED

Dothan, Aaron
    1971   "Masorah." In *Encyclopaedia Judaica*, 16:1403–14. Jerusalem: Keter.
Faur, Jose
    1986   *Golden Doves with Silver Dots: Semiotics and Textuality in Rabbinic Tradition.* Bloomington: Indiana University Press.
Fishbane, Michael
    1986   "Inner Biblical Exegesis: Types and Strategies of Interpretation in Ancient Israel." In Hartman and Budick, 19–37.
Greer, Rowan A.
    1986   "The Christian Bible and Its Interpretation." In *Early Biblical Interpretation*, 107–203, by James L. Kugel and Rowan A. Greer. Philadelphia: The Westminster Press.
Handelman, Susan
    1982   *The Slayers of Moses: The Emergence of Rabbinic Interpretation in Modern Literary Theory.* Albany: State University of New York Press.
Hartman, Geoffrey
    1986   "The Struggle for the Text." In Hartman and Budick, 3–18.
Hartman, Geoffrey, and Sanford Budick, eds.
    1986   *Midrash and Literature.* New Haven and London: Yale University Press.
Kermode, Frank
    1986   "The Plain Sense of Things." In Hartman and Budick, 179–94.
Kugel, James
    1986   "Early Interpretation: The Common Background of Late Forms of Biblical Exegesis." In *Early Biblical Interpretation*, 9–106, by James L. Kugel and Rowan A. Greer. Philadelphia: Westminster Press.
Lieberman, Saul
    1939   *Tosepheth Rishonim*, Part IV. Jerusalem: Mossad Rabbi Kook.
Loewe, Raphael
    1964   "The 'Plain' Meaning of Scripture in Early Jewish Exegesis." In *Papers of the Institute of Jewish Studies, London*, vol. 1:141–85, ed. J. G. Weiss. Jerusalem: Magnes Press.

McGrath, William
1986   *The Politics of Hysteria*. Ithaca: Cornell University Press.
Neusner, Jacob
1971   *A History of the Mishnaic Law of Purities*, vol. XIX. Leiden: E. J. Brill.
1983   *Midrash in Context: Exegesis in Formative Judaism*. Philadelphia: Fortress Press.
1986   *The Oral Torah: The Sacred Books of Judaism*. San Francisco: Harper & Row.
Porton, Gary
1981   "Defining Midrash." In *The Study of Ancient Judaism*, vol. 1:55–92, ed. Jacob Neusner. New York: Ktav.
Preus, James Samuel
1969   *From Shadow to Promise*. Cambridge: The Belknap Press of Harvard University Press.
Ricoeur, Paul
1981   "What is a text? Explanation and understanding." In *Paul Ricoeur, Hermeneutics and the Human Sciences*, 145–64, ed. and trans. John B. Thompson. Cambridge: Cambridge University Press.
Scharlemann, Robert P.
1987   "Theological Text." In *Semeia* 40, ed. Charles Winquist.
Schiffman, Lawrence H.
1983   *Sectarian Law in the Dead Sea Scrolls*. Chico, CA: Scholars Press.
Vermes, Geza
1975   "Bible and Midrash: Early Old Testament Exegesis." In *Post-Biblical Jewish Studies*, 59–91, by Geza Vermes. Leiden: E. J. Brill.

3

Writing without and with Scripture

WRITING WITHOUT SCRIPTURE

Before asking what it means to write with scripture, let me spell out the alternative. Writing without scripture means presenting ideas as essentially autonomous of any other document, such as a received scripture, and requiring no validation through citation of proof texts drawn from such another document, e.g., the ancient Israelite scriptures. The first document of the Judaism of the dual Torah, the Mishnah, a rather philosophical law code produced at ca. A.D. 200, shows us how an authorship wrote without sustained resort to scripture. On the surface, scripture plays little role in the Mishnaic system. The Mishnah rarely cites a verse of scripture, refers to scripture as an entity, links its own ideas to those of scripture, or lays claim to originate in what scripture has said, even by indirect or remote allusion to a scriptural verse of teaching. So, superficially, the Mishnah is totally indifferent to scripture. That impression, moreover, is reinforced by the traits of the language of the Mishnah. The framers of Mishnaic discourse, amazingly, never attempt to imitate the language of scripture, as do those of the Essene writings at Qumran. The very redactional structure of scripture, found to be serviceable to the writer of the Temple scroll, remarkably, is of no interest whatever to the organizers of the Mishnah and its tractates, except in a very few cases (Leviticus 16, Yoma; Exodus 12; Pesahim). That then shows us what it means for an authorship to write without resort of scripture.

Formally, redactionally, and linguistically, therefore, the Mishnah stands in splendid isolation from scripture. It is not possible to point to many parallels, that is, cases of anonymous books of any Judaism in antiquity received as holy, in which the forms and formulations (specific

24

verses) of scripture play so slight a role. Judaic writers in ancient times who wrote holy books commonly imitated the scripture's language. They cited concrete verses. They claimed at the very least that direct revelation had come to them, as in the angelic discourses of IV Ezra and Baruch, so that what they say stands on an equal plane with scripture. The internal evidence of the Mishnah's 62 usable tractates (excluding Abot), by contrast, in no way suggests that anyone pretended to talk like Moses and write like Moses, claimed to cite and correctly interpret things that Moses has said, or even alleged to have had a revelation like that of Moses and so to stand on the mountain with Moses. There is none of this. So the claim of scriptural authority for the Mishnah's doctrines and institutions is difficult to locate within the internal evidence of the Mishnah itself.

That is not to suggest that scripture made no contribution to the program of the authorship of the Mishnah. That is not true. If we examine the topical program of the Mishnah's tractates, we see the facts. First, there are tractates that simply repeat in their own words precisely what scripture has to say and, at best, serve to amplify and complete the basic ideas of scripture. For example, all the cultic tractates of the second division, the one on Appointed Times, which tell what one is supposed to do in the Temple on the various special days of the year, and the bulk of the cultic tractates of the fifth division, which deals with Holy Things, simply restate facts of scripture. For another example, all of those tractates of the sixth division, on Purities, which specify sources of uncleanness, depend completely on information supplied by scripture. I have demonstrated in detail that every important statement in Niddah, on menstrual uncleanness, and the most fundamental notions of Zabim, on the uncleanness of the person with flux referred to in Leviticus 15, as well as every detail in Negaim, on the uncleanness of the person or house suffering the uncleanness described at Leviticus 13 and 14—all of these tractates serve only to restate the basic facts of scripture and to complement those facts with other important ones.

There are, second, tractates that take up facts of scripture but work them out in a way in which those scriptural facts cannot have led us to predict. A supposition concerning what is important about the facts, utterly remote from the supposition of scripture, explains why the Mishnah tractates under discussion say the original things they say in confronting those scripturally provided facts. For one example scripture takes for granted that the red cow will be burned in a state of unclean-ness, because it is burned outside the camp-Temple. The priestly writers cannot have imagined that a state of cultic cleanness was to be attained outside of the cult. The absolute datum of tractate Parah, by contrast, is that cultic cleanness not only can be attained outside the "tent of meeting." The red cow was to be burned in a state of cleanness even exceeding that cultic cleanness required in the Temple itself. The problematic that generates the intellectual agendum of Parah, therefore, is how to work out the conduct of the rite of burning the cow in relationship to the Temple: Is it to be done in exactly the same way, or in exactly the opposite way? This mode of contrastive and analogical thinking helps us to understand the generative problematic of such tractates as Erubin and Besah, to mention only two.

Third, there are, predictably, many tractates that either take up problems in no way suggested by scripture or begin from facts at best merely relevant to facts of scripture. In the former category are Tohorot, on the cleanness of foods, with its companion, Uqsin; Demai, on doubtfully tithed produce; Tamid, on the conduct of the daily whole-offering; Baba Batra, on rules of real estate transactions and certain other commercial and property relationships; and so on. In the latter category are Ohalot, which spins out its strange problems within the theory that a tent and a utensil are to be compared with one another; Kelim, on the susceptibility to uncleanness of various sorts of utensils; Miqvaot, on the sorts of water that effect purification from uncleanness; Ketubot and Gittin, on the documents of marriage and divorce; and many others. These tractates draw on facts of scripture. But the problem confronted in these tractates in no way responds to problems important to scripture. What we have here is a prior program of inquiry, which makes ample provision for facts of scripture in an inquiry to begin with generated essentially outside of the framework of scripture. First comes the problem or topic, then—if possible—comes attention to scripture.

So some tractates merely repeat what we find in scripture. Some are totally independent of scripture. And some fall in between. When an authorship writes without scripture, it does not cite verses of scripture for any purpose at all. But in the Mishnah scripture forms a prevailing presence, not everywhere, but surely not merely episodically. The Mishnah in no way is so remote from scripture as its formal omission of citations of verses of scripture suggests. In no way can it be described as contingent upon and secondary to scripture, as many of its third-century apologists claimed. Scripture confronted the framers of the Mishnah as revelation, not merely as a source of facts. But in presenting the Mishnah as an authoritative statement, the authorship of the Mishnah joined the authorships of scriptural books in writing what would be received as

Torah—and the Mishnah found a place for itself as part of the same Torah as scripture. Having briefly reviewed what it means to write without scripture, meaning without citation of verses of scripture or even constant allusion to their contents, let me now examine the case of a document that constantly, and in diverse ways, writes with scripture.

ILLUSTRATION, EXEGESIS, PROPOSITIONAL DISCOURSE

I begin with a theoretical proposal, then test the suggested classification against a single document. An inductive inquiry permits us to sort out data among diverse classifications. One such taxonomic system visible to the naked eye instructs us to look for evidence that a verse of the Israelite scriptures illustrates theme, that is to say, provides information on a given subject. A second tells us that a verse of the Israelite scriptures defines a problem on its own, in its own determinate limits and terms. Yet a third—the classification at the center of interest in this book—points toward that utilization of Israelite scriptures in the formation and expression of a proposition independent of the theme or even the facts contained within—proved by—those scriptures. Where, to take up the first classification, a given theme requires illustration, the ancient scriptures provide a useful fact. Indeed, those scriptures may well form the single important treasury of facts. But the amplification of the verses of scripture takes second place to the display of the facts important to the topic at hand; the purpose of composition is the creation of a scrapbook of materials relevant to a given theme. The verse of received scripture serves not to validate a proposition but only to illustrate a theme. Where, second, the sense or meaning or implications of a given verse of scripture defines the center of discourse, then the verse takes over and dictates the entire character of the resulting composition, and that composition we may call exegetical (substituting "eisegetical" is a mere conceit). And when, finally, an authorship proposes to make a strong case for a given proposition, appealing to a variety of materials, there Israelite scriptures take a subordinate position within discourse determined by a logic all its own.

Let us take up examples of each of these three ways in which Israelite scripture may serve an authorship of Judaism or Christianity. For our source of examples, I turn to a single document, Sifré to Deuteronomy. We consider three pisqaot, or completed statements, as signified by the received textual tradition. One of these shows us Israelite scripture in its role as illustration of a theme, in a larger composition to be categorized as an anthology or a scrapbook. The second presents us with an instance in which the exegesis of a given verse defines the center of interest and dictates the principle of cogent discussion. That is to say, if we wish to understand the point of an exegetical composition, what holds that composite together and renders it intelligible, we find ourselves required to focus upon the verse at hand, its meanings, whether actual or merely potential, its context and focus and address. The third shows us how an authorship writes with Scripture and leads us to the problem we shall wish to explore in the remaining chapters of this book. My examples derive from Sifré to Deuteronomy, a compilation of materials relevant, as the title indicates, to the Book of Deuteronomy. We have no grounds on which to date the compilation. In this context it serves as simply another test case in the canonical repertoire of Judaism. Can we find examples of the three types of relationship to scripture that I have proposed? Indeed we can.

SCRIPTURE AND ANTHOLOGY

One way of forming a comprehensible statement is to draw together information on a single theme. The theme then imposes cogency on facts, which are deemed to illuminate aspects of that theme. Such a statement constitutes a topical anthology. The materials in the anthology do not, all together, add up to a statement that transcends detail. For example, they do not point toward a conclusion beyond themselves. They rather comprise a series of facts, e.g., fact 1, fact 2, fact 3. But put together, these three facts do not yield yet another one, nor do they point toward a proposition beyond themselves. They generate no generalization, prove no point, propose no proposition. Here is an example of a writing that forms an anthology, the theme being the righteous in the firmament or in the paradise.

Sifré to Deuteronomy X:I

1. A. " . . . The Lord your God has multiplied you until you are today as numerous as the stars in the sky" (Deut. 1:9–13);
   B. "Lo, you are established as is the day."

All we have is the amplification of the "today" of the cited verse. Next comes a completely independent statement, joined to the foregoing by meaningless joining language, 2.A. Then we have a set of facts about classes of the righteous in paradise, each established by a fact constituted by a verse of scripture. The point for our larger inquiry is that the verse of scripture constitutes not proof of a proposition but a simple fact.

2. A. On this basis they have said:

    B. There are seven classes of righteous in the Garden of Eden, one above the last.

    C. First: "Surely the righteous shall give thanks to your name; the upright shall dwell in your presence" (Ps. 140:14).

    D. Second: "Happy is the man whom you choose and bring near" (Ps. 65:5).

    E. Third: "Happy are those who dwell in your house" (Ps. 84:5).

    F. Fourth: "Lord, you shall dwell in your tabernacle" (Ps. 15:1).

    G. Fifth: "Who shall dwell upon your holy mountain" (Ps. 15:1).

    H. Sixth: "Who shall ascend the mountain of the Lord" (Ps. 24:3).

    I. Seventh: "And who shall stand in his holy place" (Ps. 24:3).

The seven facts are coextensive with the seven verses of scripture. Were we to deal with atomic weights or facts of history, such as on July 4, 1776, the colonies declared their independence, we should have in hand nothing different from the facts before us. The source, scripture, validates the facts, which are revealed truths to be sure—but that function, as is clear, is nothing more than data. The following component of the larger composition on the righteous in paradise or heaven or the age to come follows suit. It has no proposition in common with the foregoing; it makes no point beyond itself, it is a simple statement of fact, formed of a set of other facts that are drawn together for the purpose of establishing the generalization given at 1.A following.

X:II

1. A. R. Simeon b. Yohai says, "Like seven sources of joy with the faces of the righteous appear in the age to come:

    B. "The sun, moon, firmament, stars, lightning, lilies [*shoshannim*], and candelabrum of the Temple.

    C. "How do we know that that is the case for the sun? 'But they who love him shall be as the sun when it goes forth in its might' (Jud. 5:31);

    D. "the moon: 'Fair as the moon' (Song 6:10);

    E. "the firmament: 'And they who are wise shall shine as the brightness of the firmament' (Dan. 12:3);

    F. "the stars: 'And they who turn the many to righteousness as the stars' (Dan. 12:3);

    G. "the lightning: 'They run to and fro like lightnings' (Nah. 2:5);

    H. "the lilies: 'For the leader, upon shoshannim' (Ps. 45:1);

    I. "the candelabrum of the temple: 'And two olive trees by it, one on the right side of the bowl, the other on the left side thereof' (Zech. 4:3)".

Now to see the exercise as a whole: because of the use of the comparative, "as at this day," No. 1 amplifies the comparison of Israel with the day, then No. 2 picks up on the theme of the stars, hence the firmament, and X:II is tacked on for the same thematic connection to form an anthology on a theme. There is no intersection with the verse at hand and no point of interest in the substance of the passage. This composition was formed with its own principle of topical cogency, not in relationship to the exegetical interests, if any, of the framers of a compilation concerning the Book of Deuteronomy.

SCRIPTURE AND THE EXEGESIS OF SCRIPTURE

That is not to suggest that the compositors of the compilation as a whole displayed no interest in exegesis, by which I mean explaining the meanings of words and phrases. Quite to the contrary, occasionally we do have composites of materials that find cogency solely in the words of a given verse of scripture but in no other way. These materials string together, upon the necklace of words or phrases of a verse, diverse comments; the comments do not fit together or point to any broader conclusion; they do not address a single theme or form an anthology. Cogency derives from the (external) verse that is cited; intelligibility begins—and ends—in that verse and is accomplished by the amplification of the verse's contents. Without the verse before us, the words that follow form gibberish. But reading the words as amplifications of a sense contained within the cited verse, we can make good sense of them. That then is an example of not writing with scripture but explaining ("exegeting") scripture.

Sifré to Deuteronomy XXI:I

1. A. "I approved of the plan and so I selected twelve of your men, one from each tribe. They made for the hill country, came to the wadi Eshcol, and spied it out. They took some of the fruit of the land with them and brought it down to us. And they gave us this report, 'It is a good land that the Lord our God is giving to us'" (Deut. 1:22–25):
   B. "I approved of the plan"—but the Omnipresent did not.
2. A. But if he approved the plan, then why was it written along with the words of admonition?
   B. The matter may be compared to the case of someone who said to his fellow, "Sell me your ass."
   C. The other said, "All right."
   D. "Will you let me try it out?"
   E. "All right. Come along, and I'll show you how much it can carry in the hills, how much it can carry in the valley."

F.   When the purchaser saw that there was nothing standing in the way, he said, "Woe is me! It appears that the reason he is so obliging is to take away my money."

G.   That is why it is written, "I approved of the plan."

I see two distinct views of the cited verse. No. 1 finds a "no" in Moses' "yes," and No. 2 shows Moses' true intent. He did not really approve what the people wanted to do, but he went along in order to get what he wanted. We can read No. 1 without No. 2, but not No. 2 without No. 1. The upshot is that No. 1 forms a cogent statement only within the framework of the cited verse, and No. 2 gains intelligibility only as an amplification of what is said in No. 1—hence a two-stage exegesis, first, of the cited verse, second, of the exegesis itself.

XXI:II

1.   A.   ". . . and so I selected twelve of your men:"

B.   . . . from the most select among you, from among the most seasoned among you.

2.   A.   ". . .one from each tribe:"

B.   Why tell me this? Is it not already stated, ". . . I selected twelve of your men"? [So I know that there was one from each tribe.]

C.   It is to indicate that a representative of the tribe of Levi was not among the spies.

The phrase-by-phrase clarification continues to underline Moses' dubiety about the project. But there is no effort at generalization or a statement, in the form of a proposition, of an idea. Nor can we suppose that the authorship at hand has put these matters together to make a simple point, introduced, e.g., at No. 1, expanded at No. 2, then amplified at No. 3. Since that fact is self-evident—that is, there is no cogency to the whole, beyond the verse upon which all materials comment—it follows that we have not a propositional statement nor even a topical anthology but solely an exegesis, that is, a set of exegeses upon a cited verse. Such compositions do occur in the document at hand, but they are uncommon.

WRITING WITH SCRIPTURE

What I mean by writing with scripture is simple. An authorship that wishes to establish an important proposition may do so by juxtaposing sequences of verses or biblical cases (heroes, events) and, through the juxtaposition, make a point, establish a proposition, not contained within any one of the verses or cases but implicit in them all. Writing in a propositional manner we state our proposition and cite our evidence and display our argumentation. Writing with or through Scripture, we do these things:

1. state our proposition implicitly, by citing our evidence without necessarily spelling out what we mean to prove through it, and

2. conduct our argumentation with the reader by asking the reader to perceive the commonalities that, all together, point to the conclusion we wish to reach.

Here is an example of a sustained composition, cogent beginning to end, that makes its points through the medium of writing with Scripture. When we see how that medium delivers its message, we understand that the rabbinic canon, exemplified by the document at hand, undertakes a mode of discourse in an idiom very much its own, but within a logic of intelligible discourse entirely familiar to our own philosophical tradition, deriving as it does from the Greco-Roman heritage.

Sifré to Deuteronomy I:I

1. A. "These are the words that Moses spoke to all Israel in Transjordan, in the wilderness, that is to say in the Arabah, opposite Suph, between Paran on the one side and Tophel, Laban, Hazeroth, and Dizahab on the other" (Deut. 1:1):

    B. ["These are the words that Moses spoke" (Deut. 1:1):] Did Moses prophesy only these alone? Did he not write the entire Torah?

    C. For it is said, "And Moses wrote this Torah" (Deut. 31:9).

    D. Why then does Scripture say, "These are the words that Moses spoke" (Deut. 1:1)?

    E. It teaches that [when Scripture speaks of the words that one spoke, it refers in particular to] the words of admonition.

    F. So it is said [by Moses], "But Jeshurun waxed fat and kicked" (Deut. 32:15).

The proposition is stated at E. It is a philological one. "Speaking" in a specific sense implies a measure of rebuke or admonition. We are not offered the proposition as an introductory statement, e.g., a syllogism to be proved. The proposition occurs only in another way, at E–F. Let us proceed to follow the way in which the proposition is (1) stated, (2) illustrated and exemplified, and (3) proved—all through a barrage of cited verses of scripture. The form is so fixed that there is no need to comment on the individual entries. Discourse requires conventional rhetoric (deemed to persuade), conventional logic (deemed to operate self-evidently and to bear its own compelling force), and the topic particular to the case at hand but part of a larger program as well. Here the rhetoric is established by repetition. The logic is worked out through the repeated appeal to "obvious" or "self-evident" truths. The topic—the proposition—recurs at every paragraph, and the whole coalesces into a single, remarkably cogent statement.

2.   A.   So too you may point to the following:
     B.   "The words of Amos, who was among the herdmen of Tekoa, which he saw concerning Israel in the days of Uzzirah, king of Judah, and in the days of Jeroboam, son of Joash, king of Israel, two years before the earthquake" (Amos 1:1):
     C.   Did Amos prophesy only concerning these [kings] alone? Did he not prophesy concerning a greater number [of kings] than any other?
     D.   Why then does Scripture say, "These are the words of Amos [who was among the herdmen of Tekoa, which he saw concerning Israel in the days of Uzzirah, king of Judah, and in the days of Jeroboam, son of Joash, king of Israel, two years before the earthquake]" (Amos 1:1)?
     E.   It teaches that [when Scripture speaks of the words that one spoke, it refers in particular to] the words of admonition.
     F.   And how do we know that they were words of admonition?
     G.   As it is said, "Hear this word, you cows of Bashan, who are in the mountain of Samaria, who oppress the poor, crush the needy, and say to their husbands, 'Bring, that we may feast'" (Amos 4:1).
     H.   ["And say to their husbands, 'Bring that we may feast'"] speaks of their courts.

3.   A.   So too you may point to the following:
     B.   "And these are the words that the Lord spoke concerning Israel and Judah" (Jer. 30:4).
     C.   Did Jeremiah prophesy only these alone? Did he not write two [complete] scrolls?
     D.   For it is said, "Thus far are the words of Jeremiah" (Jer. 51:64).
     E.   Why then does Scripture say, "And these are the words [that the Lord spoke concerning Israel and Judah]" (Jer. 30:4)?
     F.   It teaches that [when the verse says, "And these are the words that the Lord spoke concerning Israel and Judah" (Jer. 30:4)], it speaks in particular of the words of admonition.
     G.   And how do we know they were words of admonition?
     H.   In accord with this verse: "For thus says the Lord, 'We have heard a voice of trembling, of fear and not of peace. Ask you now and see whether a man does labor with a child? Why do I see every man with his hands on his loins, as a woman in labor? and all faces turn pale? Alas, for the day is great, there is none like it, and it is a time of trouble for Jacob, but out of it he shall be saved" (Jer. 30:5-7).

4.   A.   So too you may point to the following:
      B.   "And these are the last words of David" (2 Sam. 23:1).
      C.   And did David prophesy only these alone? And has it furthermore not
            been said, "The spirit of the Lord spoke through me, and his word was
            on my tongue" (2 Sam. 23:2)?
      D.   Why then does it say, "And these are the last words of David" (2 Sam.
            23:1)?
      E.   It teaches that, [when the verse says, "And these are the last words of
            David" (2 Sam. 23:1)], it refers to words of admonition.
      F.   And how do we know that they were words of admonition?
      G.   In accord with this verse: "But the ungodly are as thorns thrust away,
            all of them, for they cannot be taken with the hand" (2 Sam. 23:6).
5.   A.   So too you may point to the following:
      B.   "The words of Qohelet, son of David, king in Jerusalem" (Qoh. 1:1).
      C.   Now did Solomon prophesy only these words? Did he not write three
            and a half scrolls of his wisdom in proverbs?
      D.   Why then does it say, "The words of Qohelet, son of David, king in
            Jerusalem" (Qoh. 1:1)?
      E.   It teaches that, [when the verse says, "The words of Qohelet, son of
            David, king in Jerusalem" (Qoh. 1:1)], it refers to words of admoni-
            tion.
      F.   And how do we know that they were words of admonition?
      G.   In accord with this verse: "The sun also rises, and the sun goes down
            . . . the wind goes toward the south and turns around to the north, it
            turns round continually in its circuit, and the wind returns again—
            that is, east and west [ ] to its circuits. All the rivers run into the sea"
            (Qoh. 1:5–7).
      H.   [Solomon] calls the wicked sun, moon, and sea, for [the wicked] have
            no reward [coming back to them].

Let us stand back and see the matter whole. The focus is upon the
exegesis of the opening word of Deuteronomy, "words. . . ." The
problem is carefully stated. And yet, without the arrangement within
what is going to be a commentary on Deuteronomy, we should have no
reason to regard the composition as exegetical at all. In fact, it is a
syllogism, aiming at proving a particular proposition concerning word
usages. Standing by itself, what we have is simply a very carefully
formalized syllogism that makes a philological point, which is that the
word "words of . . ." bears the sense of "admonition" or "rebuke." Five
proofs are offered. We know that we reach the end of the exposition
when, at 5.H, there is a minor gloss, breaking the perfect form. That is a
common mode of signaling the conclusion of discourse on a given point.

I:II

1. A.   "... to all Israel:"

   B.   [Moses spoke to the entire community all at once, for] had he admonished only part of them, those who were out at the market would have said, "Is this what you heard from the son of Amram? And did you not give him such-and-such an answer? If we had been there, we should have answered him four or five times for every word he said!"

2. A.   Another matter concerning "... to all Israel:"

   B.   This teaches that Moses collected all of them together, from the greatest to the least of them, and he said to them, "Lo, I shall admonish you. Whoever has an answer—let him come and say it."

We proceed to the next word in the base verse, but now our comment is particular to the verse. The explanation of why Moses spoke to everyone is then clear. On the one hand, it was to make certain that there was no one left out, so No. 1. On the other, it was to make certain that everyone had a say, so No. 2. These two points then complement one another. The relevance to the established proposition concerning the centrality of admonition or rebuke on all acts of "speaking" is self-evident. The theme of the proposition persists—and, for the purposes of argument, at this point, it suffices. What in fact is happening is a broadening of a philological proposition into a broader philosophical point. That point now comes to the fore.

I:III

1. A.   Another matter concerning "... to all Israel:"

   B.   This teaches that all of them were subject to admonition but quite able to deal with the admonition.

2. A.   Said R. Tarfon, "By the Temple service! [I do not believe] that there is anyone in this generation who can administer an admonition."

   B.   Said R. Eleazar ben Azariah, "By the Temple service! [I do not believe] that there is anyone in this generation who can accept admonition."

   C.   Said R. Aqiba, "By the Temple service! [I do not believe] that there is anyone in this generation who knows how to give an admonition."

   D.   Said R. Yohanan b. Nuri, "I call to give testimony against me heaven and earth, [if it is not the case that] more than five times was R. Aqiba criticized before Rabban Gamaliel in Havney, for I would lay complaints against him, and [Gamaliel therefore] criticized him. Nonetheless, I know that [each such criticism] added to [Aqiba's] love for me.

   E.   "This carries out the verse, 'Do not criticize a scorner, lest he hate you, but reprove a wise person, and he will love you' (Prov. 9:8)."

Nos. 1 and 2 are quite separate units of thought, each making its own point. Shall we say that all we have, at **I:I–III**, is a sequence of three quite disparate propositions? In that case, the authorship before us had presented nothing more than a scrapbook of relevant comments on discrete clauses. I think otherwise. It seems to us that in **I:I–III** as the distinct and complete units of thought unfold we have a proposition, fully exposed, composed by the setting forth of two distinct facts, which serve as established propositions to yield the syllogism of No. 3. But the syllogism is not made explicitly, rather it is placed on display by the (mere) juxtaposition of fact 1 and fact 2 and then the final proposition, **I:III.1**, followed by a story making the same point as the proposition. The exegesis now joins the (established) facts (1) that Moses rebuked Israel and (2) that all Israel was involved. The point is (3) that Israel was able to deal with the admonition and did not reject it. No. 2 then contains a story that makes explicit and underlines the virtue spun out of the verse. Aqiba embodies that virtue, the capacity—the wisdom—to accept rebuke. The upshot, then, is that the authorship wished to make a single point in assembling into a single carefully ordered sequence **I:I–III**, and it did so by presenting two distinct propositions, at **I:I, I:II**, and then, at **I:III**, recast the whole by making a point drawing upon the two original, autonomous proofs. Joining **I:I** and **I:II** then led directly to the proposition at which the authorship was aiming. We have much more than an assembly of information on diverse traits or points of verses, read word by word. It is, rather, a purposeful composition, made up of what clearly are already available materials.

I:IV

1. A. "On the other side of the Jordan" (Deut. 1:1):
    B. This teaches that he admonished them concerning things that they had done on the other side of the Jordan.

The paragraphing is misleading here, since the proposition continues in the following and on through **I:VII**.

I:V

1. A. "In the wilderness" (Deut. 1:1):
    B. This teaches that he admonished them concerning things that they had done in the wilderness.
2. A. Another matter concerning "In the wilderness" (Deut. 1:1):
    B. This teaches that they would take their little sons and daughters and toss them into Moses' bosom and say to him, "Son of Amram, 'what ration have you prepared for these? What living have you prepared for these?'"

C. R. Judah says, "Lo, Scripture says [to make this same point], 'And the children of Israel said to them, "Would that we had died by the hand of the Lord in the land of Egypt [when we sat by the fleshpots, when we ate bread . . . for you have brought us forth to this wilderness to kill the whole assembly with hunger]" (Exod. 16:3).'"

3. A. Another matter concerning "In the wilderness" (Deut. 1:1):
　 B. This encompasses everything that they had done in the wilderness.

The exposition continues, with the insertion of No. 2 as an illustration of what is at issue.

I:VI

1. A. "In the Plain" (Deut. 1:1):
　 B. This teaches that he admonished them concerning things that they had done in the Plains of Moab.
　 C. So Scripture says, "And Israel dwelt in Shittim [and the people began to commit harlotry with the daughters of Moab" (Num. 25:1).

I:VII

1. A. "Over against Suph [the sea]" (Deut. 1:1):
　 B. This teaches that he admonished them concerning things that they had done at the sea.
　 C. For they rebelled at the sea and turned their back on Moses for three journeys.

2. A. R. Judah says, "They rebelled at the sea, and they rebelled within the sea.
　 B. "And so Scripture says, 'They rebelled at the sea, even in the sea itself' (Ps. 106:7)."

3. A. Is it possible to suppose that he admonished them only at the outset of a journey? How do we know that he did so between one journey and the next?
　 B. Scripture says, "Between Paran and Tophel" (Deut. 1:1).

4. A. "Between Paran and Tophel" (Deut. 1:1):
　 B. [The word Tophel bears the sense of] disparaging words with which they disparaged the manna.
　 C. And so does Scripture say, "And our soul loathes this light bread (Num. 21:5).
　 D. [God] said to them, "Fools! Even royalty choose for themselves only light bread, so that none of them should suffer from vomiting or diarrhea. For your part, against that very act of kindness that I have done for you you bring complaints before me.
　 E. "It is only that you continue to walk in the foolishness of your father, for I said, 'I will make a help meet for him' (Gen. 2:18), while he said, 'The woman whom you gave to be with me gave me of the tree and I ate' (Gen. 3:12)."

The words of admonition, now fully exposed, apply to a variety of actions of the people. That is the main point of I:IV-VII. The matter is stated in a simple way at I:IV, V.1 (with an illustration at I:V.2), I:V.3, I:VI, I:VII. After the five illustrations of the proposition that the admonition covered the entire past, we proceed to a secondary expansion, I:VII.2, 3, which itself is amplified at I:VII.4. The main structure is clear, and the proposition is continuous with the one with which we began: Moses admonished Israel, all Israel, which could take the criticism, and covered the entire list of areas where they had sinned, which then accounts for the specification of the various locations specified by Deut. 1:1. When we realize what is to come, we understand the full power of the proposition, which in fact is syllogistic although in form merely exegetical. It is to indicate the character and encompassing program of the Book of Deuteronomy—nothing less.

I.VIII

1. A. "And Hazeroth" (Deut. 1:1):
    B. [God] said to them, "Ought you have not learned from what I did to Miriam in Hazeroth?
    C. "If to that righteous woman, Miriam, I did not show favor in judgment, all the more so to other people!"
2. A. Another matter: Now if Miriam, who gossiped only against her brother, who was younger than herself, was punished in this way, one who gossips against someone greater than himself all the more so!"
3. A. Another matter: Now if Miriam, whom when she spoke, no person heard, but only the Omnipresent alone, in line with this verse, "And the Lord heard . . ." (Num. 12:2), was punished, one who speaks ill of his fellow in public all the more so!"

The basic point is made at the outset and the case is then amplified. The sin concerning which Moses now admonished the people was that of gossiping, and the connection to Miriam is explicit. The argument that each place-name concerns a particular sin thus is carried forward. The entire discourse exhibits remarkable cogency.

I:IX

1. A. "And Dizahab (Deut. 1:1):
    B. [Since the place-name means, "of gold," what he was] saying to them [was this:] "Lo, [following Finkelstein] everything you did is forgiven. But the deed concerning the [golden] calf is worst of them all." [Hammer: "I would have overlooked everything that you have done, but the incident of the golden calf is to me worse than all the rest put together."]

2. A. R. Judah would say, "There is a parable. To what may the case be compared? To one who made a lot of trouble for his fellow. In the end he added yet another. He said to him, 'Lo, everything you did is forgiven. But this is the worst of them all.'

    B. "So said the Omnipresent to Israel, 'Lo, everything you did is forgiven. But the deed concerning the [golden] calf is worst of them all.'"

The place-name calls to mind the sin of the golden calf. This is made explicit as a generalization at No. 1, and then, at No. 2, Judah restates the matter as a story.

I:X

1. A. R. Simeon says, "There is a parable. To what may the case [of Israel's making the calf of gold] be compared? To one who extended hospitality to sages and their disciples, and everyone praised him.

    B. "Gentiles came, and he extended hospitality to them. Muggers came and he extended hospitality to them.

    C. "People said, 'That is so-and-so's nature—to extend hospitality [indiscriminately] to anyone at all.'

    D. "So did Moses say to Israel, '[Di zahab, meaning enough gold, yields the sense,] There is enough gold for the tabernacle, enough gold also for the calf!'

2. A. R. Benaiah says, "The Israelites have worshiped idolatry. Lo, they are liable to extermination. Let the gold of the tabernacle come and effect atonement for the gold of the calf."

3. A. R. Yose b. Haninah says, "'And you shall make an ark cover of pure gold' (Exod. 25:17).

    B. "Let the gold of the ark cover come and effect atonement for the gold of the calf."

4. A. R. Judah says, "Lo, Scripture states, 'In the wilderness, in the plain.'

    B. "These are the ten trials that our fathers inflicted upon the Omnipresent in the wilderness.

    C. "And these are they: two at the sea, two involving water, two involving manna, two involving quails, one involving the calf, and one involving the spies in the wilderness."

    D. Said to him R. Yose b. Dormasqit, "Judah, my honored friend, why do you distort verses of Scripture for us? I call to testify against me heaven and earth that we have made the circuit of all of these places, and each of the places is called only on account of an event that took place there [and not, as you say, to call to mind Israel's sin].

    E. "And so Scripture says, 'And the herdsmen of Gerar strove with herdsmen of Isaac, saying, "The water is ours." And he called the name of the well Esek, because "they contended with him"' (Gen. 26:20). 'And he called it Shibah' (Gen. 26:33)."

I:X.1–3 carries forward the matter of DiZahab and amplifies upon the theme, not the proposition at hand. No. 4 then presents a striking restatement of the basic proposition, which has been spelled out and restated in so many ways. It turns out that Judah takes the position implicit throughout and made explicit at **I:X.4.** There is then a contrary position, at D. We see, therefore, how the framers have drawn upon diverse materials to present a single, cogent syllogism, the one then stated in most succinct form by Judah. The contrary syllogism, that of Yose, of course is not spelled out, since amplification is hardly possible. Once we maintain that each place has meaning only for what happened in that particular spot, the verse no longer bears the deeper meaning announced at the outset—admonition or rebuke, specifically for actions that took place in various settings and that are called to mind by the list of words (no longer place-names) of Deut. 1:1.

I:XI

1. A. Along these same lines [of dispute between Judah and Yose:]
   B. R. Judah expounded, "'The burden of the word of the Lord. In the land of Hadrach, and in Damascus, shall be his resting-place, for the Lord's is the eye of man and all the tribes of Israel" (Zech. 9:1):
   C. "[Hadrach] refers to the Messiah, who is sharp [had] toward the nations, but soft [rakh] toward Israel."
   D. Said to him R. Yose b. Dormasqit, "Judah, my honored friend, why do you distort verses of Scripture for us? I call to testify against me heaven and earth that I come from Damascus, and there is a place there which is called Hadrach."
   E. He said to him, "How do you interpret the clause, 'and in Damascus, shall be his resting-place'?"
   F. [Yose] said to him, "How do we know that Jerusalem is destined to touch the city-limits of Damascus? As it is said, 'and in Damascus, shall be his resting-place.' And 'resting-place' refers only to Jerusalem, as it is said, 'This is my resting-place forever' (Ps. 132:14)."
   G. [Judah] said to him, "How then do you interpret the verse, 'And the city shall be built upon its own mound' (Jer. 30:18)?"
   H. [Yose] said to him, "That it is not destined to be moved from its place."
   I. [Yose continued,] saying to him, "How do I interpret the verse, 'And the side chambers were broader as they wound about higher and higher; for the winding about of the house went higher and higher round about the house, therefore the breadth of the house continued upward' (Ezek. 41:7)? It is that the Land of Israel is destined to expand outward on all sides like a fig tree that is narrow below and broad above. So the gates of [Jer]usalem are destined to reach Damascus.

J. "And so too Scripture says, 'Your nose is like the tower of Lebanon, which looks toward Damascus' (Song 7:5).

K. "And the exiles will come and encamp in it, as it is said, 'And in Damascus shall be his resting-place' (Zech. 9:1).

L. "And it shall come to pass in the end of days that the mountain of the Lord's house shall be established at the top of the mountains and shall be exalted above the hills, and all nations shall flow into it, and many peoples shall go and say . . .' (Isa. 2:2–3)."

I:XII

1. A. Along these same lines [of dispute between Judah and Yose:]

B. R. Judah expounded, "'And he made him to ride in the second chariot which he had, and they cried before him, "Abrech"' (Gen. 41:43):

C. "[Abrech] refers to Joseph, who is a father [ab] in wisdom but soft [rakh] in years."

D. Said to him R. Yose b. Dormasqit, "Judah, my honored friend, why do you distort verses of Scripture for us? I call to testify against me heaven and earth that the meaning of Abrech pertains to knees and is simply, 'I shall cause them to bend their knees' [appealing to the causative applied to the root for knee].

E. "For everyone came and went under his authority, as Scripture says, 'And they set him over all of Egypt' (Gen. 41:43)."

I:XI–XII simply lay out further instances of the same hermeneutical dispute between Judah and Yose. All three items—**I:X–XII**—form a single cogent dispute on its own terms. Then the composite establishes a distinct statement, which concerns figurative, as against literal, interpretation. Once worked out, the whole found an appropriate place here, at **I:X.4.** What has been said suffices to make clear, without further exposition, how people write through scripture.

THE USES OF SCRIPTURE IN THE TORAH

The one fact I have established in that authorships who wrote with scripture entered into a more complex and profound relationship with scripture than is suggested by the rubric "proof texts." To suggest that authorships intended to prove propositions by appealing to scripture obscures the nuances and depths of the conversation that they undertook with scripture. This protracted illustration of ways in which authorships write without and with scripture should not obscure the main point. When we examine the uses of scripture in documents that claim to form part of a statement that encompasses, also, scripture, we address a more profound issue. It is in two parts. First, we wish to know how, in general, the authorships of a given canon interpreted scripture within their larger systemic statement. Second, we want to find out how those same authorships proposed to make intelligible statements of their own, that is to say, the principles of rhetoric and logic to which they appealed in writing their books. Chapters 4, 5, and 6 respond to that issue.

4

Making Intelligible Statements

THE CASE OF LEVITICUS RABBAH

WRITING WITH SCRIPTURE
AND THINKING WITH SCRIPTURE

When we see people writing through scripture, we always know what they are doing, since the very form of their writing testifies to their rhetorical convention. But at a deeper level, authorships in the canon of the Judaism of the dual Torah performed a more profound act of creative encounter with scripture. They not only wrote with scripture, they also *thought* with scripture. Scripture formed a treasury of facts to be marshaled in argument; it provided a source of propositions to be shaped for vigorous advocacy; it provoked reflection on a range of theological possibilities that demanded exploration. In the compilation under study, which is Leviticus Rabbah, we deal with a biblical book to be sure. But the authorship approaches that book with a fresh plan, one in which exegesis does not dictate rhetoric and in which amplification of an established text (whether scripture or Mishnah) does not supply the underlying logic by which sentences are made to compose paragraphs and paragraphs, completed thoughts.

To state matters affirmatively, thinking with scripture, the framers of Leviticus Rabbah treat topics, not particular verses. They make generalizations that are free-standing. They express cogent propositions through extended compositions, not episodic ideas. Earlier, things people wished to say were attached to predefined statements based on an existing text, constructed in accord with an organizing logic independent of the systematic expression of a single, well-framed idea. Our rapid review of Sifré to Deuteronomy shows how bound an authorship was to the sequence of verses of Scripture—even when that authorship proposed to establish a proposition of its own. Now—in Leviticus Rabbah—the authors so collect and arrange their materials that an abstract proposition emerges. That proposition is not expressed only or mainly through episodic restatements, assigned, as we said, to an order established by a base text. Rather, it emerges through a logic of its own. What is new is the move from an exegetical mode of organizing and presenting logical discourse to a fundamentally philosophical one. It is the shift from discourse framed around an established (hence, old) text to syllogistic argument organized around a proposed (hence, new) theorem or proposition. What changes, therefore, is the way in which cogent thought takes place, as people move from discourse contingent on some prior principle of organization to discourse autonomous of a ready-made program inherited from an earlier paradigm.

A SAMPLE PARASHAH OF LEVITICUS RABBAH

Before proceeding, let me give a concrete sample of the document as a whole, with some brief discussion to give a reader a sense for how the writing works overall. Then the generalizations to follow, on how its authorship conveys intelligible statements, will prove concrete and subject to testing against an actual sample of the writing. For this purpose I present Parashah 30, in my own translation.

Leviticus Rabbah Parashah 30

XXX:I

1. A. "[On the fifteenth day of the seventh month, when you have gathered in the produce of the land, you shall keep the feast of the Lord seven days . . .] And you shall take on the first day [the fruit of goodly trees, branches of palm trees and boughs of leafy trees and willows of the brook, and you shall rejoice before the Lord your God for seven days]" (Lev. 23:39–40).

   B. R. Abba bar Kahana commenced [discourse by citing the following verse]: "Take my instruction instead of silver, [and knowledge rather than choice of gold]" (Prov. 8:10).

   C. Said R. Abba bar Kahana, "Take the instruction of the Torah instead of silver.

   D. "'Why do you weigh out money? Because there is no bread' (Isa. 55:2).

   E. "'Why do you weigh out money to the sons of Esau [Rome]? [It is because] "there is no bread," because you did not sate yourselves with the bread of the Torah.

   F. "'And [why] do you labor? Because there is no satisfaction' [Isa. 55:2].

   G. "'Why do you labor while the nations of the world enjoy plenty?' 'Because there is no satisfaction,' that is, because you have not sated yourselves with the wine of the Torah.

H. "For it is written, 'Come, eat of my bread, and drink of the wine I have mixed'" (Prov. 9:15).

2. A. R. Berekhiah and R. Hiyya, his father, in the name of R. Yos b. Nehori, said, "It is written, 'I shall punish all who oppress him' [Jer. 30:20] even those who collect funds for charity [and in doing so, treat people badly], except [for those who collect] the wages to be paid to teachers and repeaters of Mishnah traditions.

    B. "For they receive [as a salary] only compensation for the loss of their time, [which they devote to teaching and learning rather than to earning a living].

    C. "But as to the wages [for carrying out] a single matter in the Torah, no creature can pay the [appropriate] fee in reward."

3. A. It has been taught: On the New Year, a person's sustenance is decreed [for the coming year],

    B. except for what a person pays out [for food in celebration] of the Sabbath, festivals, the celebration of the New Month,

    C. and for what children bring to the house of their master [as his tuition].

    D. If he adds [to what is originally decreed], [in Heaven] they add to his [resources], but if he deducts [from what he should give], [in Heaven] they deduct [from his wealth]. [Marguiles, p. 688, n. to 1.5, links this statement to Prov. 8:10.]

4. A. R. Yohanan was going up from Tiberias to Sepphoris. R. Hiyya bar Abba was supporting him. They came to a field. He said, "This field once belonged to me, but I sold it in order to acquire merit in the Torah."

    B. They came to a vineyard, and he said, "This vineyard once belonged to me, but I sold it in order to acquire merit in the Torah."

    C. They came to an olive grove, and he said, "This olive grove once belonged to me, but I sold it in order to acquire merit in the Torah."

    D. R. Hiyya began to cry.

    E. Said R. Yohanan, "Why are you crying?"

    F. He said to him, "It is because you left nothing over to support you in your old age."

    G. He said to him, "Hiyya, my disciple, is what I did such a light thing in your view? I sold something which was given in a spell of six days [of creation] and in exchange I acquired something which was given in a spell of forty days [of revelation].

    H. "The entire world and everything in it was created in only six days, as it is written, 'For in six days the Lord made heaven and earth' [Exod. 20:11].

    I. "But the Torah was given over a period of forty days, as it was said, 'And he was there with the Lord for forty days and forty nights' [Exod. 34:28].

J.   "And it is written, 'And I remained on the mountain for forty days and forty nights'" (Deut. 9:9).

5.   A.   When R. Yohanan died, his generation recited concerning him [the following verse of Scripture]: "If a man should give all the wealth of his house for the love" (Song 8:7), with which R. Yohanan loved the Torah, "he would be utterly destitute" (Song 8:7).

B.   When R. Hoshaiah of Tiria died, they saw his bier flying in the air. His generation recited concerning him [the following verse of Scripture]: "If a man should give all the wealth of his house for the love," with which the Holy One, blessed be he, loved Abba Hoshaiah of Tiria, "he would be utterly destitute" (Song 8:7).

C.   When R. Eleazar b. R. Simeon died, his generation recited concerning him [the following verse of Scripture]: "Who is this who comes up out of the wilderness like pillars of smoke, perfumed with myrrh and frankincense, with all the powders of the merchant?" (Song 3:6).

D.   What is the meaning of the clause, "With all the powders of the merchant"?

E.   [Like a merchant who carries all sorts of desired powders,] he was a master of Scripture, a repeater of Mishnah traditions, a writer of liturgical supplications, and a poet.

6.   A.   Said R. Abba bar Kahana, "On the basis of the reward paid for one act of 'taking,' you may assess the reward for [taking] the palm branch [on the festival of Tabernacles].

B.   "There was an act of taking in Egypt: 'You will take a bunch of hyssop' [Exod. 12:22].

C.   "And how much was it worth? Four *manehs*.

D.   "Yet that act of taking is what made Israel inherit the spoil at the sea, the spoil of Sihon and Og, and the spoil of the thirty-one kings.

E.   "Now the palm-branch, which costs a person such a high price, and which involves so many religious duties—how much the more so [will a great reward be forthcoming on its account]!"

F.   Therefore Moses admonished Israel, saying to them, "And you shall take on the first day . . ." (Lev. 23:40).

1.B seems to me to employ Isa. 55:2 as an intersecting verse for the base verse of Prov. 8:10. That, at any rate, is the force of the exegesis of 1.C–G. Then the citation of Prov. 9:5 presents a secondary expansion of what has been said about Isa. 55:2; that is, 1.F–G lead us directly to H. What has happened to Lev. 23:39? In fact, 1.B–H are inserted whole because of the use of the key word, "take," at Lev. 23:39 and Prov. 8:10. From that point, Lev. 23:39 plays no role whatsoever. It is only at No. 6 that Lev. 23:39—with stress on the word "take"—recurs. The theme of the intervening passages is established in 1.B; namely, Torah and the value and importance of study of Torah. Nos. 2, 3, 4, and 5 all present variations on amplifications of that theme. I cannot follow Margulies in linking No. 3 to the intersecting verse. No. 5 is attached because of No. 4, and No. 4 because of its homily on the Torah. Since No. 6 ignores all that has gone before, and since No. 6 alone alludes to 1.A, we have to regard as remarkable the insertion of the rather sizable construction, 1.B through 5.E. In some other passages we see subtle connections between the base verse or, at least, the theme of the base verse, and the exegesis of the intersecting verse, and the secondary exegetical expansions of verses introduced in connection with the intersecting one. But here I see none. Even the key word "take" does not recur beyond the intersecting verse. So the editorial principle accounting for the inclusion of 1.B–5.E is the occurrence of a single shared word, that alone. That seems to me uncommon in our document. As to No. 6, of course, the homily rests on the key word "take" and that is made explicit. But No. 6 does not rest upon the exegesis of any intersecting verse; it is a simple exegetical homily. 6.F, of course, is secondary, a redactional filling we shall see again.

XXX:II

1. A. "You show me the path of life, [in your presence] there is fullness of joy" (Ps. 16:11).

   B. Said David before the Holy One, blessed be he, "Show me the open gateway to the life of the world to come."

2. A. R. Yudan said, "David said before the Holy One, blessed be he, 'Lord of the ages, "Show me the path of life."'"

   B. "Said the Holy One, blessed be he, to David, 'If you seek life, look for fear, as it is said, "The fear of the Lord prolongs life"'" (Prov. 10:27).

   C. R. Azariah said, "The Holy One, blessed be he, said to David, 'David, if you seek life, look for suffering (YYSWRYN), as it is said, "The reproofs of discipline (MWSR) are the way of life"'" (Prov. 6:23).

   D. Rabbis say, "The Holy One, blessed be he, said to David, 'David, if you seek life, look for Torah,' as it is said, 'It is a tree of life to those that hold fast to it'" (Prov. 3:18).

   E. R. Abba said, "David said before the Holy One, blessed be he, 'Lord of the ages, "Show me the path of life."'"

   F. "Said to him the Holy One, blessed be he, 'Start fighting and exert yourself! Why are you puzzled? [Lieberman, p. 880, to p. 692]. Work and eat: "Keep my commandments and live"'" (Prov. 4:4).

3. A. "The fullness (SWB') of joy" (Ps. 16:11):

   B. Satisfy (SB'NW) us with five joys: Scripture, Mishnah, Talmud, Supplements, and Lore.

4. A. Another matter: "In your presence is the fullness of joy" (Ps. 16:11):

    B.   Read not "fullness (SWB')" but "seven (SB')." These are the seven groups of righteous men who are going to receive the face of the Presence of God.

    C.   And their face is like the sun, moon, firmament, stars, lightning, lilies, and the pure candelabrum that was in the house of the sanctuary.

    D.   How do we know that it is like the sun? As it is said, "Clear as the sun" (Song 6:10).

    E.   How do we know that it is like the moon? As it is said, "As lovely as the moon" (Song 6:10).

    F.   How do we know that it is like the firmament? As it is said, "And they that are wise shall shine as the brightness of the firmament" (Dan. 12:3).

    G.   How do we know that it is like the stars? As it is said, "And they that turn the many to righteousness as the stars forever and ever" (Dan. 12:3).

    H.   And how do we know that it is like the lightning? As it is said, "Their appearance is like torches, they run to and fro like lightning" (Nah. 2:5).

    I.   How do we know that it is like lilies? As it is said, "For the leader: upon the lilies" (Ps. 80:1).

    J.   How do we know that it will be like the pure candelabrum? As it is said, "And he said to me, 'What do you see?' And I said, 'I looked and behold [there was] a candelabrum all of gold'" (Zech. 4:2).

5.   A.   "At your right hand is bliss for evermore" (Ps. 16:11).

    B.   Said David before the Holy One, blessed be he, "Lord of the ages, now who will tell me which group is the most beloved and blissful of them all?"

    C.   There were two Amoras [who differed on this matter]. One of them said, "It is the group that comes as representative of the Torah and commandments, as it is said, 'With a flaming fire at his right hand'" (Deut. 33:2).

    D.   And the other said, "This refers to the scribes, the Mishnah repeaters, and those who teach children in their fear, who are going to stand at the right hand of the Holy One, blessed be he.

    E.   "That is in line with the following verse of Scripture: 'I keep the Lord always before me, because he is at my right hand, I shall not be moved'" (Ps. 16:8).

    F.   "[You show me the path of life, in your presence there is fullness of joy,] in your right hand are pleasures for evermore'" (Ps. 16:11).

6.   A.   Another matter: "You show me the path of life" (Ps. 16:11) speaks of Israel.

    B.   Israel stated before the Holy One, blessed be he, "Lord of the ages, 'Show me the path of life.'"

    C.   Said to them the Holy One, blessed be he, "Lo, you have the ten days of repentance between the New Year and the Day of Atonement."

7.   A.   "In your presence there is fullness (SWB') of joy" (Ps. 16:11):

B. Read only "seven (SB‘) joys." These are the seven religious duties associated with the Festival [Tabernacles].

C. These are they: the four species that are joined in the palm branch, [the building of] the Tabernacle, [the offering of] the festal sacrifice, [the offering of] the sacrifice of rejoicing.

8. A. What is the meaning of the phrase, "In your right hand are pleasures for evermore (NSH)" (Ps. 16:11)?

B. Said R. Abin, "This refers to the palm branch. It is comparable with one who is victor (NWSH) and so takes the branch as [a sign of his victory].

C. "The matter may be compared with two who came before a judge. Now we do not know which one of them is the victor. But it is the one who takes the palm branch in his hand who we know to be the victor.

D. "So is the case of Israel and the nations of the world. The [latter] come and draw an indictment before the Holy One, blessed be he, on the New Year, and we do not know which party is victor.

E. "But when Israel goes forth from before the Holy One, blessed be he, with their palm branches and their citrons in their hands, we know that it is Israel that are the victors."

F. Therefore Moses admonishes Israel, saying to them, "And you shall take on the first day . . . [branches of palm trees]" (Lev. 23:40).

The base verse is not explicitly cited, but the interesting verse—Ps. 16:11—leads us to it, after a long and majestic sequence of exegeses of the three elements of the intersecting verse. When we do reach the base verse, the connection turns out to be tight and persuasive. Nos. 6–8 show us the ideal form, that is, a clause-by-clause reading of the intersecting verse within a coherent hermeneutic. If then we look back to the earlier materials, Nos. 2–5, we find a somewhat less cogent exegesis of the three clauses. No. 2 reads the verse as a statement by David. No. 4 would look to be interpolated, were it not for No. 5, which brings us back to David, and that refers to the materials exposition of No. 4. Then the original repertoire of key words—Torah, commandments, and the like—is reviewed. Nos. 6–8 go over the same verse with respect to Israel, introducing the matter of the New Year, Day of Atonement, and Festival. Then each clause suitably links to the several themes at hand. 8.F of course is tacked on.

XXX:III

1. A. "He will regard the prayer of the destitute [and will not despise their supplication]" (Ps. 102:17).

B. Said R. Abin, "We are unable to make sense of David's character. Sometimes he calls himself king, and sometimes he calls himself destitute.

C. "How so? When he foresaw that righteous men were going to come from him, such as Asa, Jehoshaphat, Hezekiah, and Josiah, he would call himself king as it is said, 'Give the king your judgments, O God' [Ps. 72:1].

D.   "When he foresaw that wicked men would come forth from him, for example, Ahaz, Manasseh, and Amon, he would call himself destitute, as it is said, 'A prayer of one afflicted, when he is faint [and pours out his complaint before the Lord]' [Ps. 102:1].

2.   A.   R. Alexandri interpreted the cited verse (Ps. 102:1) to speak of a worker. [The one afflicted is the worker. The word for faint, 'TP, bears the meaning cloak oneself, hence, in prayer. The worker then has delayed his prayer, waiting for the overseer to leave, at which point he can stop and say his prayer. So he postpones his prayer (Margulies).] [So Alexandri says], "Just as a worker sits and watches all day long for when the overseer will leave for a bit, so he is late when he says [his prayer], [so David speaks at Ps. 102:1: 'Hear my prayer, O Lord; let my cry come to you']."

B.   "That [interpretation of the word 'TP] is in line with the use in the following verse: 'And those that were born late belonged to Laban'" (Gen. 30:42).

C.   What is the meaning of "those that were born late"?

D.   R. Isaac bar Haqolah said, "The ones that tarried."

3.   A.   Another interpretation: "He will regard the prayer of the destitute individual [and will not despise their supplication]" (Ps. 102:17):

B.   Said R. Simeon b. Laqish, "As to this verse, the first half of it is not consistent with the second half, and vice versa.

C.   "If it is to be, 'He will regard the prayer of the destitute [individual],' he should then have said, 'And will not despise his supplication.'

D.   "But if it is to be, 'He will not despise their supplication,' then he should have said, 'He will regard the prayer of those who are destitute.'

E.   "But [when David wrote,] 'He will regard the prayer of the individual destitute,' this [referred to] the prayer of Manasseh, king of Judah.

F.   "And [when David wrote,] 'He will not despise their supplication,' this [referred to] his prayer and the prayer of his fathers.

G.   "That is in line with the following verse of Scripture: 'And he prayed to him, and he was entreated (Y'TR) of him'" (2 Chron. 33:13).

H.   What is the meaning of the phrase, "He was entreated of him"?

I.   Said R. Eleazar b. R. Simeon, "In Arabia they call a breach an athirta [so an opening was made for his prayer to penetrate to the Throne of God]" (Slotki, p. 385 n. 3).

J.   "And he brought him back to Jerusalem, his kingdom" (2 Chron. 33:13).

K.   How did he bring him back?

L.   R. Samuel b. R. Jonah said in the name of R. Aha, "He brought him back with a wind.

M. "That is in line with the phrase, 'He causes the wind to blow.'"

N. At that moment: "And Manasseh knew that the Lord is God" (2 Chron. 33:13). Then Manasseh said, "There is justice and there is a judge."

4. A. Another interpretation: "He will regard the prayer of the destitute" (Ps. 102:17) refers to the generation of Mordecai.

B. "And will not despise their supplication"—for he did not despise either his prayer or the prayer of his fathers.

5. A. R. Isaac interpreted the verse to speak of these generations that have neither king nor prophet, neither priest nor Urim and Thummim, but who have only this prayer alone.

B. "Said David before the Holy One, blessed be he, 'Lord of the ages, "Do not despise their prayer. 'Let this be recorded for a generation to come'" [Ps. 102:18].'

C. "On the basis of that statement, [we know that] the Holy One, blessed be he, accepts penitents.

D. "'So that a people yet unborn may praise the Lord' [Ps. 102:18].

E. "For the Holy One, blessed be he, will create them as a new act of creation."

6. A. Another interpretation: "Let this be recorded for a generation to come" (Ps. 102:18):

B. This refers to the generation of Hezekiah, which was tottering toward death.

C. "So that a people yet unborn may praise the Lord" (Ps. 102:18): for the Holy One, blessed be he, created them in a new act of creation.

7. A. Another interpretation: "Let this be recorded for a generation to come" (Ps. 102:18);

B. This refers to the generation of Mordecai, which was tottering toward death.

C. "So that a people yet unborn may praise the Lord" (Ps. 102:18): for the Holy One, blessed be he, created them in a new act of creation.

8. A. Another interpretation: "Let this be recorded for a generation to come" (Ps. 102:18):

B. This refers to these very generations, which are tottering to death.

C. "So that a people yet unborn may praise the Lord" (Ps. 102:18):

D. For the Holy One, blessed be he, is going to create them anew, in a new act of creation.

9. A. What do we have to do [in order to reach that end]? Take up the palm branch and citron and praise the Holy One, blessed be he.

B. Therefore Moses admonishes Israel, saying, "You shall take on the first day . . ." (Lev. 23:30).

Until the very final lines, No. 9, we have no reason at all to associate the exegesis of Ps. 102:17–18 with the theme of the Festival. On the contrary, all the materials stand autonomous of the present "base verse," and none of them hints at what is to come at the end. On that basis I regard the construction as complete prior to its insertion here, with a redactional hand contributing only No. 9 to validate the inclusion of an otherwise irrelevant exegetical exercise. The established pattern—the tripartite exegesis of Ps. 102:17, 18—is worked out at No. 1 (supplemented by Nos. 2 and 3), then Nos. 4–8.

XXX:IV

1. A.   "'Let the field exult and everything in it.' [Then shall all the trees of the wood sing for joy before the Lord, for he comes, for he comes to judge the earth]" (Ps. 96:12–13).

    B.   "Let the field exult" refers to the world, as it is said, "And it came to pass, when they were in the field" (Gen. 4:8) [and determined to divide up the world between them].

    C.   "And everything in it" refers to creatures.

    D.   That is in line with the following verse of Scripture: "The earth is the Lord's, and all that is in it" (Ps. 24:1).

    E.   "Then shall all the trees of the wood sing for joy" (Ps. 96:12).

    F.   Said R. Aha, "The forest and all the trees of the forest.

    G.   "The forest refers to fruit-bearing trees.

    H.   "'And all the trees of the forest' encompasses those trees that do not bear fruit."

    I.   Before whom? "Before the Lord" (Ps. 96:14).

    J.   Why? "For he comes" on New Year and on the Day of Atonement.

    K.   To do what? "To judge the earth: He will judge the world with righteousness, and the peoples with his truth" (Ps. 96:13).

    L.   On that basis what do we have to do? We take a citron, boughs of leafy trees, a palm branch, and a willow [branch], and give praise before the Holy One, blessed be he: "And you shall take on the first day . . ." (Lev. 23:40).

Ps. 96:12–14 supplies direct connections to the theme of Tabernacles, with its reference to trees of the wood, exultation and rejoicing, judgment, and the like. These topics are explicitly read into the intersecting verse at the end, but I am inclined to see the whole as a single and unified construction, with 1.F–H as an interpolated comment.

XXX:V

1. A.   "I wash my hands in innocence [and go about your altar, O Lord, singing aloud a song of thanksgiving, and telling all your wondrous deeds]" (Ps. 26:6–7).

    B.   [What I require I acquire] through purchase, not theft.

    C.   For we have learned there: "A stolen or dried up palm branch is invalid. And one deriving from an *asherah* or an apostate town is invalid" (M. Suk. 3:1A–B).

D. "And go about your altar, O Lord" (Ps. 26:7).
E. That is in line with what we have learned there (M. Suk. 4:5): Every day they circumambulate the altar one time and say, "We beseech you, O Lord, save now. We beseech you, O Lord, make us prosper now" [Ps. 118:25]. R. Judah says, "I and him, save now." On that day they circumambulate the altar seven times.

2. A. "Singing aloud a song of thanksgiving" (Ps. 26:7)—this refers to the offerings.
B. "And telling all your wondrous deeds" (Ps. 26:7):
C. Said R. Abin, "This refers to the *Hallel* Psalms [Pss. 113—18], which contain [praise for what God has done] in the past, also [what he has done] during these generations, as well as what will apply to the days of the Messiah, to the time of Gog and Magog, and to the age to come.
D. "'When Israel went forth from Egypt' [Ps. 114:1] refers to the past.
E. "'Not for us, O Lord, not for us' [Ps. 115:1] refers to the present generations.
F. "'I love for the Lord to hear' [Ps. 116:1] refers to the days of the Messiah.
G. "'All the nations have encompassed me' [Ps. 118:10] speaks of the time of Gog and Magog.
H. "'You are my God and I shall exalt you' [Ps. 118:28] speaks of the age to come."

No. 1 makes a point quite distinct from No. 2. "The innocence" of Ps. 26:6 refers to the fact that one must not steal the objects used to carry out the religious duty of the waving of the palm branch at Tabernacles. I assume that the allusion to Tabernacles in Ps. 26:6–7 is found in the referring to circumambulating the altar, such as is done in the rite on that day, as 1.C makes explicit. No. 2 then expands on the cited verse in a different way. To be sure, the *Hallel* Psalms are recited on Tabernacles, but they serve all other festivals as well. Only No. 1 therefore relates to the established context of Lev. 23:40. It follows that the exegeses of Ps. 26:6–7 were assembled and only then utilized—both the relevant and the irrelevant parts—for the present purpose.

XXX:VI

1. A. "And you will take for yourselves" (Lev. 23:40).
B. R. Hiyya taught, "[You take the required species] through purchase and not through thievery."
C. "For yourselves"—for every one of you. They must be yours and not stolen.
2. A. Said R. Levi, "One who takes a stolen palm branch—to what is he comparable? To a thief who sat at the crossroads and mugged passersby.

B. "One time a legate came by, to collect the taxes for that town. [The thug] rose before him and mugged him and took everything he had. After some time the thug was caught and put in prison. The legate heard and came to him. He said to him, 'Give back what you grabbed from me, and I'll argue in your behalf before the king.'

C. "He said to him, 'Of everything that I robbed and of everything that I took, I have nothing except for this rug that is under me, and it belongs to you.'

D. "He said to him, 'Give it to me, and I'll argue in your behalf before the king.'

E. "He said to him, 'Take it.'

F. "He said to him, 'You should know that tomorrow you are going before the king for judgment, and he will ask you and say to you, "Is there anyone who can argue in your behalf," and you may say to him, "I have the legate, Mr. So-and-so, to speak in my behalf," and he will send and call me, and I shall come and argue in your behalf before him.'

G. "The next day they set him up for judgment before the king. The king asked him, saying to him, 'Do you have anyone to argue in your behalf?'

H. "He said to him, 'I have a legate, Mr. So-and-so, to speak in my behalf.'

I. "The king sent for him. He said to him, 'Do you know anything to say in behalf of this man?'

J. "He said to him, 'I do indeed have knowledge. When you sent me to collect the taxes of that town, he rose up before me and mugged me and took everything that I had. That rug that belongs to me gives testimony against him.'

K. "Everyone began to cry out, saying, 'Woe for this one, whose defense attorney has turned into his prosecutor.'

L. "So a person acquires a palm branch to attain merit through it. But if it was a stolen one, [the branch] cries out before the Holy One, blessed be he, 'I am stolen! I am taken by violence.'

M. "And the ministering angels say, 'Woe for this one, whose defense attorney has turned into his prosecutor!'"

The theme of the preceding, the prohibition against using a stolen palm branch, is given two further treatments. Except in a formal way, none of this pretends to relate to the specific verses of Lev. 23:40ff., nor do we find an intersecting verse.

XXX:VII

1. A. "[On the fifteenth day of the seventh month, when you have gathered the produce of the land, you shall keep the feast of the Lord seven days;] on the first day [shall be a solemn rest]" (Lev. 23:40).

B. This in fact is the fifteenth day, yet you speak of the first day!

C. R. Mana of Sheab and R. Joshua of Sikhnin in the name of R. Levi said, "The matter may be compared with the case of a town that owed arrears to the king, so the king went to collect [what was owing]. [When he had reached] ten *mils* [from the town], the great men of the town came forth and praised him. He remitted a third of their [unpaid] tax. When he came within five *mils* of the town, the middle-rank people came out and acclaimed him, so he remitted yet another third [of what was owning to him]. When he entered the town, men, women, and children, came forth and praised him. He remitted the whole [of the tax].

D. "Said the king, 'What happened happened. From now on we shall begin keeping books [afresh].'

E. "So on the eve of the New Year, the great men of the generation fast, and the Holy One, blessed be he, remits a third of their [that is, Israel's] sins. From the New Year to the Day of Atonement outstanding individuals fast, and the Holy One, blessed be he, remits a third of their [that is, Israel's] sins. On the Day of Atonement all of them fast, men, women, and children, so the Holy One, blessed be he, says to Israel, 'What happened happened. From now on we shall begin keeping books [afresh].'"

2. A. Said R. Aha, "'For with you there is forgiveness' [Ps. 80:4]. From the New Year forgiveness awaits you.

B. "Why so long? 'So that you may be feared' [Ps. 80:4]. To put your fear into creatures.

C. "From the Day of Atonement to the Festival, all the Israelites are kept busy with doing religious duties. This one takes up the task of building his tabernacle, that one preparing his palm branches. On the first day of the Festival, all Israel stand before the Holy One, blessed be he, with their palm branches and citrons in their hands, praising the name of the Holy One, blessed be he. The Holy One, blessed be he, says to them, 'What happened happened. From now on we shall begin keeping books [afresh].'"

D. Therefore Moses admonished Israel: "And you shall take on the first day . . ." (Lev. 23:40).

Nos. 1 and 2 go over the same matter. It seems to me that Aha's version puts into concrete terms the basic point of Levi's. 2.D is out of place, since it ignores the antecedent materials and takes as its proof text a formula in no way important in the preceding. Once more the ultimate redactor's hand is in evidence.

XXX:VIII

1. A. "On the first day" (Lev. 23:40):

B. By day and not by night.

C. "On the . . . day"—even on the Sabbath.

D. "On the *first* day"—only the first day [of the Festival] overrides the restrictions [of Sabbath rest. When the Sabbath coincides with other than the first day of the Festival, one does not carry the palm branch.]

2. A. "[And you shall take . . .] the fruit of a goodly tree [branches of palm trees and boughs of leafy trees and willows of the brook]" (Lev. 23:40).

B. R. Hiyya taught, "'A tree': the taste of the wood and fruit of which is the same. This is the citron."

C. "Goodly (HDR): Ben Azzai said, "[Fruit] that remains [HDR] on its tree from year to year."

D. Aqilas the proselyte translated [HDR] as, "That which dwells by water (Greek: *hudor*)."

E. "Branches of a palm tree" (Lev. 23:40): R. Tarfon says, "[As to branch of palm tree (KPWT)], it must be bound. If it was separated, one has to bind it up."

F. "Boughs of leafy trees:" The branches of which cover over the wood. One has to say, "This is the myrtle."

G. "Willows of the brook:" I know only that they must come from a brook. How do I know that those that come from a valley or a hill [also are valid]? Scripture says, "*And* willows of a brook."

H. Abba Saul says, "'*And* willows of the brook' refers to the requirement that there be two, one willow for the palm branch, and a willow for the sanctuary."

I. R. Ishmael says, "'The fruit of goodly trees' indicates one; 'branches of palm tree' also one; 'boughs of leafy trees,' three; 'willows of the brook,' two. Two [of the myrtles] may have the twigs trimmed at the top, and one may not."

J. R. Tarfon says, "Even all three of them may be trimmed."

We have a mass of exegetical materials, linking laws of the Festival to the verses of scripture at hand. No. 1 conducts an inquiry into law, and No. 2 provides a word-for-word exegesis of the cited verse.

XXX:IX

1. A. Another interpretation: "The fruit of goodly (HDR) trees:" this refers to the Holy One, blessed be he, concerning whom it is written, "You are clothed with glory and majesty (HDR)" (Ps. 104:1).

B. "Branches of palm trees:" this refers to the Holy One, blessed be he, concerning whom it is written, "The Righteous One shall flourish like a palm tree" (Ps. 92:13).

C. "Boughs of leafy trees:" this refers to the Holy One, blessed be he, concerning whom it is written, "And he stands among the leafy trees" (Zech. 1:8).

D. "And willows of the brook:" this refers to the Holy One, blessed be he, concerning whom it is written, "Extol him who rides upon the willows, whose name is the Lord" (Ps. 68:5).

The base text is systematically read in line with intersecting verses referring to God. The species are read as symbolizing, in sequence, God, the patriarchs and matriarchs, Torah institutions, and Israel.

XXX:X

1. A. Another interpretation: "The fruit of goodly (HDR) trees" (Lev. 23:40):
    B. This refers to Abraham, whom the Holy One, blessed be he, honored (HDR) with a goodly old age,
    C. as it is said, "And Abraham was an old man, coming along in years" (Gen. 24:1).
    D. And it is written, "And you will honor (HDR) the face of an old man" (Lev. 19:32).
    E. "Branches (KPWT) of palm trees" (Lev. 23:40):
    F. This refers to Isaac, who was tied (KPWT) and bound upon the altar.
    G. "And boughs of leafy trees" (Lev. 23:40):
    H. This refers to Jacob. Just as a myrtle is rich in leaves, so Jacob was rich in children.
    I. "Willows of the brook" (Lev. 23:40):
    J. This refers to Joseph. Just as the willow wilts before the other three species do, so Joseph died before his brothers did.
2. A. Another interpretation: "The fruit of goodly trees" (Lev. 23:40):
    B. This refers to Sarah, whom the Holy One, blessed be he, honored with a goodly old age, as it is said, "And Abraham and Sarah were old" (Gen. 18:11).
    C. "Branches of palm trees" (Lev. 23:40): this refers to Rebecca. Just as a palm tree contains both edible fruit and thorns, so Rebecca produced a righteous and a wicked son [Jacob and Esau].
    D. "Boughs of leafy trees" (Lev. 23:40): this refers to Leah. Just as a myrtle is rich in leaves, so Leah was rich in children.
    E. "And willows of the brook" (Lev. 23:40): this refers to Rachel. Just as the willow wilts before the other three species do, so Rachel died before her sister.

The powerful result of the exegesis is to link the species of the Festival to the patriarchs and matriarchs of Israel. It is continuous with the foregoing, linking the species to God, and with what is to follow, as the species will be compared with Israel's leadership, on the one side, as well, finally, to ordinary people, on the other.

XXX:XI

1. A. Another interpretation: "The fruit of goodly trees" (Lev. 23:40): this refers to the great Sanhedrin of Israel, which the Holy One, blessed be he, honored (HDR) with old age, as it is said, "You will rise up before old age" (Lev. 19:32).

B. "Branches (KPWT) of palm trees" (Lev. 23:40): this refers to disciples of sages, who compel (KWPYN) themselves to study Torah from one another.

C. "Boughs of leafy trees:" this refers to the three rows of disciples who sit before them.

D. "And willows of the brook" (Lev. 23:40): this refers to the court scribes, who stand before them, one on the right side, the other on the left, and write down the opinions of those who vote to acquit and those who vote to convict.

The reading of the symbols of the Festival as a parable of Israel's life continues, as noted above, now with reference to the (imaginary) national government.

XXX:XII

1. A. Another interpretation: "The fruit of goodly trees" refers to Israel.

B. Just as a citron has both taste and fragrance, so in Israel are people who have [the merit of both] Torah and good deeds.

C. "Branches of palm trees" (Lev. 23:30): refers to Israel. Just as a palm has a taste but no fragrance, so in Israel are people who have [the merit of] Torah but not of good deeds.

D. "Boughs of leafy trees:" refers to Israel. Just as a myrtle has a fragrance but no taste, so in Israel are people who have the merit of good deeds but not of Torah.

E. "Willows of the brook:" refers to Israel. Just as a willow has neither taste nor fragrance, so in Israel are those who have the [merit] neither of Torah nor of good deeds.

F. What does the Holy One, blessed be he, do for them? Utterly to destroy them is not possible.

G. Rather, said the Holy One, blessed be he, "Let them all be joined together in a single bond, and they will effect atonement for one another.

H. "And if you have done so, at that moment I shall be exalted."

I. That is in line with the following verse of Scripture: "He who builds his upper chambers in heaven" (Amos 9:6).

J. And when is he exalted? When they are joined together in a single bond, as it is said, "When he has founded his bond upon the earth" (Amos 9:6).

K. Therefore Moses admonishes Israel: "And you shall take . . ." (Lev. 23:40).

The final exegesis reaches its climax here, concluding, then, with the redactional subscript. The composition follows a single program, beginning to end, as it rehearses the several intersecting realms of Judaic symbol systems. Always at the climax come Torah and good deeds. 1.K is tacked on.

XXX:XIII

1. A.   R. Judah in the name of R. Simeon b. Pazzi commenced [discourse by citing the following verse of Scripture:] "'Hear my son and take my sayings' [Prov. 4:10].

    B.   "[God speaks,] 'Many acts of taking have I commanded you, so as to give you opportunities for attaining merit.

    C.   "'I said to you, "That they take for you a red cow" [Num. 19:2]. Now could it be for my sake? No. It is in order to purify you, as it is said, "And the clean person will sprinkle the unclean" (Num. 19:19).

    D.   "'I said to you, "And they shall take up heave offering for me" (Exod. 25:2). Is it not so that I might dwell with you: "And make me a sanctuary"' (Exod. 25:8).

    E.   "It is as if the Holy One, blessed be he, had said, 'Take me and I shall dwell among you.' It is not written here, 'And they will take up heave offering,' but rather, 'And they shall take up heave offering for me.' [That is to say,] 'It is I whom you are taking.'

    F.   "'I said to you, "And you shall take for yourself pure olive oil, beaten for the light" [Exod. 27:20]. Now do I really need light from you? Is it not the case that "Light dwells with him" [Dan. 2:22]. But it was in order to give you the opportunity to attain merit and to effect atonement for your souls, which are compared with light, as it is written, "God is the light for the soul of man" (Prov. 20:27).

    G.   "'And now I have said to you, "And you shall take for yourself on the first day . . ."' (Lev. 23:40), so as to give you the opportunity to attain merit for yourself, to bring down rain for you.'

    H.   "On that account it is said, 'And you will take for yourself . . .'" (Lev. 23:40).

Simeon b. Pazzi's catalogue of commandments introduced by the word "take" makes the point that, in each case, the act of taking benefits the one who does it, specifying the particular benefit in each instance, and so too with respect to Tabernacles.

XXX:XIV

1. A.   Another interpretation: "And you will take for yourself" (Lev. 23:40):

    B.   R. Mani opened [discourse by citing the following verse of Scripture:] "'All my bones shall say, ["Lord, who is like you"]' [Ps. 35:10].

    C.   "This verse is stated only on account of the palm branch.

    D.   "The spine of the palm branch is like the spinal column of a man.

    E.   "The [leaf of the] myrtle is like the eye, the willow, the mouth, the citron, the heart.

F. "Said David, 'None among all the limbs is of greater importance than these, which outweigh the entire body.'

G. "Accordingly, [with the species of the Festival], 'All my bones shall say . . .'" (Ps. 35:10).

The species are now made to serve as an analogy for the human body, so that, when a person takes them up on the Festival, it is as if the entire body praises God. Psalm 35:10 is not subjected to extensive exegesis on its own terms, leading us back to the base verse, so we cannot cite this as an example of an intersecting base verse construction.

XXX:XV

1. A. Another matter: Despite all that wisdom which is ascribed to Solomon, "Wisdom and knowledge are granted to you" (2 Chron. 1:12), "And Solomon's wisdom excelled" (1 Kings 5:10), "For he was wiser than all men" (1 Kings 5:11), [Solomon] sat and pondered these four species.

B. For it is said, "There are three things which are too wonderful for me" (Prov. 30:18), the Passover, unleavened bread, bitter herbs.

C. "And four which I do not know" (Prov. 30:18), that is, the four species, [the meaning of] which he sought to fathom.

D. [Solomon said], "'The fruit of goodly trees' [Lev. 23:40]: Who can say that this is the citron? Every tree produces goodly fruit.

E. "'Branches of palm trees' [Lev. 23:40]: The Torah has said, 'Take two branches of palm trees with which to give praise, and a person takes only the palm branch, the core of the palm tree [alone].'

F. "'And boughs of leafy trees' [Lev. 23:40]: Who can tell me that it is a myrtle? Lo, it says elsewhere, 'Go to the mountain and fetch olive branches, oil-tree branches, myrtle branches' [Neh. 8:15].

G. "'Willows of the brook' [Lev. 23:40]: All trees grow by water.

H. "[Thus"] 'Four which I do not know'" (Prov. 30:18).

I. [Then] he went and mentioned them elsewhere, [for it says,] "They are three which are stately in their march, and four which are stately in going" (Prov. 30:29).

J. Four refers to the four species that every Israelite runs to purchase in order to give praise to the Holy One, blessed be he.

K. Now they appear to be small things in peoples' sight, but they are great before the Holy One, blessed be he.

L. And who explained to Israel that these four species are, in fact, the citron, the palm branch, the myrtle, and the willow?

M. It was the sages (HKMYM), as it was said, "They are exceedingly wise (HKMYM)" (Prov. 30:24).

The exegetical question of how do we know scripture speaks of the particular species that are required is framed in a dramatic setting. The question is phrased in a strong way, first in relationship to Prov. 30:18 for the symbols of Passover and Tabernacles, then in a specific argument applied to Lev. 23:40. The answer proves less concrete than the question, Prov. 30:29 providing little help. Then the final answer derives from Prov. 30:24, placing the entire matter in the lap of sages.

XXX:XVI

1. A.   R. Berekhiah in the name of R. Levi: "[God speaks], 'Through the merit [attained in fulfilling the commandment], "And you will take for yourself on the first day . . ." [Lev. 23:40], lo, I shall be revealed to you first; I shall exact punishment for you from the first one; I shall build for you first; and bring to you the first one.'"

   B.   "'I shall be revealed for you first,' as it is said, 'I the Lord am first' [Isa. 41:4].

   C.   "'I shall exact punishment for you from the first one' refers to the wicked Esau, as it is written, 'And the red one came forth first' [Gen. 24:24].

   D.   "'And I shall build for you first' refers to the house of the sanctuary, concerning which it is written, 'You throne of glory, on high from the first' [Jer. 17:12].

   E.   "And I shall bring to you the first one, namely, the king messiah, concerning whom it is written, 'The first to Zion I shall give'" (Isa. 41:27).

The eschatological-salvific character of the Festival is now spelled out in specific detail. Esau, that is, Rome, will be punished, the Temple will be rebuilt, and the Messiah will come, all by virtue of the merit attained in observing the Festival. Now to generalize on the results of this survey of one concrete discourse.

IMPLICIT PROPOSITIONS IN LEVITICUS RABBAH

Accordingly, when we listen to the framers of Leviticus Rabbah, we see how statements in the document at hand thus become intelligible not contingently, that is, on the strength of an established text, but a priori, that is, on the basis of a deeper logic of meaning and an independent principle of rhetorical intelligibility. How so? Leviticus Rabbah is topical, not exegetical. Each of its 37 *parashiyyot* pursues its given topic and develops points relevant to that topic. It is logical, in that (to repeat) discourse appeals to an underlying principle of composition and intelligibility, and that logic inheres in what is said. Logic is what joins one sentence to the next and forms the whole into paragraphs of meaning, intelligible propositions, each with its place and sense in a still larger, accessible system. Because of logic one mind connects to another, public discourse becomes possible, debate on issues of general intelligibility takes place, and an anthology of statements about a single subject becomes a composition of theorems about that subject. In this sense, after the Mishnah, Leviticus Rabbah constitutes the next major logical composition in the rabbinic canon. Accordingly, with Leviticus Rabbah rabbis take up the problem of saying what they wish to say not in an exegetical, but in a syllogistic and freely discursive logic and rhetoric.

The document at hand constitutes not a mere collection of unrelated or random statements, but a set of related and purposeful ones. Now we must explain what defines the relationship and how we shall make sense of the purpose. To answer that question we must uncover the fundamental logic of organization and topic: the logos of both intellect and aesthetics that account for the whole; the topics that render the book as we have it a sustained syllogism. My thesis is that Leviticus Rabbah falls into the classification of syllogistic compositions, not of exegetical collections. The proposition is that Leviticus Rabbah constitutes not a compilation of random sentences, but a purposeful and sustained composition, comparable with the Mishnah in its principles of organization and aggregation of materials. On what basis do we claim that the document in hand constitutes a single and systematic statement? We shall state matters both negatively and positively. What would constitute adequate proof that we have an anthology or a typical compilation, lacking a logic of either form or topic? What would constitute decisive proof that we have a sustained composition, exhibiting in detail an inner, animating, and encompassing logic? If we cannot falsify, we also cannot validate or propose. Accordingly, we lay forth what we conceive to be evidence and argumentation to guide us on whether we are right or wrong.

The negative: If we wished to demonstrate that a text in the rabbinic canon comprised nothing more than a compilation of discrete sentences, in no way constituting paragraphs, chapters, propositions, and syllogisms, we should begin with these questions: (1) Can we show that no external, formal pattern governed the formulation of sentences? It would then follow that the sentences were made up with no interest in composing a stylistically balanced and formally cogent paragraph or chapter. (2) Can we demonstrate that no single issue or problem occupied the mind of the authors of the sentences at hand? It would then follow that the compilation of sentences in no way flowed from a single generative problematic or addressed a cogent problem or proposition. On that basis, we should stand on firm ground in alleging that at hand was a topical anthology, a compilation of this-and-that, and not a sustained and cogent composition.

True, someone made the compilation as we have it. No one alleges that, crawling across the far reaches of rabbinical tradents, random sentences somehow made their way to a given pericope on their own. Every document reached closure and entered circulation in something very like the condition in which we now have it (making provision for enormous variations in the wording of sentences). But the person who made the compilation followed a simple principle in selecting the aggregation of materials that he gave us: shared topic, common theme. Whether or not through the shared topic he wished to deliver anything more than simply the aggregation of sentences, in no clear logical order and making no obvious single point, we cannot say. Why not? Because the parts do not add up to more than the sum of the whole. The decisive criterion is simple: The order to sentences of such an anthology makes no intelligible difference, because one could have arranged the sentences in any other sequence and gained as little, or as much, meaning from the compilation as a whole.

The positive: Beginning the account of the criteria by which we identify a composition as distinct from a compilation, a purposeful essay in contrast to an anthology on a single topic, we begin with this same point, the order of sentences. In a syllogistic paragraph, the order of sentences matters a great deal. It would not be possible to arrange matters other than in the sequence in which they occur, for each sentence depends upon the other for sense and meaning, one standing fore, the other aft, of the statement at hand. Such an orderly composition in no way serves as a mere anthology of diverse sayings on a single topic. Quite the opposite, the sentences gain their full sense and meaning only in the order dictated by the logic of the syllogism at hand.

THE CONFLUENCE OF RHETORIC AND LOGIC

In the rabbinic canon, moreover, sentences that are meant to be coherent with one another very commonly follow a single syntactic formula and resort to shared forms of rhetoric. The Mishnah, we have demonstrated, joins form to meaning. When a given topic is at hand, the sentences that spell out the rules on that topic prove cogent not only in theme and even in detailed principle but also in syntax and rhetoric. When, then, the subject changes, the syntactical and rhetorical pattern and form also change. So we shall talk about one thing in some one way, then the next thing in some other.

Whereas the logic of a syllogism therefore comes to detailed expression in both aesthetic, or formal, and literary ways, and also in intellectual, or substantive, ones, the shortest path into the center of a syllogism lies through form. How so? In the literature at hand, if we discern patterns of formal expression, we may reasonably look for patterns of substantive discourse as well. If we find no effort at formalization, we may find it more difficult, also, to demonstrate the intent of delivering cogent and substantive propositions. (Self-evidently, repeated recourse to a single form may also produce gibberish, as in the Hekhalot writings. But that fact is inconsequential in this context, since we make no claim that patterned language all by itself proves we have in hand syllogistic propositions too.) So the way forward lies through the discovery of the logic of Leviticus Rabbah, logic of expression, logic of composition, logic of proposition.

Let me now link what has been said about formal cogency to the larger claim that Leviticus Rabbah expresses a cogent logic, a logic of form and a logic of substance, a logic of context as well. What has formal cogency to do with logic? The question may be reframed as follows: How shall we recognize—and so demonstrate the presence of—logic? Since logic constitutes what orders and renders intelligible a set of sentences or propositions, so laying down the principle of composition for discourse and the rules by which discourse takes place, we look throughout for regularities. Our perception of order emerges from our discovery of repeated choices, first of form, and only second of proposition. If we can demonstrate a single program of formal choices, we may also try to show that the author or authors of the document—the people who in the end made it what is now is—did some one thing rather than some other. Then through systematic classification we may describe what they chose to do. That taxonomic description constitutes the statement of the formal logic of the document as a whole.

By contrast, if we can discover in a text of the character of this one no repeated patterns in the way people express their ideas—no sustained logic of rhetoric and syntax, for example—we have slight warrant for supposing that in substance or in topical program we deal with a composition, a proportioned statement, a cogent syllogism. We shall have then to concede that what we have in hand is what people generally suppose we have—a composite, not a composition. We shall have to agree that Leviticus Rabbah is a collection of diverse and episodic sentences, this-and-that about what-not, not a coherent syllogism, a statement and intelligible judgment addressed to the age in which the composition reached closure. Leviticus Rabbah, located by the scholarly consensus at ca. A.D. 400–450, contends with the context of its age, addresses Israel's condition with syllogisms of substance and meaning, not merely with ad hoc sayings equally relevant—because of their very discrete and episodic character—everywhere but also nowhere in particular.

In Leviticus Rabbah, we have a composition in which outsiders, not the authors but other people, provided "completed units of thought" that are whole paragraphs, and in which the authors also provided "completed units of thought," also whole paragraphs. When we speak of these "completed units of thought" and invoke the analogy of the sentence, therefore, in fact we refer not to atomic but to molecular units of thought, that is to say, composites that, all together, make a single point or statement. What then forms the arena for analysis, and where do we claim to locate the boundaries of discourse? The answer is simple. We speak of the parashah as the proposition. Then there are 37 of them. Our entire mode of analysis is to claim that each parashah constitutes not merely an assembly of relevant materials about a topic, but something much more cogent and purposive, that is, a composition that makes a specific polemical point about a topic. We further propose that the main points of the polemic on the bulk, although not all, of the parashiyyot and their topics, cohere and add up to a single proposition concerning Israel's salvation. So the parts make points and the whole makes a point. And, in the nature of things (since we claim to contribute to the study of the history of the formation of the ideas of Judaism), the point that is made concerns the world to which the framers speak.

The burden of proof lies on the one who alleges we deal with a composition and not a composite. Either a document is exegetical and so depends upon some other for its cogency and order, or it is syllogistic and therefore provides its own inner connections and relations. The former sort of document, by definition, constitutes a timeless exegesis out of all distinctive historical and social context. It depends upon, therefore it meant to amplify, some other document, of some other age; hence, provides an exegesis of something other than itself. The latter sort of document, by definition, constitutes a timely syllogism, a free-standing statement made intelligible in two complementary ways. These are, first, by its own inner correspondences and proportions, a set of relationships joined from within and, second, by a socially defined logic, a cogent address directed to a given world by a specific intellect and therefore meant to be intelligible at some one time (if, also, for all time too).

A deep cogency characterizes the formulary and redactional systems of Leviticus Rabbah. What of that logic—that mode of thought, of formulating and answering questions, of deciding what is fit and right and proportionate—that inheres in the whole and emerges in each of the parts? Surely we have reason to ask whether the formal traits of discourse correspond to the substantive purposes. So far as style and aesthetic dictate one mode, rather than some other, of saying what the author wants, do they also signal limits to what one may appropriately say in that mode? We ask the question, but in phrasing matters this way, we also dictate the selection of data to lead us to the answer of a still more encompassing inquiry into the mode of thought, the manner of the construction, in mind, of reality out there. Accordingly, we shall try to find a route to the fundamental layers of the intellect that animates and generates the accessible layers of formal expression of doctrine and deliberation.

METHOD AND MESSAGE IN LEVITICUS RABBAH

Since we hypothesize that form and substance cohere, we start back with the points of formal cogency of the document. It is there, at the repeated literary structures, that we should be able to point to the evidences of a fundamentally coherent way of seeing things, a mode of thought expressed throughout. What people wished to say and the way in which they chose to say it together constituted the document as we now know it. So, as is clear, we turn to the one to teach us how to analyze the other.

We begin, then, once more with the paramount and dominant exegetical construction, the base-verse/intersecting verse exegesis characteristic of our document. In such an exercise, what in fact do we do? We read one thing in terms of something else. To begin with, it is the base verse in terms of the intersecting verse. But, as the reader observes in the text itself, it also is the intersecting verse in other terms as well—a multiple layered construction of analogy and parable. The intersecting verse's elements always turn out to stand for, to signify, to speak of, something other than that to which they openly refer. If water stands for Torah, the skin disease for evil speech, the reference to something for some other thing entirely, then the mode of thought at hand is simple. One thing symbolizes another, speaks not of itself but of some other thing entirely.

How shall we describe this mode of thought? It seems to me we may call it an as-if way of seeing things. That is to say, it is as if a common object or symbol really represented an uncommon one. Nothing says what it means. Everything important speaks metonymically, elliptically, parabolically, symbolically. All statements carry deeper meaning, which inheres in other statements altogether. The profound sense, then, of the base verse emerges only through restatement within and through the intersecting verse—as if the base verse spoke of things that, on the surface, we do not see at all. Accordingly, if we ask the single prevalent literary construction to testify to the prevailing frame of mind, its message is that things are never what they seem. All things demand interpretation. Interpretation begins in the search for analogy, for that to which the thing is likened, hence the deep sense in which all exegesis at hand is parabolic. It is a quest for that for which the thing in its deepest structure stands.

Exegesis as we know it in Leviticus Rabbah (and not only there) consists in an exercise in analogical thinking—something is like something else, stands for, evokes, or symbolizes that which is quite outside itself. It may be the opposite of something else, in which case it conforms to the exact opposite of the rules that govern that something else. The reasoning is analogical or it is contrastive, and the fundamental logic is taxonomic. The taxonomy rests on those comparisons and contrasts we should call metonymic and parabolic. In that case what lies on the surface misleads. What lies beneath or beyond the surface—there is the true reality, the world of truth and meaning. To revert to the issue of taxonomy, the tracts that allow classification serve only for that purpose. They signify nothing more than that something more.

How shall we characterize people who see things this way? They constitute the opposite of ones who call a thing as it is. Self-evidently, they have become accustomed to perceiving more—or less—than is at hand. Perhaps that is a natural mode of thought for the Jews of this period (and not then alone), so long used to calling themselves God's first love, yet now seeing others with greater worldly reason claiming that same advantaged relationship. Not in mind only, but still more, in the politics of the world, the people that remembered its origins along with the very creation of the world and founding of humanity, that recalled how it alone served, and serves, the one and only God, for more than 300 years had confronted a quite different existence. The radical disjuncture between the way things were and the way Scripture said things were supposed to be—and in actuality would some day become—surely imposed an unbearable tension. It was one thing for the slave born to slavery to endure. It was another for the free man sold into slavery to accept that same condition. The vanquished people, the nation that had lost its city and its temple, that had, moreover, produced another nation from its midst to take over its scripture and much else, could not bear too much reality. That defeated people will then have found refuge in a mode of thought that trained vision to see other things otherwise than as the eyes perceived them. Among the diverse ways by which the weak and subordinated accommodate to their circumstance, the one of iron-willed pretense in life is most likely to yield the mode of thought at hand: things never are, because they cannot be, what they seem.

THE MESSAGE OF LEVITICUS RABBAH

If we now ask about further recurring themes or topics in Leviticus Rabbah, there is one so commonplace that we should have to list the majority of paragraphs of discourse in order to provide a complete list. It is the list of events in Israel's history, meaning, in this context, Israel's history solely in scriptural times, down through the return to Zion. The one-time events of the generation of the flood, Sodom and Gomorrah, the patriarchs and the sojourn in Egypt, the exodus, the revelation of the Torah at Sinai, the golden calf, the Davidic monarchy and the building of the Temple, Sennacherib, Hezekiah, and the destruction of northern Israel, Nebuchadnezzar and the destruction of the Temple in 586, the life of Israel in Babylonian captivity, Daniel and his associates, Mordecai and Haman—these events occur over and over again. They turn out to serve as paradigms of sin and atonement, steadfastness and divine intervention, and equivalent lessons. We find, in fact, a fairly standard repertoire of scripture heroes or villains, on the one side, and conventional lists of Israel's enemies and their actions and downfall, on the other. The boastful, for instance, include **VII:VI** the generation of the flood, Sodom and Gomorrah, Pharaoh, Sisera, Sennacherib, Nebuchadnezzar, the wicked empire (Rome)—contrasted to Israel, "despised and humble in this world." The four kingdoms recur again and again, always ending, of course, with Rome, with the repeated message that after Rome will come Israel. But Israel has to make this happen through its faith and submission to God's will. Lists of enemies ring the changes on Cain, the Sodomites, Pharaoh, Sennacherib, Nebuchadnezzar, Haman.

Accordingly, the mode of thought brought to bear upon the theme of history remains exactly the same as in the Mishnah: list-making, with data exhibiting similar taxonomic traits drawn together into lists based on common monothetic traits or definitions. These lists then, through the power of repetition, make a single enormous point or prove a social law of history. The catalogues of exemplary heroes and historical events serve a further purpose. They provide a model of how contemporary events are to be absorbed into the biblical paradigm. Since biblical events exemplify recurrent happenings, sin and redemption, forgiveness and atonement, they lose their one-time character. At the same time and in the same way, current events find a place within the ancient, but eternally present paradigmatic scheme. So no new historical events, other than exemplary episodes in lives of heroes, demand narration because, through what is said about the past, what was happening in the times of the framers of Leviticus Rabbah would also come under consideration. This mode of dealing with biblical history and contemporary events produces two reciprocal effects. The first is the mythicization of biblical stories, their removal from the framework of ongoing, unique patterns of history and sequences of events, and their transformation into accounts of things that happen all the time. The second is that contemporary events too lose all of their specificity and enter the paradigmatic framework of established mythic existence. So (1) the scripture's myth happens every day, and (2) every day produces reenactment of the scripture's myth.

In seeking the substance of the mythic being invoked by the exegetes at hand, who read the text as if it spoke about something else and the world as if it lived out the text, we uncover a simple fact. At the center of the pretense, that is, the as-if mentality of Leviticus Rabbah and its framers, we find a simple proposition. Israel is God's special love. That love is shown in a simple way. Israel's present condition of subordination derives from its own deeds. It follows that God cares, so Israel may look forward to redemption on God's part in response to Israel's own regeneration through repentance. When the exegetes proceeded to open the scroll of Leviticus, they found numerous occasions to state that proposition in concrete terms and specific contexts. The sinner brings on his or her own sickness. But God heals through that very ailment. The nations of the world govern in heavy succession, but Israel's lack of faith guaranteed their rule and its moment of renewal will end it. Israel's leaders—priests, prophets, kings—fall into an entirely different category from those of the nations, as much as does Israel. In these and other concrete allegations, the same classic message comes forth.

Accordingly, at the foundations of the pretense lies the long-standing biblical-Jewish insistence that Israel's sorry condition in no way testifies to Israel's true worth—the grandest pretense of all. All the little evasions of the primary sense in favor of some other testify to this, the great denial that what is, is what counts. Leviticus Rabbah makes that statement with art and imagination. But it is never subtle about saying so.

BIBLICAL EXEGESIS OR THEOLOGICAL SYLLOGISM?
THE TESTIMONY OF LEVITICUS RABBAH

The message of Leviticus Rabbah attaches itself to the Book of Leviticus, as if that book had come from prophecy and addressed the issue of salvation. But it came from the priesthood and spoke of sanctification. The paradoxical syllogism—the as-if reading, the opposite of how things seem—of the composers of Leviticus Rabbah therefore reaches simple formulation. In the very setting of sanctification we find the promise of salvation. In the topics of the cult and the priesthood we uncover the national and social issues of the moral life and redemptive hope of Israel. The repeated comparison and contrast of priesthood and prophecy, sanctification and salvation, turn out to produce a complement, which comes to most perfect union in the text at hand.

Nearly all of the *parashiyyot* of Leviticus Rabbah turn out to deal with the national, social condition of Israel, and this in three contexts: (1) Israel's setting in the history of the nations, (2) the character of the inner life of Israel itself, and (3) the future history of Israel. So the biblical book that deals with the holy Temple now is shown to address the holy people. Leviticus really discusses not the consecration of the cult but the sanctification of the nation—its conformity to God's will, laid forth in the Torah, and God's rules.

So when we review the document as a whole and ask what is that something else that the base text is supposed to address, it turns out that the sanctification of the cult stands for the salvation of the nation. So the nation now is like the cult then, the ordinary Israelite now like the priest then. The holy way of life lived now, through acts to which merit accrues, corresponds to the holy rites then. The process of metamorphosis is full, rich, complete. When everything stands for something else, the something else repeatedly turns out to be the nation. This is what our document spells out in exquisite detail, yet never missing the main point.

The authors of Leviticus Rabbah express their ideas, first, by selecting materials already written for other purposes and using them for their own, second, by composing materials, and third, by arranging both in *parashiyyot* into an order through which propositions may reach expression. As we sifted and resifted traits of organization and topics of discourse, we reached two complementary conclusions, which yield a third point as well.

1. The formal conclusion was that the principal mode of thought required one thing to be read in terms of another, one verse in light of

a different verse (or topic, theme, symbol, idea), one situation in light of another.

2. The substantive conclusion was that the principal subject of our composition is the moral condition of Israel, on the one side, and the salvation of Israel, on the other.

3. The single unifying proposition—the syllogism at the document's deepest structure—was that Israel's salvation depends upon its condition.

In these three statements we are able to account for the literary character and the topical contents of the document and, further, to express its single paramount proposition. The context in which the work of selection, arrangement, and composition went on, of course, is one (if not uniquely) in which Israel's salvation framed the issue of the times. At the outset we alleged that we have at hand a syllogistic statement, by which we mean a statement of logical, not merely rhetorical, coherence. We promised to specify the logic that defines the underlying principle to account for the unity and cogency of the whole. The logic in substance has now been identified. Our reason for maintaining that Leviticus Rabbah constitutes not merely diverse thoughts but a single, sustained composition is fully exposed. But the question remains, in the context of logical discourse, what sort of syllogism do we have in hand? It is to this matter that we now turn. The question demands attention, because when we answer it, we shall know how the framers communicate. We shall claim to understand how, through selecting existing materials and including compositions of new ones, they develop their points and establish a discourse sufficiently cogent and logical to make an important point.

EXEGESIS AND SYLLOGISTIC DISCOURSE: THE ROLE OF SCRIPTURE

Since we claim that the authors do state propositions, we have at the end to make that claim stick by showing how they do so. It is, in a word, through a rich tapestry of unstated propositions that only are illustrated, delineated at the outset, by the statement of some propositions that also are illustrated. It is, in a word, a syllogism by example—that is, by repeated appeal to facts—rather than by argument alone. For in context, an example constitutes a fact. The source of many examples or facts is scripture, the foundation of all reality. Accordingly, in the context of Israelite life and culture, in which scripture recorded facts, we have a severely logical, because entirely factual, statement of how rightly organized and classified facts sustain a proposition. In context that proposition is presented as rigorously and critically as the social rules of discourse allowed.

Precisely what sort of syllogism does our document set forth? In my view, it is a perfectly simple one (which biblical historians and prophets used all the time as at Leviticus 26—27): if X, then Y; if not X, then not Y. If Israel carries out its moral obligations, then God will redeem Israel. If Israel does not, then God will punish Israel. This simple statement is given innumerable illustrations, for example, Israel in times past repented, therefore God saved them. Israel in times past sinned, therefore God punished them. Other sorts of statements follow suit. God loves the humble and despises the haughty. Therefore God saves the humble and punishes the haughty. In the same terms, if she or he is humble, then God will save her or him, and if one is haughty, then God will punish her or him. Accordingly, if one condition is met, then another will come about. And the opposite also is the fact. True, the document does not express these syllogisms in the form of arguments at all. Rather they come before us as statements of facts, and the facts upon which numerous statements rest derive from scripture. So, on the surface, there is not a single statement in the document that a Greco-Roman logician would have understood, since the formal patterns of Greco-Roman logic do not make an appearance. Yet once we translate the statements the authors do make into the language of abstract discourse, we find exact correspondences between the large-scale propositions of the document and the large-scale syllogisms of familiar logic.

Along these same lines, we may find numerous individual examples in which, in exquisite detail, the syllogistic mode at hand—if X, then Y; if not X, then not Y—defines the pattern of discourse. The logic at hand, at its deepest layers, accords with the formal logic of the Stoic logic of propositions (described by Berchman in appendix 1). We find both brief and simple propositions that make sense of large-scale compositions, e.g., on humility and arrogance, and also an overall scheme of proposition and argument, a micro- and a macro-syllogistic discourse, with the small and the large corresponding to one another.

The place of scripture is such a logical system now requires explanation. To understand how scripture functions, we have to grasp clearly the larger logical matrix. In light of the account of the syllogistic possibilities at hand, we may identify the theorems of argumentation operative in our document (and not alone here, of course). What is important is that the logic at hand proves subject to verification on grounds other than those supplied by the proof texts alone. How so? The appeal is to an autonomous realm, namely, reason confirmed by experience. The repeated claim is not that things are so merely because scripture says what it says, but that things happened as they happened in accord with laws we may verify or test (as scripture, among other sources of facts, tells us). The emphasis is on the sequence of events, the interrelationship exhibited by them. How does scripture in particular participate? It is not in particular at all. Scripture serves as a source of information, much as any history of the world or of a nation would provide sources of information: facts. Who makes use of these facts? In our own time it is the social scientist, seeking the rules that social entities are supposed to exhibit. In the period at hand it was the rabbinical philosopher, seeking the rules governing Israel's life. So far as people seek rules and regularities, the search is one of logic, of philosophy. It follows that our document rests upon logical argumentation. Its framers, rabbis, served as philosophers in the ancient meaning of the term. And, in consequence, scripture for its part is transformed into the source of those facts that supply both the problem, chaos, and the solution, order, rule, organized in lists. So scripture in the hands of the rabbis of our document corresponds to nature in the hands of the great Greek philosophers.

The Mishnah makes its principal points by collecting three or five examples of a given rule. The basic rule is not stated, but it is exemplified through the several statements of its application. The reader then may infer the generalization from its specific exemplifications. Sometimes, but not often, the generalization is made explicit. The whole then constitutes an exercise in rhetoric and logic carried out through list-making. And the same is true in Leviticus Rabbah. But it makes lists of different things from those of the Mishnah: events, not everyday situations. The framers of Leviticus Rabbah revert to sequences of events, all of them exhibiting the same definitive traits and the same ultimate results, e.g., arrogance, downfall, not one time but many; humility, salvation, over and over again; and so throughout. Indeed, if we had to select a single paramount trait of argument in Leviticus Rabbah, it would be the theorem stated by the making of a list of similar examples. The search for the rules lies through numerous instances that, all together, yield the besought rule.

In context, therefore, we have in Leviticus Rabbah the counterpart to the list-making that defined the labor of the philosophers of the Mishnah. Through composing lists of items joined by a monothetic definitive trait, the framers produce underlying or overriding rules always applicable. Here too, through lists of facts of history, the foundations of social life rise to the surface. All this, we see, constitutes a species of a molecular argument, framed in very definite terms, e.g., Nebuchad- nezzar, Sennacherib, David, Josiah did so-and-so with such-and-such result. So, as we said, the mode of argument at hand is the assembly of instances of a common law. The argument derives from the proper construction of a statement of that law in something close to a syllogism. The syllogistic statement often, though not invariably, occurs at the outset, all instances of so-and-so produce such-and-such, followed by the required catalogue. A final point is in order. The conditional syllogisms of our composition over and over again run through the course of history. The effort is to demonstrate that the rule at hand applies at all times, under all circumstances. Why so? It is because the conditional syllogism must serve under all temporal circumstances. The recurrent listing of events subject to a single rule runs as often as possible through the course of all of human history, from creation to the fourth monarchy (Rome), which, everyone knows, is the end of time prior to the age that is coming. Accordingly, the veracity of rabbinic conditional arguments depends over and over again on showing that the condition holds at all times.

To summarize: the proposition of the syllogistic argument at hand derives from clear statements of scripture, the conditional part: if X, then Y; if not X, then not Y. Leviticus 26 (which receives strikingly slight attention in our composition) states explicitly that if the Israelites keep God's rules, they will prosper, and if not, they will suffer. The viewpoint is commonplace, but its appearance at Leviticus in particular validates the claim that it is topically available to our authors. The two further stages in the encompassing logic of the document do represent a step beyond the simple and commonplace theorem. The first is the con- struction of the molecular argument, encompassing a broad range of subjects. The second, and the more important of the two, is the insis- tence of the temporal character of the list. That is why the recurrent reference to sequences of figures, events, or actions, all listed in accord with a monothetic definitive trait, forms so central a component in the argument of the document as a whole.

What Leviticus Rabbah does not contribute is the basic proposition at hand. Why not? Because, as we said, it is one that would not have surprised most of the framers of the important components of scripture itself. When an authorship thinks *with* scripture, that is what happens. What the authors of the document do originate (along with authors in the Talmud of the Land of Israel) is the proof through review of examples deriving from a wide range of times and places. That logical contribution explains why our document differs from all but one of its contemporaries and all of its predecessors, except, of course, for one. As we explained, the Mishnah too composes its arguments through the laying down of basic principles—syllogisms—sustained by lists of specific instances in the validation and clarification of those principles. So too the authors of Leviticus Rabbah collect and arrange, since they do not propose to invent facts, but to interpret them by discovering the rules the facts obey. The facts with which they work are indifferently scriptural or contemporary (although mostly the former). The propositions they propose to demonstrate through these facts, however, are eternal.

So, in a word, Leviticus Rabbah takes up the modes of thought and argumentation characteristic of the Mishnah (and, in one measure or other, of the larger Greco-Roman philosophical setting) and accomplishes the logically necessary task of applying them to society. Speaking of society, the authors turn to, among other records, the history book, scripture, which provides examples of the special laws governing Israel, the physics of Israel's fate. In scripture, but not only there, the authors find rules and apply them to their own day. Greek science focused upon physics. Then the laws of Israel's salvation serve as the physics of the sages. But Greek science derived facts and built theorems on the basis of other sources besides physics; the philosophers also, after all, studied ethnography, ethics, politics, and history. For the sages at hand, along these same lines, parables, exemplary tales, and completed paragraphs of thought deriving from other sources (not to exclude the Mishnah, Tosefta, Sifra, Genesis Rabbah, and such literary compositions that had been made ready for the Talmud of the Land of Israel)—these too make their contribution of data subject to analysis. All these sources of truth, all together, were directed toward the discovery of philosophical laws for the understanding of Israel's life, now and in the age to come.

What we have in Leviticus Rabbah, therefore, is the result of the mode of thought not of prophets or historians, but of philosophers and scientists. The framers propose not to lay down, but to discover, rules governing Israel's life. We state with necessary emphasis: As we find the rules of nature by identifying and classifying facts of natural life, so we find rules of society by identifying and classifying the facts of Israel's social life. In both modes of inquiry we make sense of things by bringing together like specimens and finding out whether they form a species, then bringing together like species and finding out whether they form a genus—in all, classifying data and identifying the rules that make possible the classification. That sort of thinking lies at the deepest level of list-making, which is work of offering a proposition and facts (for social rules) as much as a genus and its species (for rules of nature). Once discovered, the social rules of Israel's national life of course yield explicit statements, such as that God hates the arrogant and loves the humble. As we have seen, the readily assembled syllogism follows: If one is arrogant, God will hate her or him, and if she or he is humble, God will love her or him. The logical status of these statements, in context, is as secure and unassailable as the logical status of statements about physics, ethics, or politics, as these emerge in philosophical thought. What differentiates the statements is not their logical status—as sound, scientific philosophy—but only their subject matter, on the one side, and distinctive rhetoric, on the other.

5

The Four Logics
of Cogent Discourse
and the Role of Scripture
in Sifré to Deuteronomy

THE ISSUE OF RHETORIC AND LOGIC

Theological syllogism, such as predominates in Leviticus Rabbah, requires linguistic and syntactic forms capable of bearing the burden of proposition. That mode of writing with scripture further demands the framing of discourse in such a way as to convey sense, order, proportion, above all, the self-evidence of what is argued. In a literature such as that produced by the sages of the dual Torah, which persistently appeals to patterned language and formalized, conventional modes of making statements, the traits of systematic ordering of words in one way, rather than in another—or in random ways—we may expect in rhetorical patterns evidence for syllogistic discourse. So too, in a document that proposes not merely to collect things relevant to a common theme but to make an important statement about a theme, there should be an operative logic that facilitates not merely joining thoughts because of a common, extrinsic point of relevance, but for narrowly syllogistic purposes. That is to say, two distinct thought-units, e.g., sentences, should connect to one another not solely because both refer to the same thing but because together the two sentences make a point that transcends them both, add up, so to speak, to more than the sum of the parts.

My claim concerning the syllogistic intent of the framers of Leviticus Rabbah requires testing against the data of yet another document. If, as I maintain, authorships in the Judaism of the dual Torah propose not merely to amplify verses of scripture but also to make important statements of their own by resorting, in part, to verses of scripture, then, in the highly stereotypical language of the canonical writings, we should find evidence of the formation of rhetorical forms, patterns of syntax and linguistic arrangement, to facilitate propositional discourse. And, along these same lines, the modes of joining one sentence to another to make a cogent statement out of two discrete thought units—which in the abstract we may call the logic of intelligible discourse—ought to give evidence of the intent to form discourse in syllogistic propositions, not merely discrete and unrelated statements concerning verses, or clauses of verses, of scripture. Rather than amplify these ways of testing our hypothesis, let us turn directly to a concrete case, and having reviewed its evidence, revert to the dual experiment at hand, the one concerning rhetoric, the other logic.

The document is Sifré to Deuteronomy, of indeterminate origin in time, but certainly coming after the formation of the Mishnah, in ca. A.D. 200, and before the closure of the Talmud of Babylonia or Bavli, in ca. A.D. 600. The authorship cites the Mishnah verbatim, and the document is cited in the Bavli. An educated guess would place this compilation in the same general time as that of Sifra and Sifré to Numbers, and a convenience date of 300–400 is not wholly without justification. But the point, within the unfolding of the canonical writings of the Judaism of the dual Torah, at which this one reached closure has no bearing upon our problem; our concern is with the fixed structures of rhetoric and logic characteristic of its authorship, not with the larger social and political world in which the authorship did its work.

SYLLOGISTIC AND EXEGETICAL FORMS IN SIFRÉ TO DEUTERONOMY

This document's authorship, overall, utilizes two distinct kinds of rhetorical forms or modes of patterned language. One establishes a syllogism, makes a point, and the other serves only to amplify a cited formula, e.g., a verse or a clause of a verse. The latter is formally simple and indeed serves, also, as a building block for varieties of the form. It consists only of "clause + phrase," that is, a cited formula from a document other than the one subject to composition by the present authorship, followed by a statement, ordinarily a phrase of a sentence or at most a whole sentence, by the authorship of the document at hand. The whole then adds up to a sentence, explicit or merely implied, which we may present in a simple symbol: $3 = X$, that is, a clause from an external source (thus 3) bears the sense of the phrase presented by "us," that is, this authorship maintains that the unknown sense of the cited clause in fact is the sense stated by us. That strict exegetical form produces a good sentence, such as just now exemplified, "Moses spoke" means "Moses admonished." To move rapidly to the syllogistic form, an authorship then may wish to make a more general statement. It may wish, for instance, to maintain that "spoke" always bears the sense of "admonish," and to do so, it will then catalogue numerous other verses of clauses or verses in which "spoke" bears the clear sense, established in context (not always cited verbatim but commonly merely subject to allusion), of "admonish." Then we have a proposition, argued in the normal philosophical way. That of course represents only one among many possible propositional forms of discourse. (Later in this chapter we shall see the counterpart, in logics, of "exegetical form" and "propositional form.") Let us forthwith present the repertoire of rhetorical forms in our document.

There is, in the rhetoric of this document, a variety of syllogistic demonstrations, in all cases the matter being made explicit. What they have in common is that each proposes an encompassing generalization. Exegetical form, by contrast, is single and atomistic. It invariably makes possible only ad hoc amplification of a verse or a phrase. What we have in the propositional forms, however varied, always are two or more sentences formed into a proposition and an argument. Exegetical form, by contrast, comprises singleton sentences, rather than components of a more sustained discourse. They invariably deal with a detail and bear no implications for any phrase or issue beyond themselves. There is, further, a mode of linguistic patterning, closely joined to the sense conveyed by the pattern, that is a subdivision of the propositional mode of discourse. This form serves to pattern language in such a way as to illustrate a prevailing structural trait of mind, but not a proposition yielded by a particular case. These items ordinarily deal with matters of proper conduct or right action, hence *halakhic* issues. There is a two-layer discourse in them, since, at the superficial level, they yield only a detail of a law, that is, thus and so is the rule here; but at the deep layer of thought, they demonstrate a prevailing and global proposition, that applies—it is implied—throughout, and not only to a single case. Hence, over all, rhetorical analysis of Sifré to Deuteronomy draws our attention to modes of stating a middle-level proposition, affecting a variety of verses and their cases, in the present list. Then we move onward, to the low-level proposition, that pertains only to a single case, and, finally, we turn to a global proposition, that affects a broad variety of cases, left discrete, but homogenizes them. Let us now describe in greater detail the forms at hand, which show that all but one of the recurrent rhetorical forms of Sifré to Deuteronomy serve propositional, and only one, exegetical discourse. That will indicate how the authorship of this document so worded its statements as consistently to establish arguments and make of two or more sentences cogent points. On the fact of it, therefore, we have a rhetoric of proposition, not one of exegesis. When we consider the principles of logical cogency, we shall see the same result.

The Proposition and Its Syllogistic Argument

All paragraphs or sustained and complex units of thought made up of simple sentences, in one way or another, set forth propositions and demonstrate them by amassing probative facts, e.g., examples. The patterning of the individual sentences of course varies. But the large-scale rhetoric, involving the presentation of a proposition, in general terms, and then the amassing of probative facts (however the sentences are worded), is essentially uniform.

The Proposition Based on the Classification of Probative Facts

The prevailing pattern here is not vastly changed. This is different from the foregoing only in a minor matter. In this case we prove a proposition, e.g., the meaning of a word, by classifying facts that point toward that proposition. In the foregoing, the work of proof is accomplished through listing proofs made up of diverse facts. The difference between the one and the other is hardly very considerable, but we think we can successfully differentiate among the formal patterns through the stated criterion. However, one may reasonably argue that this catalogue and the foregoing list essentially the same formal patterns of language or argument. Here we have a complex development of a simple exegesis, and it is at the complexity—the repeated use of a simple pattern—that the propositional form(s) reaches full exposure.

The Proposition Based on the Recurrent Opinions of Sages

This is another variation, in that the nature of the evidence shifts, and, it follows, also the patterning of language. Here we shall have the attributive constantly present, e.g., X says, and that does form an important rhetorical indicator. We may say flatly that this form is not characteristic of our authorship and accomplishes none of their goals. It is a commonplace in the Mishnah, inclusive of tractate Avot, and in the

Tosefta; large-scale compositions in the Yerushalmi and the Bavli follow the same pattern; and other large-scale compositions will be drawn together because a sequence of simple declarative sentences on diverse topics, whether or not related in theme, bears the same attributive.

The Narrative and Its Illustrated Proposition. The Scripture Story. The Parable as Illustration of an Established Proposition.

The construction in which a proposition is established and then illustrated in a narrative, whether parable, scriptural story, or other kind of narrative, for the present purpose is treated in a single rubric. The formal-structural uniformity justifies doing so. We may find varieties of patterns of sentences, e.g., parables as against stories. But the narrative is always marked by either, "he said to him . . . he said to him . . . ," for the story, or counterpart indications of a select pattern of forming and arranging sentences, for the parable. Our authorship has resorted to a very limited repertoire of patterns of language even for "narrative," although that category admittedly is gross and hardly refined. Narratives, viewed as an encompassing formal category, do not play a large role in defining (therefore differentiating) the rhetorical-logical program of our authorship. But all narratives in our document serve to state or to prove propositions, and none serves a narrowly exegetical purpose, e.g., merely amplifying or clarifying the sense of a verse of scripture.

The (Implicit) Proposition Based on Facts Derived from Exegesis

These items involve lists of facts, but lack that clear statement of the proposition that the facts establish. What we have here are complexes of tightly joined declarative sentences, many of them (in the nature of things) in that atom pattern, "commentary form," but all of them joined into a much larger set of (often) highly formalized statements.

Exegetical Form with No Implicit Proposition

These items present in simple exegetical form a single fact, a discrete sentence, left without further development and without association or affinity with surrounding statements—once more, "exegetical form." The form is as defined: clause + phrase. That same form in the propositional compositions rarely occurs without development, and if we had to specify the one fundamental difference between nonpropositional exegetical form and all other forms, it is in the simplicity of the one as against the complexity of the other. Or, to state matters more bluntly, excluding narrative, the sole rhetorical building block of any consequence in Sifré to Deuteronomy is the simple exegetical one, consisting of clause + phrase = sentence. What happens then is that all other forms develop the simple atom into a complex molecule, but the "exegetical form with no implicit proposition" remains at the atomic level (if not an even smaller particle than the atom) and never gains the molecular one. These therefore constitute entirely comprehensible sense units, that is, on their own, simple sentences, never formed into paragraphs, and define the lowest rhetorical form of our document. The other rhetorical forms build these simple sense units or sentences into something more complex. That fact of rhetoric accounts, also, for our having—willy-nilly—to appeal to considerations of logical cogency in our analysis of rhetoric and form.

Dialectical Exegesis with No Implicit Proposition Pertinent
to the Case at Hand but with Bearing on Large-Scale Structural Issues

In formal terms, compositions of the present category are made up of a series of closely joined thought units or sentences. Hence they present us with two or more sentences that constitute joined, propositional paragraphs. But their rhetorical traits are so much more particular, and their net effect so much more distinctive, that we treat them as a quite distinct rhetorical phenomenon. Moreover, these are the most patterned, the most formed, of all formal compositions at hand. They require sustained exposition of a proposition, not a simple proposition plus probative facts. They all make two points, as we have already pointed out, one at the surface, the other through the deep structure. Strictly speaking, as sustained and complex forms, all these items conform most exactly to the fundamental definition of a rhetorical form, language that coheres to a single pattern. And the pattern is one of both rhetoric and logic. Two subdivisions of such patterns are, first, the systematic analytical exercise of restricting or extending the application of a discrete rule, ordinarily signified through stereotypical language; second, the demonstration that logic without revelation in the form of a scriptural formulation and exegesis produces unreliable results. There are other recurrent patterns of complex linguistic formation matched by sustained thought that conform to the indicative traits yielded by these two distinct ones. The formal traits are fairly uniform, even though the intent—the upshot of the dialectical exegesis—varies from instance to instance. Very often these amplifications leave the base verse far behind, since they follow a program of their own, to which the base verse and its information is at best contributory. One of the ways in which this formalization of language differs from the foregoing is that the exegesis that is simple in form always is closely tied to the base verse, whereas the one that pursues larger-scale structural issues very frequently connects only very loosely to the base verse. Another persistent inquiry, external to any given verse and yielding, in concrete terms, no general rule at all, asks how to harmonize two verses, the information of which seems to conflict. The result is a general proposition that verses are to be drawn into alignment with one another.

This brief account of the formal preferences of Sifré to Deuteronomy suffices to indicate that all but one recurrent rhetorical pattern serve propositional, not solely exegetical purposes. They make possible the presentation of propositions of an encompassing character, not merely the ad hoc and episodic statement of the sense of a verse or clause of a verse of scripture. We may say that the rhetorical structure of our document presupposes an other-than-exegetical intent for the whole. That draws us onward to the more profound issue of the inner logic of cogency characteristic of the document.

THE LOGIC OF INTELLIGIBLE DISCOURSE

By "logic of intelligible discourse" we mean a very specific thing. It concerns how two or more sentences are seen by an authorship to relate to one another and to form a cogent statement. The issue of determining what connects one sentence to another and how cogency is established is critical to our understanding of how this authorship addressed scripture, that is, made use of scripture in its presentation of its ideas. When we know and can describe the character of the connections between one thing and another, one fact and another—which can be quite diverse— we point to the logics of intelligible discourse for our authorship. It is that repertoire of logics that makes the thought of one person or authorship intelligible to some other person(s). When we have reached the end of our examination of the repertoire of these logics, we shall spell out what we conceive to be at stake in finding out how in Sifré to Deuteronomy two or more sentences join together to form a cogent statement. At that final point we shall see how probative for defining the character of the document as a whole is the issue of the logics of cogent discourse implicit within this writing. Then we shall understand the full weight of evidence behind our claim that, for the sages of the Judaism of the dual Torah, scripture formed an instrument of writing, a principal part of speech, but not the structure and construction of discourse.

COGENCY AND THE ISSUE OF CONNECTION:
THE FOUR LOGICS OF INTELLIGIBLE DISCOURSE
IN SIFRÉ TO DEUTERONOMY

One sentence—in modes of intelligible discourse familiar to us—not only stands beside, but generates another; a consequent statement follows from a prior one. We share a sense of connection, pertinence, relevance—the aptness of joining thought A to thought B to produce proposition 1. These (only by way of example) form intelligible discourses, turning facts into statements of meaning and consequence. To conduct intelligible discourse, therefore, people make two or more statements that, in the world in which they say their piece, are deemed self-evidently to hang together and form a proposition understood by someone else in that same world. It is the matter of self-evident cogency and intelligibility, in the document at hand, that now gains our attention. When people write with scripture, they appeal to a logic of cogency that is independent of the cogency established by the sequence of verses of scripture. When they propose to present what is an essentially exegetical discourse, then scripture forms the premise, implicit throughout, of cogency, self-evidently joining otherwise unrelated sentences to one another and into a sizable discourse utterly lacking in a single purposive proposition of any kind. But in so stating, we have moved far ahead of our argument. Let us begin from the first principle.

Discourse shared by others begins when one sentence joins to a second one in framing a statement (whether or not presenting a proposition) in such a way that others understand *the connection* between the two sentences.[1] In the document at hand we see four different logics by which two sentences are deemed to cohere and to constitute a statement of consequence and intelligibility. One is familiar to us as philosophical logic, the second is equally familiar as the logic of cogent discourse attained through narrative. These two, self-evidently, are logics of a propositional order, evoking a logic of a philosophical character. Now the third is not propositional, and, as a matter of fact, it also is not ordinarily familiar to us at all. It is a mode of joining two or more statements—sentences—not on the foundation of meaning or sense or proposition but on the foundation of a different order altogether. It presents the greatest difficulty in exposition, although numerous examples will show beyond doubt that our authorship took for granted the

1. At the end I shall propose that what is shared among many documents of the Judaism of the dual Torah is the mode of connection common among them all. The system reaches definition in the interstice between sentence and sentence.

mode of connection we shall define and describe. And the fourth, distinct from the prior three, is a mode of establishing connections at the most abstract and profound level of discourse, the level of methodical analysis of many things in a single way, and that forms the single most commonplace building block of thought in our document. It is, as a matter of fact, stunning in its logical power. But, in a limited sense, it also is not propositional, although it yields its encompassing truths of order, proportion, structure, and self-evidence.

Let us first consider the two familiar modes of turning two sentences into a coherent statement with weight and meaning that connects the two sentences, forming them into a whole that in meaning and intelligible proposition transcends the sum of the parts. Then we shall point to the third and fourth logics before us. In the next sections we shall offer examples of each of the four kinds of cogent and therefore intelligible discourse in our document.

PHILOSOPHICAL DISCOURSE:
PROPOSITIONS AND ARGUMENTS FROM FACTS AND REASON

Let us first give one example of the philosophical mode of stating and proving propositions, that is, repeatedly deriving one thing from many things. Then we shall offer a more general description of the logic at hand.

CCCXXVI:I

1. A. ["For the Lord will vindicate his people and repents himself [JPS: take revenge] for his servants, when he sees that their might is gone, and neither bond nor free is left. He will say, 'Where are their gods, the rock in whom they sought refuge, who ate the fat of their offerings and drank their libation wine? Let them rise up to your help and let them be a shield unto you. See, then, that I, I am he; there is no god beside us. I deal death and give life; I wounded and I will heal, none can deliver from our hand. Lo, I raise my hand to heaven and say, As I live forever, when I whet my flashing blade and my hand lays hold on judgment, vengeance will I wreak on my foes, will I deal to those who reject me, will I make my arrows drunk with blood, as my sword devours flesh—blood of the slain and the captive, from the long-haired enemy chiefs.' O nations, acclaim his people, for he will avenge the blood of his servants, wreak vengeance on his foes, and cleanse the land of his people" (Deut. 32:36–43).]

    B. "For the Lord will vindicate his people:"

    C. When the Holy One, blessed be he, judges the nations, it is a joy to him, as it is said, "For the Lord will vindicate his people."

D.   But when the Holy One, blessed be he, judges Israel, it is—as it were—a source of grace to him.

E.   For it is said, ". . . and repents himself [JPS: take revenge] for his servants.

F.   Now "repents" can only mean "regret," for it is said, "For I regret that I made them" (Gen. 6:7),

G.   and further, "I regret that I made Saul king" (1 Sam. 15:11).

The contrast between the meaning of words when they apply to gentiles and to Israel forms the basis for the familiar proposition before us. We shall now see a systematic demonstration of the proposition that, when things are at their worst and the full punishment impends, God relents and saves Israel.

CCCXXVI:II

1.   A.   ". . . when he sees that their night is gone, and neither bond nor free is left:"

    B.   When he sees their destruction, on account of the captivity.

    C.   For all of them went off.

2.   A.   Another teaching concerning the phrase, ". . . when he sees:"

    B.   When they despaired of redemption.

3.   A.   Another teaching concerning the phrase, ". . . when he sees [that their might is gone, and neither bond nor free is left]:"

    B.   When he sees that the last penny is gone from the purse,

    C.   in line with this verse: "And when they have made an end of breaking in pieces the power of the holy people, all these things shall be finished" (Dan. 12:7) [Hammer's translation].

4.   A.   Another teaching concerning the phrase, ". . . when he sees that their might is gone, and neither bond nor free is left:"

    B.   . When he sees that among them are no men who seek mercy for them as Moses had,

    C.   in line with this verse: "Therefore he said that he would destroy them, had not Moses his chosen one stood before him in the breach" (Ps. 106:23). . . .

6.   A.   Another teaching concerning the phrase, ". . . when he sees that their might is gone, and neither bond nor free is left:"

    B.   When he sees that among them are no men who seek mercy for them as Aaron had,

    C.   in line with this verse: "And he stood between the dead and the living and the plague was stayed" (Num. 17:13).

7.   A.   Another teaching concerning the phrase, ". . . when he sees that their might is gone, and neither bond nor free is left:"

    B.   When he sees that there are no men who seek mercy for them as Phineas had,

C. in line with this verse: "Then stood up Phineas and wrought judgment and so the plague was stayed" (Ps. 106:30).
8. A. Another teaching concerning the phrase, ". . . when he sees that their
might is gone, and neither bond nor free is left:"
B. None shut up, none [Hammer:] at large, none helping Israel.

The completion of what God sees is diverse but on the whole
coherent. No. 1 introduces the basic theme invited by the base verse,
namely, Israel's disheartening condition. Then the rest of the items
point to the unfortunate circumstance of Israel and the absence of
effective leadership to change matters. Whereas philosophers in the
Greco-Roman tradition will have made their points concerning other
topics entirely, modes of proof will surely have proved congruent to the
systematic massing of probative facts, all of them pertinent, all of them
appropriate to the argument and the issue.

Now to frame matters in more general terms: In the canonical writings
of the Judaism of the dual Torah, represented by Sifré to Deuteronomy,
authorships present their propositions in ways that are familiar to us, as
well as in one way that we do not, in general, find in our own intellectual
world. Overall, writers rely upon one of four available means of linking
sentence to sentence in paragraphs. The first is to establish propositions
that rest upon philosophical bases, e.g., through the proposal of a thesis
and the composition of a list of facts that prove the thesis. This—to us
entirely familiar, Western—mode of scientific expression through the
classification of data that, in a simple way, we may call the science of
making lists (*Listenwissenschaft*) is best exemplified by the Mishnah, but
it dominates in such profoundly philosophical-syllogistic documents as
Leviticus Rabbah as well. Within the idiom of the canonical writings of
the dual Torah, those documents bring us closest to the modes of
thought with which we are generally familiar. When, in later sections of
this chapter, we review how the authorship of Sifré to Deuteronomy
proposes to link two or more sentences into intelligible discourse, we
shall see, in a distinctive idiom of expression to be sure, a broad range of
philosophical modes of stating and then proving or establishing propositions. No philosopher in antiquity will have found unintelligible these
types of units of thought.

The issue at hand is one of connection, that is, not of fact (such as is
conveyed by the statement of the meaning of a verse or a clause of a
verse) but of the relationship between one fact and another. That relationship, e.g., connection, is shown in a conclusion, different from the
established facts of two or more sentences, that we propose to draw when

we set up as a sequence two or more facts and claim out of that sequence to propose a proposition different from, transcending, the facts at hand. We demonstrate propositions in a variety of ways, appealing to both a repertoire of probative facts and also a set of accepted modes of argument. In this way we engage in a kind of discourse that gains its logic from what, in general, we may call philosophy: the rigorous analysis and testing of propositions against the canons of an accepted reason. Philosophy accomplishes the miracle of making the whole more—or less—than the sum of the parts, that is, in the simple language we have used up to now, showing the connections between fact 1 and fact 2, in such wise as to yield proposition A. We begin with the irrefutable fact; our issue is not how facts gain their facticity, rather, how, from givens, people construct propositions or make statements that are deemed sense and not nonsense or gibberish. So the problem is to explain the connections between and among facts, so accounting for the conclusions people draw, on the one side, or the acceptable associations people tolerate, on the other, in the exchange of language and thought.

One mode of making connections in the philosophical mode—and the most familiar—is the linking of one sentence to another so as to make a statement that transcends both contributing statements. This logic is called syllogistic. This syllogism conveys and also proves a proposition, e.g., the variant on a famous syllogistic argument:

1. All Greeks are philosophers;
2. Demosthenes is a Greek;
3. Therefore Demosthenes is a philosopher.

At issue is not mere facticity, rather broadly speaking, the connections between facts. The problem subject to analysis here then is how one thing follows from something else, or how one thing generates something else, thus, as we said, connection. And by "logic," we mean simply what in the context of the mind of the authorship of Sifré to Deuteronomy connects one thing to something else. But for the present purpose we appeal not to the philosophical statement in the sages' peculiar idiom, such as we have already noted and shall presently examine once again, rather to the more familiar and accessible Western idiom of abstraction.

In that context, then, the sentences 1, 2, and 3, standing entirely by themselves, convey not a proposition but merely statements of a fact, which may or may not be true, and which may or may not bear sense and meaning beyond itself. Sentence 1 and sentence 2 by themselves state facts but announce no proposition. But the logic of syllogistic discourse joins the two into No. 3, which indeed does constitute a proposition and also (by the way) shows the linkage between sentence 1 and sentence 2. But there are more ways for setting forth propositions, making points, and thus for undertaking intelligible discourse, besides the philosophical and syllogistic one with which we are familiar in the West. We know a variety of other modes of philosophical-propositional discourse, that is to say, presenting, testing, and demonstrating a proposition through appeal to fact and argument.

Another way is to offer a proposition, lay out the axioms, present the proofs, test the proposition against contrary argument, and the like. A third way (not necessarily distinct from the second) is the demonstration we know, in general, as *Listenwissenschaft*, that is, a way to classify and so establish a set of probative facts, which compel us to reach a given conclusion. These probative facts may derive from the classification of data, all of which point in one direction and not in another. A catalogue of facts, for example, may be so composed that, through the regularities and indicative traits of the entries, the catalogue yields a proposition. A list of parallel items all together point to a simple conclusion; the conclusion may or may not be given at the end of the catalogue, but the catalogue—by definition—is pointed. All the catalogued facts are taken to bear self-evident connections to one another, established by those pertinent shared traits implicit in the composition of the list, therefore also bearing meaning and pointing through the weight of evidence to an inescapable conclusion. The discrete facts then join together because of some trait common to them all. This is a mode of classification of facts to lead to an identification of what the facts have in common and—it goes without saying—an explanation of their meaning. These and other modes of philosophical argument are entirely familiar to us all. In calling all of them "philosophical," we mean only to distinguish them from the other three logics we shall presently examine.

NARRATIVE DISCOURSE:
PROPOSITIONS PROVED BY TELEOLOGY

Connection is attained, in our document, not only through the philosophical demonstration of a proposition, e.g., in syllogistic argument. For a proposition emerges not only through philosophical argument and analysis, e.g., spelling out in so many words a general and encompassing proposition, and further constructing in proof of that explicit generalization a syllogism and demonstration. We may state and demonstrate a proposition in a second way, which resorts to narrative (itself subject to a taxonomy of its own) both to establish and to explain connections between naked facts. Let us spell this out.

A proposition (whether or not it is stated explicitly) may be set forth and demonstrated by showing through the telling of a tale (of a variety of kinds, e.g., historical, fictional, parabolic, and the like) that a sequence of events, real or imagined, shows the ineluctable truth of a given proposition. The logic of connection demonstrated through narrative, rather than philosophy, is simply stated. It is connection attained and explained by invoking some mode of narrative in which a sequence of events, first this, then that, is understood to yield a proposition, first this, then that *because of this*. That sequence both states and establishes a proposition in a way different from the philosophical and argumentative mode of propositional discourse. Whether or not the generalization is stated in so many words rarely matters, because the power of well-crafted narrative is to make unnecessary explicit drawing of the moral.

That is why we argue that this second logic, besides the logic of philosophy and syllogistic argument, is one of that narrative that sees cogency in the purpose, the necessary order of events seen as causative. That is then a logic or intelligibility of connection that is attained through teleology: the claim of purpose, therefore cause, in the garb of a story of what happened because it had to happen. Narrative conveys a proposition through the setting forth of happenings in a framework of inevitability, in a sequence that makes a point, e.g., establishes not merely the facts of what happens, but the teleology that explains those facts. Then we speak not only of events—our naked facts—but of their relationship. We claim to account for that relationship teleologically, in the purposive sequence and necessary order of happenings. In due course we shall see how various kinds of narratives serve to convey highly intelligible and persuasive propositions.

The parable, as we said above, forms a subset of the narrative. The parable makes its point by telling a story in which vivid action, producing contrasts between the good way and the bad way, the desired result and the rejected result, tells the story. The parable of course—by its very definition—is general and is so told as to apply to everyone everywhere in a timeless present. What holds the parable together is both explicit and implicit. The explicit cogency derives from the power of the story itself, with its beginning, middle, and end, or with its tension and resolution. The implicit cogency is contained by the proposition that the parable is meant to illustrate. In our document it is very common for that proposition to be stated explicitly in a prior pericope, to which the parable then is attached. The parable forms a fine instance of how connection is demonstrated through the logic of narrative.

Let us turn to concrete instances of narrative as a mode of cogent discourse. All parables, among narratives, present their points through the tensions and resolutions accomplished, again by indirection, through the mode of the unfolding of the story. These points may be more than one-dimensional, and they do not always serve the purpose of the framer of the document as a whole; we find cases in which the editor announces that a parable makes a given point, whereas the parable itself states a quite different point altogether. But the discourse is wholly cogent, and all the sentences join together in a tight and united way to make a highly intelligible point. We take an example, more or less at random from The Fathers According to Rabbi Nathan, because the parable at hand operates at more than a single level and therefore serves to make two propositions, one explicit, the other implicit.

A parable is like a story, in that the narrative is centered on things people do, rather than on what they say, and the message is carried by the medium of described action, commonly with a point of tension introduced at the outset and resolved at the end. A parable is different from a story in that its author presents a totally abstract tale, not mentioning specific authorities, placing the action in concrete time and setting, or invoking an authoritative text (e.g., a proof text of scripture). Like a story, a parable does not serve to prove a point of law or supply a precedent. As to the sage story in particular, whereas a sage story centers on a sage's exemplary actions as the point of tension and resolution, a parable ordinarily focuses on wisdom or morality, which the parable's narrator proposes to illustrate. A parable teaches its lesson explicitly, a story about a sage is rarely explicit in specifying its lesson, and the implicit lesson is always the exemplary character of the sage and what he does—whatever it is, whatever its verbal formulation as a lesson. So there is a very considerable difference between the parable and the story. One example of a parable, so labeled, The Fathers According to Rabbi Nathan, is at **I:XIII.2**:

I:XIII

2.   A.   R. Simeon b. Yohai says, "I shall draw a parable for you. To what may the first Man be compared? He was like a man who had a wife at home. What did that man do? He went and brought a jug and put in it a certain number of dates and nuts. He caught a scorpion and put it at the mouth of the jug and sealed it tightly. He left it in the corner of his house.

B. "He said to her, 'My daughter, whatever I have in the house is entrusted to you, except for this jar, which under no circumstances should you touch.' What did the woman do? When her husband went off to market, she went and opened the jug and put her hand in it, and the scorpion bit her, and she went and fell into bed. When her husband came home from the market, he said to her, 'What's going on?'

C. "She said to him, 'I put our hand into the jug, and a scorpion bit us, and now I'm dying.'

D. "He said to her, 'Didn't I tell you to begin with, "Whatever I have in the house is entrusted to you, except for this jar, which under no circumstances should you touch."' He got mad at her and divorced her.

E. "So it was with the first man.

F. "When the Holy One, blessed be he, said to him, *Of all the trees of the garden you certainly may eat, but from the tree of knowledge of good and evil you may not eat, for on the day on which you eat of it, you will surely die* (Gen. 2:7),

G. "on that day he was driven out, thereby illustrating the verse, *Man does not lodge overnight in honor* (Ps. 49:24)."

Simeon's point is that by giving man the commandment, God aroused his interest in that tree and led man to do what he did. The explicit proposition is the first point, we sin at our obsession. The implicit proposition is that God bears a measure of guilt for the fall of man.[2]

The trait of the parable that draws our attention is its impersonality: The details of the narrative point toward the lesson to be drawn and, it goes without saying, not to the specificities of the name of the man and the day of the week and the place of the event. These have no bearing, obviously, because the parable is parabolic, intended to state in a concrete narrative a general point. The parable in its narrative traits is the opposite of a historical story, such as we find told about sages. The one is general, universal, pertinent to humanity wherever and whenever the narrated event takes place. The other is specific, particular, relevant to a concrete circumstance and situation and person.

---

2. I may point out that, in The Fathers According to Rabbi Nathan, the parable may be parachuted down, with slight connection to the proposition that it is supposed to prove or illustrate. In Sifré to Deuteronomy, by contrast, I cannot point to a single parable that is distinct from the proposition that it is supposed to prove, and in most cases, the statement of the parable includes an explicit proposition, start and again at the end. There are other differences among parables, as that type of narrative makes its appearance in a variety of documents, and, it follows, the description and interpretation of parables as a literary genre require the differentiation among the parables as these occur in various documents, respectively. I do not think that those who claim to work on parables have as yet recognized their analytical task.

NONPROPOSITIONAL, YET INTELLIGIBLE DISCOURSE: A NEGATIVE DEFINITION

We come, third, to the one genuinely odd mode of discourse in our document, one which, in our intellectual world and culture, is unfamiliar although not unknown. In order to avoid trivialization or misunderstanding of what, in time, became the single most commonplace mode of discourse in the world of Judaism from antiquity to the modern times, only at the end shall we propose for this logic a name. It is a phenomenon to be approached in stages, first negative, then positive. Before proceeding with a negative definition, let us give an illustrative case that derives from our document and so avoid excessively abstract description. Here we have a sequence of absolutely unrelated sentences, made up in each instance of a clause of a verse, followed by a phrase of amplification. Nothing links one sentence (completed thought) to the ones fore or aft. Yet the compositors have presented us witl what they represent side by side with sentences that do form large compositions, that is, that are linked one to the next by connection that we can readily discern. That seems to us to indicate that our authorship conceives one mode of connecting sentences to form a counterpart to another.

XXV:I

1. A. "What kind of place are we going to? Our kinsmen have taken the heart out of us, saying, ['We saw there a people stronger and taller than we, large cities with walls sky-high, and even Anakites']" (Deut. 1:25–28):
   B. They said to him, "Moses, our lord, had we heard these things from ordinary people, we should have never believed it.
   C. "But we have heard it from people whose sons are ours and whose daughters are ours."

We continue the clause-by-clause exposition. What is amplified is the reference to "our kinsmen."

XXV:II

1. A. "We saw there a people . . . taller than we:"
   B. This teaches that they were tall.
2. A. ". . . and greater . . .:"
   B. This teaches that they were numerous.

The clause-by-clause reading adds little to the obvious sense.

XXV:III

1. A. ". . . large cities with walls sky-high, and even Anakites:"

    B.   Rabban Simeon b. Gamaliel says, "In the present passage, scriptures speak in exaggerated language: 'Hear O Israel, you are going to pass over the Jordan this day to go in to dispossess nations greater and mightier than yourself, cities great and fortified up to heaven' (Deut. 9:1).

    C.   "But when God spoke to Abraham, scripture did not use exaggerated language: 'And we will multiply your seed as the stars of the heaven' (Gen. 26:4), 'And we will make your seed as the dust of the earth' (Gen. 13:16)."

Simeon's statement makes its own point and has no bearing upon the exposition of the present passage.

XXV:IV

1.   A.   ". . . and even Anakites did we see there:"

    B.   This teaches that they saw giants on top of giants, in line with this verse: "Therefore pride is as a chain about their neck" (Ps. 73:6).

The cited verse uses the word for giants.

XXV:V

1.   A.   "And we said to you:"

    B.   He stressed to them, "It is not on our own authority that we speak to you, but it is on the authority of the Holy One that we speak to you."

The point is familiar.

XXV:VI

1.   A.   "Do not be frightened and do not be afraid of them:"

    B.   On what account?

    C.   "for the Lord your God is the one who goes before you."

    D.   He said to them, "The one who did miracles for you in Egypt and all these miracles is going to do miracles for you when you enter the land:

    E.   "'According to all that he did for you in Egypt before your eyes' (Deut. 1:30).

    F.   "If you do not believe concerning what is coming, at least believe concerning what has already taken place."

Moses' argument is now spelled out in complete form. That each unit of thought, signified by a roman numeral, stands by itself hardly needs proof, since it is a self-evident fact of discourse here. That is the example. Now to its exposition. To begin with, we set forth the connection, then attempt to define it.

In our document, as in many others in the canon, we find side by side a sequence of sentences that bear no relationship or connection at all among one another. These discrete sentences have come before us in "commentary form," for instance:

"Clause 1:" "this means A."
"Clause 2:" "this refers to Q."

Nothing joins A and Q. Indeed, had we used symbols out of different classifications altogether, e.g., A, a letter of an alphabet, and #, which stands for something else than a sound of an alphabet, the picture would have proved still clearer. Nothing joins A to Q or A to # except that clause 2 follows clause 1. The upshot is that no proposition links A to Q or A to #, and so far as there is a connection between A and Q or A and # it is not propositional. Then is there a connection at all? We think the authorship of the document that set forth matters as they did assumes that there is such a connection. For there clearly is—at the very least— an order, that is, "clause 1" is prior to "clause 2," in the text that out of clauses 1 and 2 does form an intelligible statement, that is, two connected, not merely adjacent, sentences. When we give concrete examples of the phenomenon, the reader will find this abstract statement of matters entirely plausible.

Now to move ahead in the statement of the logic of connection that is not propositional and yet that is exceedingly common in the canonical writings, as common as the atom, commentary form itself. The upshot of the negative is that the connection between two facts is not established by the confluence or intersection of propositions, whether philosophically or teleologically. The upshot of the positive is that the connection is established in ways particular to the literary culture, the textual community, before us. Associations that are deemed the absolute given of all discourse are invoked, yielding no proposition at the joint of what is nonetheless an ineluctable connection.

The negative route to definition begins in the traits of the sustained discourse at hand, that is, sequences of sentences that do not relate to one another in sense or meaning or proposition at all. This third way in which two or more sentences are deemed, in the canonical literature of Judaism, to constitute a more than random, episodic sequence of unrelated allegations, A, X, Q, C, and so on, on its own, out of context, yields gibberish—no proposition, no sense, no joining between two sentences, no implicit connection accessible without considerable labor of access. But this third way can see cogent discourse even where there is no proposition at all, and even where the relationship between sentence A and sentence X does not derive from the interplay among the propositions at hand. It is hard for us even to imagine nonpropositional, yet intelligible discourse, outside the realm of feeling or inchoate attitude, and yet, as we shall see, before us is a principle of intelligible discourse that is entirely routine, clearly assumed to be comprehensible, and utterly accessible. This third logic rests on a premise of education—that is, of prior discourse attained through processes of learning a logic not accessible, as are the logics of philosophy and narrative, but through another means. We shall return to this point at the end. Let us first list the negative traits, asking for a moment of the reader's patience before we proceed in positive traits to the clear definition of the logic at hand. Now to the concrete, negative traits, which overlap.

The first negative trait of this mode of discourse is that it is not made cogent by addressing, or relating to, a given, shared proposition; hence, we underline, while fully exposed in words and not restricted to feeling or attitude or emotion, nonetheless it is a logic that is *non-propositional*. And yet, we would maintain, it is in its context deemed cogent and consecutive, as much as philosophical and narrative ways of presenting and proving propositions are received as cogent, and as much as sentences in philosophical and narrative discourse are understood as consecutive.

A second also essentially negative trait of the logic under discussion is that the burden of establishing meaning rests not upon what is said but upon some other principle of cogency entirely. A set of associations will join what is otherwise discrete. In propositional discourse, what is said by Rabbi X relates because of the substance of the matter to what is said by Rabbi Y. We have seen, in our catalogue of forms, a propositional form of this kind. Thus the point of intersection of two or more sentences lies not with attributive, Rabbi X says, but with the proposition, *what* the rabbi maintains. If we for the moment call the attributive clause the protasis and what is attributed the apodosis, then propositional discourse centers upon the apodosis and nonpropositional discourse upon the protasis. That is, two or more sentences link to a common point but not to one another, which is another way of calling this mode of discourse nonpropositional.

A third negative trait of these sequences of discrete facts, or sentences—in a measure repetitive of the first and second—deserves explication on its own. It is that the sentences do not form a proposition even though they are deemed cogent with one another. "The dog stands on the corner. Chile bombed Peru." These two facts or sentences in no way connect. And yet, facts of a similarly unrelated character, sentences as wildly incongruous as these, can stand quite comfortably side by side in what is clearly proposed as a cogent unit of thought and intelligible discourse in our document. Our authorship clearly means to appeal to a source of cogency deriving from a principle of connection other than the—to us sole—kind of cogency we can grasp, which is the propositional kind.[3]

The third logic rests upon the premise that an established sequence of words joins whatever is attached to those words into a set of cogent statements, even though it does not form of those statements propositions of any kind, implicit or explicit. The established sequence of words may be made up of names always associated with one another. It may be made up of a received text, with deep meaning of its own, e.g., a verse or a clause of scripture. It may be made up of the sequence of holy days or synagogue lections, which are assumed to be known by everyone and so to connect on their own. The fixed association of these words, whether names, whether formula such as verses of scripture, whether lists of facts, serves to link otherwise unrelated statements to one another and to form of them all not a proposition but, nonetheless, *an entirely intelligible sequence of connected or related sentences.* Even though these negative definitions intersect and in a measure cover the same ground, each requires its own specification—but we shall ask only a mite more of the reader's indulgence.

NONPROPOSITIONAL, YET INTELLIGIBLE DISCOURSE: A POSITIVE DEFINITION. THE LOGIC OF FIXED ASSOCIATION

To state matters affirmatively, the third logic is one of *fixed association.* That is, there is, in the document before us as in many other rabbinic writings, a logic that joins one sentence to another not because of what is said or the proposition at stake in what is said, but because of a fixed association among traits or formulas common to sequential sentences but external to them all. That association is always fixed and extrinsic to the passage(s) at hand. We state for the document before us, there is not a single instance in which two or more facts, that is, discrete sentences, are set side by side on a principle of the intrinsic link of the one to the next (apart from a propositional link of course), which would be appropriately called free association: "There is this, and, by the way, this reminds us of

---

3. I do not mean to ignore functional cogency, e.g., the discrete facts collected in a telephone book, but that principle of connection of sentences into sustained discourse does not function in our document. I of course do not deny that there are yet other modes of finding connections besides the four I claim to discern in Sifré to Deuteronomy.

that," when neither this nor that join to form a proposition. To take the case we gave earlier, free association would permit someone to present as a set of connected facts, lacking all proposition, something like the following:

"The dog stands on the corner."
[That reminds us:]
"Chile bombed Peru."

A well-known example of how connection makes sense of otherwise unrelated facts is this simple statement: We can make propositions out of the Providence (R.I.) or Rochester (N.Y.) telephone books simply by adding the word "begat" between each entry.

That rather odd example of a connection of fixed association raises the question of whether or not (as is sometimes claimed by the romantic or the uninformed) what forms connections is mere free association. Let us state as a matter of simple fact that there is no case in our document in which the contents of one sentence stimulate a compositor to put down the next sentence only because one thing happens to remind the compositor of something else, that is, without all reference to a principle of association external to both sentences (our "fixed association") and without all reference to a shared proposition that connects the two. Not one case! The representation of any document in the rabbinic canon as exemplary in its logic of connection of a principle of free association— which some might call simply making things up as you go along—seems to us parlous and probably unlikely. But for this document, it is wrong. Rather than expanding in abstract terms upon that painfully abstract way of expressing matters, let us give yet another concrete instance and then generalize. The one given here presents an example of the logic of fixed association comprising specific names. That is to say, a sequence of unrelated sentences form—in the mind of the framers of a unit of thought—connected sentences forming cogent discourse. What relates those unrelated sentences forms the logic of fixed (prior) association.

Our next illustrative case derives from Mishnah-tractate Avot, The Fathers, Chapter 1. The chapter is made up of three units, first, three names, then five paired names, finally, three more names. That the names are not random but meaningful, that the fixed association of name A with name B, name C with name D, name E with name F, and so on, is deemed cogent—these are the premises of all discourse in Chapter 1 of The Fathers. The premise rests on the simple fact that these names are announced as sequential, set by set—e.g., the first holds office M, the second, office N—and then in their unfolding, the first group is prior in time to the second, and so on. The order matters and conveys the information, therefore, that the compositor or author wishes to emphasize or rehearse. So when we claim that the logic of fixed association links sentences into meaningful compositions, even though it does not find cogency in the proposition at hand, we believe that claim rests upon the givens of reading the chapter at hand that universally prevail among all interpreters. No one known to us maintains that the fixed associations of the names of The Fathers Chapter 1 are lacking in consequence. But, standing by themselves, they do lack all propositional character. Let us show that fact.

The fact that the logic of fixed association appeals to an available structure to form connections between otherwise unconnected sentences becomes clear only when we see the matter in situ. Let us take up a small passage of The Fathers, so that the point will be entirely clear. We examine The Fathers 1:1-3. We present in italics the apodosis—the propositions, the things that people say, which would correspond to the propositions of a syllogistic, philosophical discourse. In plain type is the attributive or, in the less precise usage introduced earlier, the protasis.

> 1:1. Moses received the Torah at Sinai and handed it on to Joshua, Joshua to elders, and elders to prophets. And prophets handed it on to the men of the great assembly. They said three things: *Be prudent in judgment. Raise up many disciples. Make a fence for the Torah.*
>
> 1:2. Simeon the Righteous was one of the last survivors of the great assembly. He would say: *On three things does the world stand: On the Torah, and on the Temple service, and on deeds of lovingkindness.*
>
> 1:3 Antigonus of Sokho received [the Torah] from Simeon the Righteous. He would say: *Do not be like servants who serve the master on condition of receiving a reward, but [be] like servants who serve the master not on condition of receiving a reward. And let the fear of Heaven be upon you.*

Now if we ask ourselves what the italicized words have in common, how they form a cogent discourse, the answer is clear. They have nothing in common (though some may claim they are joined in overall theme) and, standing by themselves, do not establish a proposition in common. As propositions in sequence, they do not form an intelligible discourse. But—and this must stand as a premise of all argument—in the mind of the authorship of The Fathers, which has set matters forth as we see them, those same words serve intelligible discourse. But the principle of cogency, upon which intelligibility rests, does not derive from what is said. A shared topic by itself does not in our view constitute an adequate logic of connection between two otherwise discrete sentences, although, admittedly, a shared topic is better than none at all. But we can offer, in the document at hand, a range of compositions appealing clearly to the connection of fixed association, yet lacking all topics in common, for example, Chapter 5, with its sequences of lists of different things that have some trait in common but that in no way point to a shared proposition or prove a syllogism of any kind.

Since, self-evidently, we find no syllogistic statement or other philosophically formulated proposition, and since we find no narrative of any sort, we address a mode of intelligible discourse that falls into a different classification from either philosophical or narrative logic. What holds the several sentences together is—to revert to the description of the third logic of our document—the principle of fixed association. That is, in this context, the principle that things are deemed to form a fixed sequence, specifically, the list of named authorities. The premise that because Rabbi X is linked on a common list—a text, a canon of names—with Rabbi Y, and linked in that order, first X, then Y, accounts (for the authorship at hand) for the intelligibility of the writing before us: this is connected to that. That is to say, the logic joining one sentence to another in The Fathers derives from the premise of fixed associations or, stated in more general terms, an established or classic text, This formulation of fixed associations, this received text—in this case, a list of names—joins together otherwise unrelated statements. What makes two or more sequential sentences of Chapter 1 or Chapter 5 of The Fathers into an intelligible statement overall (or in its principal parts) is not *what* is said but (in this context) *who* does the saying. The list of those canonical names, in proper order, imparts cogency to an otherwise unintelligible sequence of statements (any one of which, to be sure, is as intelligible as the statement, "all Greeks are philosophers").

The upshot is that a statement that relies for intelligibility upon the premise of fixed associations, e.g., an established text (whether a list of names, whether a passage of scripture, whether the known sequence of events, as in the Pesher-writings, whether the well-known sequence of events in the life of a holy man) differs in its fundamental logic of cogency from one that relies for intelligibility upon either narrative, on the one side, or philosophical and syllogistic thought, on the other. What holds the whole together? It is knowledge shared among those to whom this writing is addressed; hence, the "fixed" part of "fixed association," as distinct from (mere) free association. Cogency therefore is social, therefore not ever the product of private, free association, any more than form ever permits individual manner of expressing ideas. Connection here rests on the premise of education or what we may call the system and structure of a textual community (using the phrase in no technical sense). That premise derives from prior discourse attained through processes of learning; it is not a logic readily accessible, as are the logics of philosophy and narrative, but one that comes only through the training of the mind, e.g., the learning of the terms that are fixed in their association with one another. Our authorship assumes that the discrete sentences form an intelligible statement (even with an unarticulated proposition, though that need not detain us), in which sentence A joins sentence B to say something important, even though that statement is not conveyed by what A says and what B says. For these sentences to form connected statements, we have then to know that these names bear meaning, in their facticity (of course), but also in the order in which they occur, in the conglomerates that they comprise.

We have carefully named this mode of logic "fixed association." The reason is twofold. First, as we have already suggested, we wish vigorously to deny that the received literature of Judaism, as exemplified by Sifré to Deuteronomy, makes a place for free association. Not a single completed unit of thought in our document is put together through the free and undisciplined, therefore subjective, association of this, that, and the other thing. So we speak of "fixed association" explicitly to reject the conception of "free association." Our sages were intellectuals of a most serious, rigorous, and disciplined kind. Their principles of association were not always stated in such a way that we immediately grasp them. But these were principles, not merely acts of indulgence of personal caprice, such as free association tolerates and even celebrates.

Second, because fixed associations derived from a variety of sources, we do not want to confuse the mode of thought, the logic of fixed association, with one form taken by that mode, which is "commentary." The fixed and conventional associations that join A to Q or A to # derive not only from prior writing, e.g., scripture; they derive also from other matters seen as sequential, e.g., holy days, historical periods or events, names of authorities (as we just saw). Hence, the "text" for fixed associations need not be textual, and in a profound sense, it is not at all textual, that is, set formulas of words received as holy writ.[4] For not only statements appealing for the logic of cogency to fixed association invoke a written text, e.g., scripture, and not only statements in the form of a commentary on a text form cogent units of discourse merely because discrete sentences refer to a single text in common. Many statements

---

4. I think that when we can define that "text" and how fixed associations take shape in this canon, we shall know how to define that "Judaism" that transcends all the canonical writings and forms the premise and foundation for each one of them.

that utilize verses of scripture and even impute meanings to those verses in fact form highly propositional compositions. Accordingly, we avoid calling this mode of fixed-associative thought (mere) commentary or exegesis, in which discrete thoughts are joined to a common text and by that common text alone, even though, in form and in volume, the discrete sentences of part of our document do attain cogency and connection, one to the next, through fixed association with the base text.

To summarize this part of the argument: "Commentary" speaks of a form, a rhetorical model, and it presupposes "text." "Fixed association" calls up a principle of linking sentence to sentence and framing intelligible discourse. "Commentary" (in this context) reduces and trivializes, assuming that for cogency discrete sentences in all discourse invariably refer back to the text that is commented upon; "fixed association" allows a broad variety of discourse, on a wide range of "texts," to be classified in a single way as a mode of logic. What is at stake is understanding how documents coalesce, which is to say, how thought and intelligible discourse are realized. And a variety of the writings of the Judaism of the dual Torah find its center of gravity in fixed associations of an other-than-exegetical form, not as "commentary" in any sense at all. The "fixed associations" that yield a text were not always textual at all, although in our document most were. Fixed association, as we said, are what impose cogency on such disparate expressions of culture as, first, the entirety of Pesiqta deRab Kahana, which holds together because we know in advance the cycle of the liturgical year, and second, the names of The Fathers, Chapter 1, and, third, the canonical sequence of facts that compose the history of Israel in the structure of Genesis Rabbah and Leviticus Rabbah, e.g., repertoires of heroes and saints, or of enemies, lists of events such as the entry into the land, building of the first temple, destruction, building of the second temple, destruction, end of days and coming of the messiah, and the like. Compositions that appeal to such fixed associations but otherwise prove disparate in failing to register a proposition are not invariably exegetical at all, because they appeal to fixed sequences of facts that are not always preserved in textual form. The sages themselves dictate the texts, some of them written, some of them oral, some of them verbal, some of them not. So there are varieties of sources of fixed associations, generally known and available for appeal in the search for that order, proportion, balance, and above all source of the self-evidence of what makes immediate sense, that, in the aggregate, form the principle that sentence A may not only juxtapose with sentence B but, lacking all propositional intersection, logically and necessarily stand next to sentence B.

NONPROPOSITIONAL, YET INTELLIGIBLE DISCOURSE:
THE COGENCY OF A FIXED ANALYTICAL METHOD
IN THE FORMATION OF INTELLIGIBLE DISCOURSE

An important qualification now is required, and this yields our fourth logic of intelligible discourse as promised at the outset. It is discourse in which one analytical method applies to many sentences, with the result that many discrete and diverse sentences are shown to constitute a single intellectual structure. Various explanations and amplifications, topically and propositionally unrelated, are joined in such a way, which is very common in our document. Here we have a fixed way of connecting diverse things, so showing that many things really conform to a single pattern or structure. It is the promiscuous application to a range of discrete facts of a single mode of thought, that is, a cogent analytical method. Let us define matters and then give a single example of the phenomenon. First the definition: Methodologically coherent analysis then imposes upon a variety of data a structure that is external to all the data, yet that imposes connection between and among facts or sentences, a connection consisting in the order and balance and meaning of them all, seen in the aggregate. One of the most common modes of intelligible discourse in our document is to ask the same question to many things and to produce a single result, wherever that question is asked: methodical analysis of many things showing pattern and therefore order where, on the surface, none exists. Now to make concrete what, lacking an illustration, proves altogether too abstract, we given an instance of the matter.

CVII:III

1. A. "... and spend the money on anything you want [cattle, sheep, wine or other intoxicant, or anything you may desire. And you shall feast there, in the presence of the Lord your God, and rejoice with your household]" (Deut. 14:22–26):

    B. R. Judah says, "Might one suppose that if what is purchased for money in the status of tithe should become unclean, it requires redemption [through the exchange with funds, and these latter funds will be used for the purchase of other food]?

    C. "And it is a matter of logic. If food in the status of second tithe that itself became unclean, lo, that food has to be redeemed, that food purchased with money that becomes unclean should surely have to be redeemed!

    D. "Scripture states, '... silver.'

    E. "The sense is, the money first exchanged, not money later on exchanged.

F.   "I know only that that applies to money in a state of cleanness. How
      about money in a state of uncleanness?
G.   "Scripture states, '. . . silver.'
H.   "The sense is, the money first exchanged, not money later on
      exchanged."

In concrete terms what we do here is investigate the logical standing
of details, asking whether they are meant to be restrictive or augmentative and expansive. Scripture refers to one detail, in its formulation of
cases. Does the detail limit the rule to itself? Or does the detail typify, by
its traits, the range to which the rule applies. Must we deal with money
in the form of silver, or does silver stand for money in general? That is,
do we form the rule, out of the case, restrictively or augmentatively and
expansively? In answering that question once, we state a mere fact. In
repeatedly asking and answering that question, we conduct a methodical
analysis. And the upshot of that analysis, throughout, is to turn the
details of scripture's statement of a case into a general rule, applicable
beyond the case. Overall, we show that many things form one thing, that
is to say, diverse cases conform to a single logic and constitute, all
together and in the aggregate, a single highly cogent and coherent
statement, even though each of the individual sentences of that statement bears slight relationship to any other of those sentences. What is
important then is not the item by itself—the unit of thought seen all
alone—but the repeated effect of imposing upon diverse units of thought
a single analytical, that is, logical program. Here is the same thing done
to something else.

CVII:IV

1. A.   ". . . spend the money on anything you want [cattle, sheep, wine or
          other intoxicant, or anything you may desire. And you shall feast
          there, in the presence of the Lord your God, and rejoice with your
          household]" (Deut. 14:22–26):
    B.   Might one suppose that it is permitted to purchase male slaves, female
          slaves, or real estate?
    C.   Scripture says, ". . . cattle, sheep."
    D.   I know only that one may purchase food. How about drink?
    E.   Scripture says, ". . . wine or other intoxicant."
    F.   I know only that one may purchase food or drink. How about things
          that improve food and drink, such as costus root, amomum, heads of
          spices, crowfoot root, asafetida, peppers, and saffron lozenges [all:
          Hammer]?
    G.   Scripture says, ". . . or anything you may desire."
    H.   Is it possible that one may purchase also water and salt?

I.   Scripture says, ". . . cattle, sheep, wine or other intoxicant"—
J.   now what distinguishes these items is that they are produce deriving from produce, growing from the earth, so I know only that things which are produce, deriving from produce, growing from the earth [may be purchased, thus excluding water and salt].

Whereas there is no proposition particular to the case, there most certainly is a recurrent methodical analysis, one that demonstrates how a great many cases really conform to a single mode of methodical analysis. True, there is no implicit proposition, all the more so an explicit one. Yet the logic does demonstrate a fundamental trait, one that is *systematically* critical, if, in detail, particular to the case at hand. So that sort of middle-level proposition that we see in the forms that demonstrate, through diverse verses or facts, a given point distinguishes the first two logics from this one. Here, as we said previously, we find another kind of generalization all together, one that encompasses principles embedded in the foundation of thought, principles of the very structure of reality— not details of that structure conveyed by propositions that apply to a variety of middle-range cases.

That methodical analysis in fact imposes stunning cogency on otherwise unrelated facts or sentences, showing one thing out of many things. For unity of thought and discourse derives not only from what is said, or even from a set of fixed associations. It may be imposed—as our two cases have shown us—by addressing a set of fixed questions, imposing a sequence of stable procedures, to a vast variety of data. That yields not a proposition, not even a sequence of facts formerly unconnected but now connected, but a different mode of cogency, one that derives from showing that many things follow a single rule or may be interpreted in a single way. It is the intelligible proposition that is general and not particular, that imposes upon the whole a sense of understanding and comprehension, even though the parts of the whole do not join together. What happens, in this mode of discourse, is that we turn the particular into the general, the case into a rule, and if we had to point to one purpose of our authorship overall, it is to turn the cases of the Book of Deuteronomy into rules that conform, overall, to the way in which the Mishnah presents its rules: logically, topically, a set of philosophically defensible generalizations.

The conception that fixed analytical methods, plans for how one was to compose cogent thought, governed sages' discourse comes to us not merely through the intrinsic traits of the writings at hand. We have, in fact, an explicit statement of one ongoing analytical task. It is to find, in the details of the Torah, encompassing rules. That search for the one thing that is implicit in the many things corresponds, in one concrete way, to the fourth logic of our catalogue, that is, the conception that sages persistently applied a single mode of methodical analysis to a wide variety of passages. In doing so, they produced cogent statements, out of many things, of some one thing. The methodical analysis, then, made possible yet another kind of intelligible discourse. This one yielded not so much proposition as a sense of proportion, order, and understanding, transcendent of any given proposition.

CCCVI:XVIII

1. A. Another teaching concerning the phrase, "May our discourse come down as the rain:"
   B. R. Nehemiah would say, "One should always draw together words of Torah and frame them as encompassing rules."
   C. Might one suppose that, just as one should always draw together words of Torah and frame them as encompassing rules, so one should express them as encompassing rules?
   D. Scripture says, ". . . our speech distill as the dew."
   E. "Distill" bears meaning in Canaanite language in accord with the following comparison:
   F. One does not say to his fellow, "Collect this *sela* for us," but rather, "Distill this *sela* for us," [that is, using the same word as is before us, meaning, spread out, break into small change].
   G. Along these same lines, one should always draw together words of Torah and frame them as encompassing rules, but then break them out and express them like drops of dew, and not like drops of rain.
   H. Not like drops of rain, which are great, but like drops of dew, which are small.

Another statement of the same notion, that many things yield one thing, and that Torah learning requires an inductive process requiring the survey of much but also the organization of much into a few general principles, is in the following as well:

CCCVI:XXIV

1. A. Another teaching concerning the phrase, "May our discourse come down as the rain, [our speech distill as the dew, like showers on young growths, like droplets on the grass]:"
   B. R. Meir would say, "One should also collect teachings of the Torah in the form of encompassing principles, for if you collect them solely as details, they will exhaust you and in the end you will not know what to do anyhow.
   C. "The matter may be compared with the case of someone who went to Caesarea and needed a hundred or two hundred *zuz* for the trip. If he

took the money as change, the coins would tire him out and he would not know what to do. But if he put them together and brought *sela*-coins with him, and then paid them out one by one wherever he wanted, [then he could manage].

D. "So too, someone who goes to Bet Ilias to the market and needed a hundred manehs or even two myriads for the expense of the trip. If he took the money as *selas*, the coins would tire him out and he would not know what to do. But if he turned them into denars of gold and then paid them out in change as he needed, [he would be all right]."

2. A. ". . . like showers on young growths:"

B. When someone goes to study the Torah, at first he does not know what to do, until he repeats two scrolls or two Divisions [of the Mishnah].

C. Then the rest will be drawn to him like showers on young growths.

CCCVI:XXV

1. A. Another teaching concerning the phrase, "May our discourse come down as the rain, [our speech distill as the dew, like showers on young growths, like droplets on the grass]:"

B. Just as rain falls on various trees and gives to each its appropriate flavor in accord with its species, to the vine in accord with its species, to the olive in accord with its species, to the fig in accord with its species,

C. so the words of the Torah are whole and one, encompassing Scripture, the Mishnah, Talmud, laws, lore.

2. A. ". . . like showers on young growths:"

B. Just as showers fall on grass and help them grow, and there are grasses that are red, green, black, white,

C. so words of the Torah reach some who are sages, some who are suitable, some who are righteous, some who are pious [and vivify them all].

The dynamic process—organize, collect, then restate in systematic disposition of detail—corresponds to that methodical analysis that we claim to find at the foundations of numerous units of thought and that imparts cogency to discrete sentences.

AN EXAMPLE OF FIXED-ASSOCIATIVE DISCOURSE
AND ITS COGENCY

The fixed-associative mode of discourse in our document appeals not to a list of names but to the equivalent of a (mere) list of names, namely, a verse of scripture—indeed, most of the verses of the Book of Deuteronomy. Let us rapidly review the criteria for the logic of fixed association. The negative ones are, first, the sentences, two or more, do not all together yield a statement that transcends the sum of the parts. Fact 1, fact 2 will not yield fact 3 (or proposition A). The two facts remain just what they were: unrelated facts. Fixed-associative compositions, it follows, do not gain cogency through statements of propositions. The sentences are cogent, but the cogency derives from a source other than shared propositions or participation in an argument yielding a shared proposition. The fixed association derives, it follows from a "text" outside of the composition at hand and known to, taken for granted by, the composition at hand. That "text" may be a list of names; it may be a received document or portion thereof. But it is the given, and its cogency is the single prevailing premise that otherwise unrelated facts belong together in some sort of established sequence and order. Here is another simple instance.

CLXXVIII:III

1. A. ". . . the prophet has uttered it presumptuously:"
    B. One is liable for acting presumptuously, and one is not liable for acting in error.
2. A. ". . . do not stand in dread of him:"
    B. Do not hesitate to hold him guilty as charged.

Each numbered unit forms a single declarative sentence. No. 1 makes a distinction important only in legal theory, and No. 2 simply exhorts people to enforce the law. Nothing joins No. 1 to No. 2 except that both rest upon clauses of the same verse. The compositor of the passage took for granted that that fixed association validated his joining No. 1 to No. 2. We must admit that our sample contains very few instances of this logic. The fourth logic by contrast is ubiquitous in our document.

AN EXAMPLE OF THE COGENT DISCOURSE ATTAINED THROUGH FIXED ANALYTICAL METHOD

One recurring exercise, which fills up much of the discussion of the legal passages of Deuteronomy in Sifré to Deuteronomy, systematically proposes to generalize the case discourse of the Book of Deuteronomy and to reframe the case into the example of a law. The "if a person does such and so," or the details of a case as spelled out in scripture, are subjected to a sustained exercise of generalization. In this exercise we do two things. Either—in the process of generalization—we restrict the rule, or we extend it. If scripture contains a detail, such as the statement of a case always demands, we ask whether that detail restricts the rule to a kind of case defined by the detail, or whether that detail represents a more general category of cases and is to be subjected, therefore, to generalization. (In the unfortunate term of contemporary philosophy, the fixed analytical method at hand investigates issues of generalizability.) Here is an example of many instances in which the authorship of a sustained discourse proposed to turn a case into a law.

CLXVI:I

1. A. "[You shall also give him] the first fruits of your new grain and wine and oil, [and the first shearing of your sheep. For the Lord your God has chosen him and his descendants, out of all your tribes, to be in attendance for service in the name of the Lord for all time]" (Deut. 18:1–6):
   B. This teaches that offerings are taken up for the priestly rations only from produce of the finest quality.

The point applies to more than the case at hand.

2. A. Just as we find that as to two varieties of produce of fruit-bearing trees, priestly rations are not taken from the one to provide the requisite gift for the other as well,
   B. so in the case of two varieties of produce of grain and vegetables, priestly rations are not taken from the one to provide the requisite gift for the other as well.

No. 2 is parachuted down and has no bearing upon anything in the cited verse. But the importance is to derive a general rule, as stated at B, that applies to a broad variety of categories of priestly gifts, just as at No. 1.

CLXV:II

1. A. ". . . the first shearing of your sheep:"
   B. not the fleece that falls off when the sheep is dipped.
2. A. ". . . the first shearing of your sheep:"
   B. excluding a sheep that suffers from a potentially fatal ailment.
3. A. ". . . the first shearing of your sheep:"
   B. whether in the land or abroad.

No. 1 is particular to our verse; Nos. 2 and 3 are general rules invoked case by case. These items are not coherent, one by one, and the three sentences in no way state a single proposition, explicit or otherwise. And yet the exercise of analysis is uniform—we could give many dozens of cases in which precisely the same distinctions are made—and the purpose is clear. It is to impose upon the case a set of generalizing issues, which yield either restrictive or expansive definitions. This is a fine instance of what we mean by attaining cogent discourse—linking one sentence to another—through an established methodical analysis of one sort or another.

CLXVI:IV

1. A. "You shall also give him:"
   B. This indicates that there should be sufficient fleece to constitute a gift.
   C. On this basis sages have ruled:
   D. How much does one give to the priest?
   E. Five *selas'* weight in Judah, equivalent to ten in Galilee, bleached but not spun,
   F. sufficient to make a small garment from it.
   G. as it is said, "You shall also give him:"
   H. This indicates that there should be sufficient fleece to constitute a gift.

The same pattern recurs as before, and the interest is in an autonomous program. This represents a different kind of methodical analysis. The framer wishes to relate a verse of scripture to a rule in the Mishnah and so asks how C–F are founded on scripture. G–H go over the ground of A–B. The work of restriction or expansion of the rule is now implicit, of course.

IS THE LOGIC OF SIFRÉ TO DEUTERONOMY AN EXEGETICAL LOGIC?

No, the prevailing logic of our authorship is not exegetical but propositional. Most units of cogent discourse in Sifré to Deuteronomy appeal for cogency to propositions, not to fixed associations, such as characterize commentaries and other compilations of exegeses of verses of scripture. Commentary, strictly speaking, has no need for propositions, although through commentary an authorship may propose to prove propositions. A document formed in order to convey exegesis attains cogency and imparts connections to two or more sentences, by appeal to fixed associations. It makes no call upon narrative, does not demand recurrent methodical analyses. The text that is subjected to commentary accomplishes the joining of sentence to sentence, and to that cogency, everything else proves secondary. At stake in what follows, therefore, is an assessment of the true character of our document. Is Sifré to Deuteronomy in its logical formations essentially a commentary? Or is it something else? If it is that something else, as we maintain it is, then we fairly claim that the logics of the document define discourse as propositional, not exegetical—a fine instance of what it means to write with scripture. Let us undertake a rough statistical summary of a survey of the logics of the units of completed thought of Sifré to Deuteronomy:[5]

Logic	Propositional Units of Cogent Discourse		Nonpropositional Units	
Fixed-associative			159	13.9%
Propositional	690	60.4%		
Narrative	61	5.3%		
Methodical-analytical	232	20.3%		
	983	86.0%	159	13.9%

More than 85% of all itemized units of discourse find cogency through one or another mode of propositional logic. That figure is confirmed by yet another. Of the propositional units of cogent discourse, 70.1% in fact constitute propositional discourse, 6.2% find cogency in narrative, and 23.6% in the methodical-analytical mode. Since that mode presents not one but two propositions, we find ourselves on firm ground in maintaining that the logic of Sifré to Deuteronomy is a logic not of exegesis but of sustained proposition of one kind or another. Our document's authorship links one sentence to another by appeal to connections of proposition, not mere theme, and only occasionally asks the structure of a verse or sequence of verses to sustain the intelligible joining of two or more sentences into a coherent and meaningful statement.

These questions then conclude the matter. First, do the rhetoric and logic of our document derive from the (supposed) purpose of the authorship of forming a commentary? Not at all. To the contrary, in general, the logic of our document is sustained, propositional, mostly philosophical, and not that of commentary. What holds things together for our authorship does not rely upon the verse at hand to impose order and cogency upon discourse. To the contrary, the authorship of this document ordinarily appeals to propositions to hold two or more sentences together. If, by definition, a commentary appeals for cogency to the text that the commentators propose to illuminate, then ours is a document that is in no essential way a commentary. The logic is not that of a commentary, and (as we saw in the opening discussion) the formal

5. This table summarizes the results of Neusner, *Sifré to Deuteronomy. An Introduction to the Rhetorical, Logical, and Propositional Program* (Atlanta: Scholars Press for Brown Judaic Studies, 1987), chapters 3 and 4.

repertoire shows strong preference for other than commentary form. So far as commentary dictates both its own rhetoric and its own logic, this is no commentary. Sifré to Deuteronomy is, in fact, a highly argumentative, profoundly well crafted and cogent set of propositions. We may indeed speak of a message, a topical program, such as, in general, a commentary that in form appeals to a clause of a verse and a phrase of a sentence and in logic holds things together through fixed associations, is not apt to set forth. A commentary makes statements about meanings of verses, but it does not make a set of cogent statements of its own. We have now shown that in rhetoric and in logic Sifré to Deuteronomy takes shape in such a way as to yield a statement or a set of cogent statements. Such a document as ours indicates that an authorship has found a need for propositions to attain cogency or impart connections to two or more sentences, calls upon narrative, demands recurrent methodical analyses.

6

Arguing through Scripture

THE USE OF SCRIPTURE
IN SIFRA'S CRITIQUE OF THE MISHNAH

Sifra, an address to the Book of Leviticus, employs a well-defined and restricted program of formal and rhetorical conventions to set forth within a single system of logical cogency an encompassing argument and determinate proposition. A framer of a pericope used in Sifra's final compilation could make use of one or more of three forms but no others. Not only so, but he ordinarily appealed to one paramount mode of logical coherence to make an intelligible point, but rarely to the other three that were available. And in the aggregate, when seen over all, the document that the framer helped to formulate again and again made a single stunning and encompassing point, an argument concerning the appropriate mode of classifying things. We can think of no more probative case of the contrast between a well-crafted, propositional document and a haphazard compilation of commonplaces than that between Sifra (and Sifré to Deuteronomy), on the one side, and Mekhilta Attributed to R. Ishmael, on the other. Whereas, as we shall shortly observe, the framers of pericopes in that Mekhilta Attributed to R. Ishmael's nine tractates used a variety of forms, appealed to all sorts of logics, and made a vast number of episodic points, or none at all, their counterparts in Sifra invoked a limited repertoire of rhetorical patterns, made cogent by a single logic of coherent discourse, to make one point, many times over. The match among rhetoric, logic, and proposition contrasts with the indifference to rhetorical, logical, and propositional congruity that we shall find characteristic of Mekhilta Attributed to R. Ishmael and its nine tractates, severally and jointly.

Three formal conventions characterize Sifra, and since a sizable repertoire of other forms were utilized by other authorships, we may state with finality that this authorship in particular made choices about the formal plan of its document. And, as we shall see, these choices corresponded to the authorship's polemical purpose in framing the document. What were these three forms? The first, the dialectical, is the demonstration that if we wish to classify things, we must follow the taxa dictated by scripture rather than relying solely upon the traits of the things we wish to classify. The second, the citation form, invokes the citation of passages of the Mishnah or the Tosefta in the setting of scripture. The third is what we call commentary form, in which a phrase of scripture is followed by an amplificatory clause of some sort. The forms of the document admirably expressed the polemical purpose of the authorship at hand. What they wished to prove was that a taxonomy resting on the traits of things without reference to scripture's classifications cannot serve. They further wished to restate the oral Torah in the setting of the written Torah. And, finally, they wished to accomplish the whole by rewriting the written Torah. The dialectical form accomplishes the first purpose, the citation form the second, and the commentary form the third.

The simple commentary form is one in which a verse, or an element of a verse, is cited, and then a very few words explain the meaning of that verse. Second come the complex forms, in which a simple exegesis is augmented in some important way, commonly by questions and answers, so that we have more than simply a verse and a brief exposition of its elements or of its meaning as a whole. The authorship of the Sifra time and again wishes to show that prior documents, Mishnah or Tosefta, cited verbatim, require the support of exegesis of scripture for important propositions, presented in the Mishnah and the Tosefta not on the foundation of exegetical proof at all. In the main, moreover, the authorship of Sifra tends not to attribute its materials to specific authorities, and most of the pericopae containing attributions are shared with Mishnah and Tosefta. As we should expect, just as in Mekhilta Attributed to R. Ishmael, Sifra contains a fair sample of pericopae that do not make use of the forms common in the exegesis of specific scriptural verses, and, mostly, do not pretend to explain the meaning of verses, but rather resort to forms typical of Mishnah and Tosefta. When Sifra uses forms other than those in which its exegeses are routinely phrased, it commonly, although not always, draws upon materials also found in Mishnah and Tosefta. It is uncommon for Sifra to make use of nonexegetical forms for materials peculiar to its compilation. As a working hypothesis, to be corrected presently, the two forms of rhetorical patterning of language in Sifra are two, simple and complex.

Every example of a complex form, that is, a passage in which we have more than a cited verse and a brief exposition of its meaning, may be called "dialectical," that is, moving or developing an idea through questions and answers, sometimes implicit, but commonly explicit. What "moves" is the argument, the flow of thought, from problem to problem. The movement is generated by the raising of contrary questions and theses. There are several subdivisions of the dialectical exegesis, so distinctive as to be treated by themselves. But all exhibit a flow of logical argument, unfolding in questions and answers, characteristic, in the later literature, of the Talmud. One important subdivision of the stated form consists of those items, somewhat few in number but all rather large in size and articulation, intended to prove that logic alone is insufficient, and that only through revealed law is a reliable view of what is required attained. The polemic in these items is pointed and obvious; logic (DYN) never wins the argument, although at a few points flaws in the text seem to suggest disjunctures in the flow of logic. There are some few instances of this form in Mekhilta Attributed to R. Ishmael.

The rhetorical plan of Sifra leads us to recognize that the exegetes, although working verse by verse, in fact have brought a considerable program to their reading of the Book of Leviticus. It concerns the interplay of the oral Torah, represented by the Mishnah, with the written Torah, represented by the Book of Leviticus. That question demanded, in their view, not an answer comprising mere generalities. They wished to show their results through details, masses of details, and like the rigorous philosophers that they were, they furthermore argued essentially through an inductive procedure, amassing evidence that in its accumulation made the point at hand. The syllogism we have identified about the priority of the revelation of the written Torah in the search for truth is nowhere expressed in so many words, because the philosopher-exegetes of the rabbinic world preferred to address an implicit syllogism and to pursue or to test that syllogism solely in a sequence of experiments of a small scale. Sifra's authorship therefore finds in the Mishnah and Tosefta a sizable laboratory for the testing of propositions. We have therefore to ask at what points do Sifra and Mishnah and Tosefta share a common agenda of interests, and at what points does one compilation introduce problems, themes, or questions unknown to the other? The answer to these questions will show that Sifra and Mishnah and Tosefta form two large concentric circles, sharing a considerable area in common. Sifra, however, exhibits interests peculiar to itself. On the criterion of common themes and interests, Mishnah and Tosefta and Sifra exhibit a remarkable unity. If we had to compare the rhetorical program of

Sifra's authorship with that of their counterparts in our document, we should say that the latter group has taken over and vastly expanded the program selected by the former. More to the point, the two documents intersect, but for Sifré to Deuteronomy, the rhetorical intersection covers only a small segment of the whole plan governing the formulation of the document. In that sense, we have to say that our authorship has made choices and has not simply repeated a restricted program available to all rabbinic authorships and utilized at random by each.

To clarify these general remarks, let us now address a particular chapter of Sifra and out of its details form a theory of the repertoire of forms on which our authorship has drawn. When we take up a sample chapter of Mekhilta Attributed to R. Ishmael, we shall find valuable the encounter with a quite different document.

Parashat Vayyiqra Dibura Denedabah Parashah 7

XIV:I

1. A.   ["If his offering to the Lord is a burnt offering of birds, he shall choose [bring near] his offering from turtledoves or pigeons. The priest shall bring it to the altar, pinch off its head, and turn it into smoke on the altar; and its blood shall be drained out against the side of the altar. He shall remove its crop with its contents and cast it into the place of the ashes, at the east side of the altar. The priest shall tear it open by its wings, without severing it, and turn it into smoke on the altar, upon the wood that is on the fire. It is a burnt offering, an offering by fire, of pleasing odor to the Lord" (Lev. 1:14–17)]:

   B.   "[The priest] shall bring it [to the altar]:"

   C.   What is the sense of this statement?

   D.   Since it is said, "he shall choose [bring near] his offering from turtledoves or pigeons," one might have supposed that there can be no fewer than two sets of birds.

   E.   Accordingly, scripture states, "[The priest] shall bring it [to the altar]" to indicate, [by reference to the "it,"] that even a single pair suffices.

Reduced to its simplest syntactic traits, the form consists of the citation of a clause of a verse, followed by secondary amplification of that clause. We may call this commentary form, in that the rhetorical requirement is citation plus amplification. Clearly, the form sustains a variety of expressions, e.g., the one at hand: "what is the sense of this statement . . . since it is said . . . accordingly scripture states. . . ." But for our purposes there is no need to differentiate within the commentary form.

2. A.   "The priest shall bring it to the altar, pinch off its head:"

   B.   Why does scripture say, "The priest . . . pinch off . . ."?

    C.   This teaches that the act of pinching off the head should be done only by a priest.

    D.   But is the contrary to that proposition not a matter of logic:

    E.   If in the case of a beast of the flock, to which the act of slaughter at the north side of the altar is assigned, the participation of a priest in particular is not assigned, to the act of pinching the neck, to which the act of slaughter at the north side of the altar is not assigned, surely should not involve the participation of the priest in particular!

    F.   That is why it is necessary for scripture to say, "The priest . . . pinch off . . .,"

    G.   so as to teach that the act of pinching off the head should be done only by a priest.

3.   A.   Might one compose an argument to prove that one should pinch the neck by using a knife?

    B.   For lo, it is a matter of logic.

    C.   If to the act of slaughter [of a beast as a sacrifice], for which the participation of a priest is not required, the use of a correct utensil is required, for the act of pinching the neck, for which the participation of a priest indeed is required, surely should involve the requirement of using a correct implement!

    D.   That is why it is necessary for Scripture to say, "The priest . . . pinch off. . . ."

4.   A.   Said R. Aqiba, "Now would it really enter anyone's mind that a nonpriest should present an offering on the altar?

    B.   "Then why is it said, 'The priest . . . pinch off. . .'?

    C.   "This teaches that the act of pinching the neck must be done by the priest using his own finger [and not a utensil]."

5.   A.   Might one suppose that the act of pinching may be done either at the head [up by the altar] or at the foot [on the pavement down below the altar]?

    B.   It is a matter of logic:

    C.   If in the case of an offering of a beast, which, when presented as a sin offering is slaughtered above [at the altar itself] but when slaughtered as a burnt offering is killed below [at the pavement, below the altar], in the case of an offering of fowl, since when presented as a sin offering it is slaughtered down below, surely in the case of a burnt offering it should be done down below as well!

    D.   That is why it was necessary for scripture to make explicit [that it is killed up by the altar itself:] "The priest shall bring it to the altar, pinch off its head, and turn it into smoke on the altar."

    E.   The altar is explicitly noted with respect to turning the offering into smoke and also to pinching off the head.

    F.   Just as the offering is turned into smoke up above, at the altar itself, so the pinching off of the head is to be done up above, at the altar itself.

The form at hand is to be characterized as a dialectical exegetical argument, in which we move from point to point in a protracted, yet very tight, exposition of a proposition. The proposition is both implicit and explicit. The implicit proposition is that "logic" does not suffice. The explicit proposition concerns the subject matter at hand. We may identify the traits of this form very simply: citation of a verse or clause + a proposition that interprets that phrase, then "it is a matter of logic" followed by the demonstration that logic is insufficient for the determination of taxa.

XIV:II

1. A. ". . . pinch off its head:"
   B. The pinching off of the head is done at the shoulder.
   C. Might one suppose that it may be done at any other location?
   D. It is a matter of logic. Lo, we shall argue as follows:
   E. Here an act of pinching off the neck is stated, and elsewhere we find the same [Lev. 5:8: "He shall bring them to the priest, who shall offer first the one for the sin offering, pinching its head at the nape without severing it"].
   F. Just as pinching off at the neck in that passage is to be done at the nape of the neck, so pinching off at the neck in the present context is to be done at the nape of the neck.
   G. Perhaps the analogy is to be drawn differently, specifically, just as the pinching stated in that other passage involves pinching the neck without dividing the bird [Lev. 5:8: "without severing it"], so the importance of the analogy is to yield the same rule here.
   H. In that case, the priest would pinch the neck without severing it.
   I. Accordingly, [the ambiguous analogy is such as to require] scripture to state, ". . . pinch off its head."

We have an example of the dialectical exegesis of the limitations of logic for definition of taxa.

2. A. "[turn it into smoke on the altar;] and its blood shall be drained out:"
   B. Can one describe matters in such a way?
   C. Specifically, after the carcass is turned into smoke, can one drain out the blood?
   D. But one pinches the neck in accord with the way in which one turns it into smoke:
   E. Just as we find that the turning of the carcass into smoke is done up to the head by itself and then the body by itself, so in the act of pinching the neck, the head is by itself and the body is by itself.
3. A. And how do we know that in the case of turning a carcass into smoke, the head is done by itself?

B. When Scripture says, "The priest [shall tear it open by its wings, without severing it,] and turn it into smoke on the altar" (Lev. 1:17),

C. lo, the turning of the body into smoke is covered by that statement.

D. Lo, when Scripture states here, "pinch off its head, and turn it into smoke on the altar," it can only mean that the head is to be turned into smoke by itself.

E. Now, just as we find that the turning of the carcass into smoke is done up to the head by itself and then the body by itself, so in the act of pinching the neck, the head is by itself and the body is by itself.

Nos. 2 and 3 present in a rather developed statement the simple exegetical form. The formal requirement is not obscured, however, since all we have is the citation of a clause followed by secondary amplification. This version of commentary form obviously cannot be seen as identical to the other; but so far as the dictates of rhetoric are concerned, there is no material difference, since the variations affect only the secondary amplification of the basic proposition, and in both cases, the basic proposition is set forth by the citation of the verse or clause followed by a sentence or two of amplification.

XIV:III

1. A. ". . . and its blood shall be drained out [against the side of the altar]:"

    B. all of its blood: he takes hold of the head and the body and drains the blood out of both pieces.

This is commentary form.

2. A. ". . .against the side of the altar:"

    B. not on the wall of the ramp up to the altar, and not on the wall of the foundation, nor on the wall of the courtyard.

3. A. It is to be on the upper half of the wall.

    B. Might one suppose it may be on the lower half of the wall?

    C. It is a matter of logic: in the case of the sacrifice of a beast, which, if done as a sin offering, has its blood tossed on the upper part of the wall, and if done as a burnt offering, has its blood tossed on the lower part of the wall,

    D. in the case of the sacrifice of a bird, since, if it is offered as a sin offering, the blood is tossed at the lower half of the wall, should logic not dictate that if it is offered as a burnt offering, its blood should be tossed on the lower part of the wall as well?

    E. That is why it is necessary for scripture to frame matters in this way:

    F. "The priest shall bring it to the altar, pinch off its head, and turn it into smoke on the altar; and its blood shall be drained out against the side of the altar,"

G. the altar is noted with respect to turning the carcass into smoke and also with reference to the draining of the blood.

H. Just as the act of turning the carcass into smoke is done at the topside of the altar, so the draining of the blood is done at the topside of the altar.

This is the dialectical exegetical form. Now we come to a third usage.

4. A. How does the priest do it?

B. The priest went up on the ramp and went around the circuit. He came to the southeastern corner. He would wring off its head from its neck and divide the head from the body. And he drained off its blood onto the wall of the altar [M. Zeb. 6:5B–E].

C. If one did it from the place at which he was standing and downward by a cubit, it is valid. R. Simeon and R. Yohanan ben Beroqah say, "The entire deed was done only at the top of the altar" [T. Zeb. 7:9C–D].

What we have now is the verbatim citation of a passage of the Mishnah or of the Tosefta, joined to its setting in the exegetical framework of Sifra by some sort of joining formula. We shall call this formal convention Mishnah-citation-form. Its formal requirement is simply appropriate joining language.

XIV:IV

1. A. "He shall remove its crop [with its contents and cast it into the place of the ashes, at the east side of the altar]:"

B. this refers to the bird's crop.

C. Might one suppose that one should extract the crop with a knife and remove it surgically?

D. Scripture says, ". . . with its contents."

E. He should remove it with its contents [including the innards, or, alternatively, the feathers].

F. Abba Yosé b. Hanan says, "He should remove the intestines with it."

A variation on commentary form, we have secondary development at C, might one suppose? I am not inclined to think a sizable catalogue of variations on commentary form will materially advance our inquiry.

We now turn to a summary of the form-analytical study of Sifra as a whole. Counting each entry as a single item presents a gross and simple picture of the proportions of the types of forms we catalogued in our analysis of the document. Since numerous entries in each of the catalogues encompass more than a single item, the understatement of the numbers of examples in any one catalogue will be balanced by understatements of the numbers of examples in the other catalogues. Overall, our count is as follows:

Form	Number of Entries	Percentage of the Whole
Commentary	121	55%
Dialectical	57	26%
Citation	42	19%
	220	100%

The rough proportions of forms can stand considerable refinement, but we may say with some certainty that Sifra's authorship planned to produce a commentary to the Book of Leviticus, and that commentary would encompass two major, although not ubiquitous, concerns. We shall presently give examples of the sustained discourse of Sifra, in which the rhetorical or formal patterns just now noted are fully exposed.

Just as a limited and fixed pattern of formal preferences characteristic of the document as a whole, so a simple logical program, consisting of three logics of cogent discourse, served for every statement. Sifra's authorship made choices about how cogent and coherent statements would be made to hold together in its document. Counting each entry as a single item presents a gross and simple picture of the proportions of the types of logics we have catalogued. Since numerous entries in each of the catalogues encompass more than a single item, the understatement of the numbers of examples in any one catalogue is balanced by understatements of the numbers of examples in the other catalogues. Overall, our count is as follows:

Type of Logic	Number of Entries	Percentage of the Whole
Propositional	73	30.4%
Teleological	1	0.4%
Fixed-associative	43	17.9%
Methodical-analytical	123	51.0%
	240	99.7%

The operative logics are mainly propositional, approximately 82%, inclusive of propositional, teleological, and methodical-analytical compositions. An authorship intending what we now call a commentary will have found paramount use for the logic of fixed association. That logic clearly served only a modest purpose in the context of the document as a whole.

Our authorship developed a tripartite program. It wished to demonstrate the limitations of the logic of hierarchical classification, such as predominates in the Mishnah; that forms a constant theme of the methodical-analytical logic. It proposed, second, to restate the Mishnah within the context of scripture, that is, to rewrite the written Torah to make a place for the oral Torah. This is worked out in the logic of propositional discourse. And, finally, it wished in this rewriting to represent the whole Torah as a cogent and unified document. Through the logic of fixed association it in fact did re-present the Torah. What the authorship of Sifra wished to prove was that a taxonomy resting on the traits of things without reference to scripture's classifications cannot serve. They further wished to restate the oral Torah in the setting of the written Torah. And, finally, they wished to accomplish the whole by rewriting the written Torah. The dialectical form accomplished the first purpose, the citation form the second, and the commentary form the third.

For its topical program the authorship of Sifra takes the Book of Leviticus. For propositions Sifra's authorship presents episodic and ad hoc sentences. If we ask how these sentences form propositions other than amplifications of points made in the Book of Leviticus itself, and how we may restate those propositions in a coherent way, so far as we can see, nothing sustained and coherent emerges. Without leading the reader through all 277 chapters of Sifra, we state simply that Sifra does not constitute a propositional document transcending its precipitating text. But that in no way bears the implication that the document's authorship merely collected and arranged this and that about the Book of Leviticus. This matter requires amplification, first negatively, then positively.

For three reasons, we must conclude that Sifra does *not* set forth propositions in the way in which the Rabbah-compilations and Sifré to Deuteronomy do. First, in general we fail to see a topical program distinct from that of scripture, nor do we find it possible to set forth important propositions that transcend the cases at hand. Sifra remains wholly within scripture's orbit and range of discourse, proposing only to expand and clarify what it found within scripture. Where the authorship moves beyond scripture, it is not toward fresh theological or philosophical thought, but rather to a quite different set of issues altogether, concerning Mishnah and Tosefta. When we describe the topical program of the document, the blatant and definitive trait of Sifra is simple: The topical program and order derive from scripture. Just as the Mishnah defines the topical program and order for Tosefta, the Yerushalmi, and the Bavli, so scripture does so for Sifra. It follows that Sifra takes as its structure the plan and program of the written Torah, by contrast to decision of the framers or compilers of Tosefta and the two Talmuds.

Second, for sizable passages, the sole point of coherence for the discrete sentences or paragraphs of Sifra's authorship derives from the base verse of scripture that is subject to commentary. That fact corresponds to the results of the form analysis and the description of the logics of cogent discourse. Whereas, as we have noted, the Mishnah holds thought together through propositions of various kinds, with special interest in demonstrating propositions through a well-crafted program of logic of a certain kind, Sifra's authorship appeals to a different logic altogether. It is one that we have set forth as fixed-associative discourse. That is not a propositional logic—by definition.

The third fundamental observation draws attention to the paramount position, within this restatement of the written Torah, of the oral Torah. We may say very simply that, in a purely formal and superficial sense, a sizable proportion of Sifra consists simply in the association of completed statements of the oral Torah with the exposition of the written Torah, the whole *re*-presenting as one whole Torah the dual Torah received by Moses at Sinai (speaking within the Torah myth). Even at the very surface we observe a simple fact. Without the Mishnah or the Tosefta, our authorship will have had virtually nothing to say about one passage after another of the written Torah. A deeper knowledge of Sifra, set forth in our complete translation, has shown, furthermore, that far more often than citing the Mishnah or the Tosefta verbatim, our authorship cites principles of law or theology fundamental to the Mishnah's treatment of a given topic, even when the particular passage of the Mishnah or the Tosefta that sets forth those principles is not cited verbatim.

It follows that the three basic and definitive traits of Sifra, are, first, its total adherence to the topical program of the written Torah for order and plan; second, its very common reliance upon the phrases or verses of the written Torah for the joining into coherent discourse of discrete thoughts, e.g., comments on, or amplification of, words or phrases; and third, its equally profound dependence upon the oral Torah for its program of thought: the problematic that defines the issues the authorship wishes to explore and resolve.

That brings us to the positive side of the picture. Sifra in detail presents no paramount propositions. But Sifra as a whole demonstrates a highly distinctive and vigorously demonstrated proposition. Although in detail we cannot reconstruct a topical program other than that of scripture, viewed in its indicative and definitive traits of rhetoric, logic, and implicit proposition, Sifra does take up a well-composed position on a fundamental issue, namely, the relationship between the written Torah, represented by the Book of Leviticus, and the oral Torah, represented by the passages of the Mishnah deemed by the authorship of Sifra to be pertinent to the Book of Leviticus. In a simple and fundamental sense, Sifra joins the two Torahs into a single statement, accomplishing a representation of the written Torah in topic and in program and in the logic of cogent discourse, and within that rewriting of the written Torah, a re-presentation of the oral Torah in its paramount problematic and in many of its substantive propositions. Stated simply, the written Torah provides the form, the oral Torah, the content. What emerges is not merely a united, dual Torah, but *The* Torah, stated whole and complete, in the context defined by the Book of Leviticus. Here the authorship of Sifra presents, through its representation, The Torah as a proper noun, all together, all at once, and, above all, complete and utterly coherent. In order to do so our authorship has constructed through its document, first, the sustained critique of the Mishnah's *Listenwissenschaft*, then, the defense of the Mishnah's propositions on the foundation of scriptural principles of taxonomy, hierarchical classification in particular.

Since in Sifra, the issue of hierarchical logic forms a principal formal pattern and a main logical principle of thought, there can be no reasonable doubt that characteristic of Sifra in rhetoric, logic, and topic is the disquisition on the logic of the Mishnah and the program of the Mishnah. In order to advance the argument, we have now to show two propositions, first, Sifra's authorship's defense of *Listenwissenschaft*; second, its critique of the Mishnah's mode of carrying out that science. Because of the distinctive nature of the proposition that, we maintain, Sifra's authorship sets forth, we shall dwell on the matter. It is fundamental to the thesis of our reading of Mekhilta, which follows this chapter, that documents can and do in the aggregate and through countless details make a single overriding point. In the case of Sifra we can show precisely how that happens. That accounts for the somewhat protracted nature of the demonstration that follows. It shows that, whereas to a topical program, our authorship presents little more than the topics dictated by scripture, it does so in such a way as to make a single point particular to itself and critical to its reconstruction of the Judaism of the dual Torah. When we come to Mekhilta Attributed to R. Ishmael, we shall therefore have a first-rate example of what might have been, against which to assess what was, done. How then does an authorship make its single overriding point through diverse topical discourses?

First, we shall observe how a sequence of cases shows how Sifra's authorship demonstrates the *Listenwissenschaft* is a self-evidently valid mode of demonstrating the truth of propositions. Second, we shall see in the same cases that *the* source of the correct classification of things is scripture and only scripture. Without scripture's intervention into the taxonomy of the world, we should have no knowledge at all of which things fall into which classifications and therefore are governed by which rules. Let us begin with a sustained example of the right way of doing things. Appropriately, the opening composition of Sifra shows the contrast between relying on scripture's classification, and the traits imputed by scripture to the taxa it identifies, and appealing to categories not defined and endowed with indicative traits by scripture.

Parashat Vayyiqra Dibura Denedabah Parashah 1

I:I

1. A. "The Lord called [to Moses] and spoke [to him from the tent of meeting, saying, 'Speak to the Israelite people and say to them']" (Lev. 1:1):
   B. He gave priority to the calling over the speaking.
   C. That is in line with the usage of scripture.
   D. Here there is an act of speaking, and in connection with the encounter at the bush [Exod. 3:4: "God called to him out of the bush, 'Moses, Moses'"], there is an act of speaking.
   E. Just as in the latter occasion, the act of calling is given priority over the act of speaking [even though the actual word "speaking" does not occur, it is implicit in the framing of the verse], so here, with respect to the act of speaking, the act of calling is given priority over the act of speaking.
2. A. No, [you cannot generalize on the basis of that case,] for if you invoke the case of the act of speaking at the bush, which is the first in the sequence of acts of speech [on which account, there had to be a call prior to entry into discourse],
   B. will you say the same of the act of speech in the tent of meeting, which assuredly is not the first in a sequence of acts of speech [so there was no need for a preliminary entry into discourse through a call]?
   C. The act of speech at Mount Sinai [Exod. 19:3] will prove to the contrary, for it is assuredly not the first in a sequence of acts of speech, yet, in that case, there was an act of calling prior to the act of speech.
3. A. No, [the exception proves nothing,] for if you invoke in evidence the act of speech at Mount Sinai, which pertained to all the Israelites, will you represent it as parallel to the act of speech in the tent of meeting, which is not pertinent to all Israel?
   B. Lo, you may sort matters out by appeal to comparison and contrast, specifically:
   C. The act of speech at the bush, which is the first of the acts of speech, is not of the same classification as the act of speech at Sinai, which is not the first act of speech.
   D. And the act of speech at Sinai, which is addressed to all Israel, is not in the same classification as the act of speech at the bush, which is not addressed to all Israel.

4. A. What they have in common, however, is that both of them are acts of speech, deriving from the mouth of the Holy One, addressed to Moses, in which case the act of calling comes prior to the act of speech,

B. so that, by way of generalization, we may maintain that every act of speech which comes from the mouth of the Holy One to Moses will be preceded by an act of calling.

5. A. Now if what the several occasions have in common is that all involve an act of speech, accompanied by fire, from the mouth of the Holy One, addressed to Moses, so that the act of calling was given priority over the act of speaking, then in every case in which there is an act of speech, involving fire, from the mouth of the Holy One, addressed to Moses, should involve an act of calling prior to the act of speech.

B. But then an exception is presented by the act of speech at the tent of meeting, in which there was no fire.

C. [That is why it was necessary for scripture on this occasion to state explicitly,] "The Lord called [to Moses and spoke to him from the tent of meeting, saying, 'Speak to the Israelite people and say to them']" (Lev. 1:1).

D. That explicit statement shows that, on the occasion at hand, priority was given to the act of calling over the act of speaking.

I:II

1. A. ["The Lord called to Moses and spoke to him from the tent of meeting, saying, 'Speak to the Israelite people and say to them'" (Lev. 1:1)]: Might one suppose that the act of calling applied only to this act of speaking alone?

B. And how on the basis of scripture do we know that on the occasion of all acts of speaking that are mentioned in the Torah [there was a prior act of calling]?

C. Scripture specifies, "from the tent of meeting,"

D. which bears the sense that on every occasion on which it was an act of speaking from the tent of meeting, there was an act of calling prior to the act of speaking.

2. A. Might one suppose that there was an act of calling only prior to the acts of speech alone?

B. How on the basis of scripture do we know that the same practice accompanied acts of saying and also acts of commanding?

C. Said R. Simeon, "Scripture says not only, '. . . spoke . . . ,' but '. . . and he spoke,' [with the inclusion of the *and*] meant to encompass also acts of telling and also acts of commanding."

The exercise of generalization addresses the character of God's meeting with Moses. The point of special interest is the comparison of the meeting at the bush and the meeting at the tent of meeting. And at stake is asking whether all acts of God's calling and talking with, or speaking to, the prophet are the same, or whether some of these acts are of a different classification from others. In point of fact, we are able to come to a generalization, worked out at I:I.5.A. And that permits us to explain why there is a different usage at Lev. 1:1 from what characterizes parallel cases. I:II.1–2 proceeds to generalize from the case at hand to other usages entirely, a very satisfying conclusion to the whole. We separate I:II from I:I because had I:I ended at 5, it could have stood complete and on its own, and therefore we see I:II as a brief appendix. The interest for our argument should not be missed. We seek generalizations, governing rules, that are supposed to emerge by the comparison and contrast of categories or of classifications. The way to do this is to follow the usage of scripture, that alone. And the right way of doing things is then illustrated. Now we seek rules that emerge from scripture's classification.

I.IV

1. A. How on the basis of scripture do we know that every act of speech involved the call to Moses, Moses [two times]?
   B. Scripture says, "God called to him out of the bush, 'Moses, Moses'" (Exod. 3:4).
   C. Now when scripture says, "And he said," it teaches that every act of calling involved the call to Moses, Moses [two times].

2. A. And how on the basis of scripture do we know, furthermore, that at each act of calling, he responded, "Here we am"?
   B. Scripture says, "God called to him out of the bush, 'Moses, Moses,' and he said, 'Here we am'" (Exod. 3:4).
   C. Now when scripture says, "And he said," it teaches that in response to each act of calling, he said, "Here we am."

3. A. "Moses, Moses" (Exod. 3:4), "Abraham, Abraham" (Gen. 22:11), "Jacob, Jacob" (Gen. 46:2), "Samuel, Samuel" (1 Sam. 3:10).
   B. This language expresses affection and also means to move to prompt response.

4. A. Another interpretation of "Moses, Moses:"
   B. This was the very same Moses both before he had been spoken with [by God] and also afterward.

The final unit completes the work of generalization that began with the opening passage. The point throughout is that there are acts of calling and speech, and a general rule pertains to them all. No. 3 and No. 4 conclude with observations outside of the besought generalization. The first of the two interprets the repetition of a name, the second, a conclusion particular to Moses personally. These seem to us tacked on. The first lesson in the rehabilitation of taxonomic logic is then clear. Let us state the proposition, which is demonstrated over and over again in rhetoric and logic: *Scripture provides reliable taxa and dictates the indicative characteristics of those taxa.*

The next step in the argument is to maintain that scripture *alone* can set forth the proper names of things: classifications and their hierarchical order. How do we appeal to scripture to designate the operative classifications? Here is a simple example of the alternative mode of classification, one that does not appeal to the traits of things but to the utilization of names by scripture. What we see is how by naming things in one way, rather than in another, scripture orders all things, classifying and, in the nature of things, also hierarchizing them.

Parashat Vayyiqra Dibura Denedabah Parashah 4

VII:V

1. A. ". . . and Aaron's sons the priests shall present the blood and throw the blood [round about against the altar that is at the door of the tent of meeting]:"
   B. Why does scripture make use of the word "blood" twice [instead of using a pronoun]?
   C. [It is for the following purpose:] How on the basis of scripture do you know that if blood deriving from one burnt offering was confused with the blood deriving from another burnt offering, blood deriving from one burnt offering with blood deriving from a beast that has been substituted therefor, blood deriving from a burnt offering with blood deriving from an unconsecrated beast, the mixture should nonetheless be presented?
   D. It is because scripture makes use of the word "blood" twice [instead of using a pronoun].
2. A. Is it possible to suppose that whereas if blood deriving from beasts in the specific classifications, it is to be presented, for the simple reasons that if the several beasts while alive had been confused with one another, they might be offered up,
   B. but how do we know that even if the blood of a burnt offering were confused with that of a beast killed as a guilt offering, [it is to be offered up]
   C. we shall concede the case of the mixture of the blood of a burnt offering confused with that of a beast killed as a guilt offering, it is to be presented, for both this one and that one fall into the classification of Most Holy Things.
   D. But how do we know that if the blood of a burnt offering were confused with the blood of a beast slaughtered in the classification of peace offerings or of a thanksgiving offering, [it is to be presented]?

E.   We shall concede the case of the mixture of the blood of a burnt offering confused with that of a beast slaughtered in the classification of peace offerings or of a thanksgiving offering, [it is to be presented,] because the beasts in both classifications produce blood that has to be sprinkled four times.

F.   But how do we know that if the blood of a burnt offering were confused with the blood of a beast slaughtered in the classification of a firstling or a beast that was counted as tenth or of a beast designated as a passover, [it is to be presented]?

G.   We shall concede the case of the mixture of the blood of a burnt offering confused with that of a beast slaughtered in the classification of firstling or a beast that was counted as tenth or of a beast designated as a passover, [it is to be presented,] because scripture uses the word "blood" two times.

H.   Then although we may make that concession, might we also suppose that if the blood of a burnt offering was confused with the blood of beasts that had suffered an invalidation, it also may be offered up?

I.   Scripture says, ". . . its blood," [thus excluding such a case].

J.   Then we shall concede the case of a mixture of the blood of a valid burnt offering with the blood of beasts that had suffered an invalidation, which blood is not valid to be presented at all.

K.   But how do we know that if such blood were mixed with the blood deriving from beasts set aside as sin offerings to be offered on the inner altar, [it is not to be offered up]?

L.   We can concede that the blood of a burnt offering that has been mixed with the blood deriving from beasts set aside as sin offerings to be offered on the inner altar is not to be offered up, for the one is offered on the inner altar, and other on the outer altar [the burnt offering brought as a free will offering, under discussion here, is slaughtered at the altar ". . . that is at the door of the tent of meeting," not at the inner altar].

M.   But how do we know that even if the blood of a burnt offering was confused with the blood of sin offerings that are to be slaughtered at the outer altar, it is not to be offered up?

N.   Scripture says, ". . . its blood," [thus excluding such a case].

In place of the rejecting of arguments resting on classifying species into a common genus, we now demonstrate how classification really is to be carried on. It is through the imposition upon data of the categories dictated by scripture: scripture's use of language. That is the force of this powerful exercise. No. 1 sets the stage, simply pointing out that the use of the word "blood" twice encompasses a case in which blood in two distinct classifications is somehow confused in the process of the conduct of the cult. In such a case it is quite proper to pour out the mixture of blood deriving from distinct sources, e.g., beasts that have served different, but comparable purposes. We then systemically work out the limits of that rule, showing how comparability works, then pointing to cases in which comparability is set aside. Throughout the exposition, at the crucial point we invoke the formulation of scripture, subordinating logic or in our instance the process of classification of like species to the dictation of scripture. We cannot imagine a more successful demonstration of what the framers wish to say.

From this simple account of the paramount position of scripture in the labor of classification, let us turn to the specific way in which, because of scripture's provision of taxa, we are able to undertake the science of *Listenwissenschaft*, including hierarchical classification, in the right way. What can we do because we appeal to scripture, which we cannot do if we do not rely on scripture? It is to establish the possibility of polythetic classification. We can appeal to shared traits of otherwise distinct taxa and so transform species into a common genus for a given purpose. Only scripture makes that initiative feasible, so our authorship maintains. What is at stake? It is the possibility of doing precisely what the framers of the Mishnah wish to do. That is to join together masses of diverse data into a single, encompassing statement, to show the rule that inheres in diverse cases.

In what follows, we shall see an enormous, coherent, and beautifully articulated exercise in the comparison and contrast of many things of a single genus. The whole holds together, because scripture makes possible the statement of all things within a single rule. That is, as we have noted, precisely what the framers of the Mishnah proposed to accomplish. Our authorship maintains that only by appeal to The Torah is this feat of learning possible. If, then, we wish to understand all things all together and all at once under a single encompassing rule, we had best revert to The Torah, with its account of the rightful names, positions, and order, imputed to all things.

Parashat Vayyiqra Dibura Denedabah Parashah 11

XXII:I

1. A. [With reference to M. Men. 5:5:] There are those [offerings which require bringing near but do not require waving, waving but not bringing near, waving and bringing near, neither waving nor bringing near: These are offerings which require bringing near but do not require waving: the meal offering of fine flour and the meal offering prepared in the baking pan and the meal offering prepared in the frying pan, and the meal offering of cakes and the meal offering of wafers, and the meal offering of priests, and the meal offering of an

anointed priest, and the meal offering of gentiles, and the meal offering of women, and the meal offering of a sinner. R. Simeon says, "The meal offering of priests and of the anointed priest—bringing near does not apply to them, because the taking of a handful does not apply to them. And whatever is not subject to the taking of a handful is not subject to bringing near,"] [scripture] says, "When you present to the Lord a meal offering that is made in any of these ways, it shall be brought [to the priest who shall take it up to the altar]:"

B.   What requires bringing near is only the handful alone. How do we know that we should encompass under the rule of bringing near the meal offering?

C.   Scripture says explicitly, "meal offering."

D.   How do we know that we should encompass all meal offerings?

E.   Scripture says, using the accusative particle, "the meal offering."

2. A.   We might propose that what requires bringing near is solely the meal offering brought as a free will offering.

B.   How do we know that the rule encompasses an obligatory meal offering?

C.   It is a matter of logic.

D.   Bringing a meal offering as a free will offering and bringing a meal offering as a matter of obligation form a single classification. Just as a meal offering presented as a free will offering requires bringing near, so the same rule applies to a meal offering of a sinner [brought as a matter of obligation], which should likewise require bringing near.

E.   No, if you have stated that rule governing bringing near in the case of a free will offering, on which oil and frankincense have to be added. Will you say the same of the meal offering of a sinner [Lev. 5:11], which does not require oil and frankincense?

F.   The meal offering brought by a wife accused of adultery will prove to the contrary, for it does not require oil and frankincense, but it does require bringing near [as is stated explicitly at Num. 5:15].

G.   No, if you have applied the requirement of bringing near to the meal offering brought by a wife accused of adultery, which also requires waving, will you say the same of the meal offering of a sinner, which does not have to be waved?

H.   Lo, you must therefore reason by appeal to a polythetic analogy [in which not all traits pertain to all components of the category, but some traits apply to them all in common]:

I.   The meal offering brought as a free will offering, which requires oil and frankincense, does not in all respects conform to the traits of the meal offering of a wife accused of adultery, which does not require oil and frankincense, and the meal offering of the wife accused of adultery, which requires waving, does not in all respects conform to the traits of a meal offering brought as a free will offering, which does not require waving.

J.   But what they have in common is that they are alike in requiring the taking up of a handful and they are also alike in that they require bringing near.

K.   We shall then introduce into the same classification the meal offering of a sinner, which is equivalent to them as to the matter of the taking up of a handful, and also should be equivalent to them as to the requirement of being drawn near.

L.   But might one not argue that the trait that all have in common is that all of them may be brought equally by a rich and a poor person and require drawing near, which then excludes from the common classification the meal offering of a sinner, which does not conform to the rule that it may be brought equally by a rich and a poor person, [but may be brought only by a poor person,] and such an offering also should not require being brought near!

M.   [The fact that the polythetic classification yields indeterminate results means failure once more, and, accordingly,] scripture states, "meal offering,"

N.   with this meaning: all the same are the meal offering brought as a free will offering and the meal offering of a sinner, both this and that require being brought near.

The elegant exercise draws together the various types of meal offerings and shows that they cannot form a classification of either a monothetic or a polythetic character. Consequently, scripture must be invoked to supply the proof for the classification of the discrete items. The important language is at H–J: These differ from those, and those from these, but what they have in common is. . . . Then we demonstrate, with our appeal to scripture, the sole valid source of polythetic classification, M. And this is constant throughout Sifra.

The strength of argument of our authorship is manifest in its capacity to demonstrate how diverse things relate through points in common, so long as the commonalities derive from a valid source. And that leads us to the central and fundamental premise of all: scripture, its picture of the classification of nature and supernature, its account of the rightful names and order of all things, is the sole source for that encompassing and generalizing principle that permits scientific inquiry into the governing laws to take place. This tripartite subject of (1) the transformation of case to rule in Leviticus through the exercise of exclusion and inclusion; (2) the movement from rule to system and structure, hence, the interest in taxonomy based on scripture's classification system; and (3) the reunification of the two Torahs into a single statement, effected in part through commentary, in part through extensive citation of passages of the Mishnah and of the Tosefta—this is what we take to be the topic addressed by Sifra, together with its simple problematic: the relationship of the two Torahs not only in form but at the deepest structures of thought.

Enough has been said to make the point that the authorship of Sifra follows its distinctive topical and propositional program, as much as a particular rhetorical and logical one. And the correspondence between the topical-propositional program and the rhetorical and logical choices is established. The entire composition is aimed at making a fundamental systemic argument concerning the correct foundations for the classification of things. That is its purpose and its point, and all things serve to make that one point. When, in Mekhilta Attributed to R. Ishmael, we ask whether the authorship of the whole or of the nine tractates has formed a coherent statement in which rhetoric, logic, and topic or proposition form a cogent and compelling proposition, the appeal to the example of Sifra justifies asking the question. And this brings us to the final step in our brief encounter with Sifra as part of the study, in the context of comparison and contrast, of Mekhilta Attributed to R. Ishmael. What we want to know is whether the message we impute to the authorship of Sifra is systemically inert or systemically active. By that we mean, does the authorship compose an argument that is a restatement of points held in common by diverse groups, or does it appear, in the setting of extant writings, that our authorship forms a cadre in the shaping of a system in process? The answer will derive from a comparison of the fundamental proposition of Sifra with that of other compilations of Midrash-exegeses.

That explains why we now ask ourselves a simple question: Is the message of Sifra or Sifré to Numbers the same as that of Leviticus Rabbah or Genesis Rabbah? The answer is no, these are four different books, each with its distinctive burden. The former two make distinct points of their own, respectively. The latter produce a coherent statement, but each with its own emphases. So, in all, the several documents make different points in answering different questions. In plan and in program they yield more contrasts than comparisons. Since these *are* different books, which *do* use different forms to deliver different messages, it must follow that each document forms and states a systemically active proposition, not one that is inert and conventional. In our view there is nothing routine or given or to be predicted about the point that the authorships of the named documents wish to make. Why not? Because it is not a point that is simply "there to be made." It is a striking and original point. How, again, do we know it? The reason is that, when the sages who produced Genesis Rabbah read Genesis, they made a different point from the one that the Book of Leviticus precipitated for the authorships of Sifra and, as a matter of fact, also Leviticus Rabbah. So contrasting the one composition with the other shows us that each composition bears its own distinctive traits—traits of mind, traits of plan, traits of program.

As a matter of fact, Sifra and the other documents of its class do not merely assemble this and that, forming a hodgepodge of things people happen to have said: scrapbooks. In the case of each document we can answer the question of topic as much as of rhetoric and logic: Why this, not that? That is to say, why discuss this topic in this pattern of language and resort to this logic of cogent discourse, rather than treating some other topic in a different set of language patterns and relying on other modes of making connections and drawing conclusions? These are questions that we have now answered for Sifra and, in the contrasts already drawn, for the other writings as well. The writings before us, seen individually and also as a group, stand not wholly autonomously but also not everywhere forming a continuity of discourse, whether in rhetoric, or in logic, or in topic and problematic. They are connected. They intersect at a few places but not over the greater part of their territory. For they are not compilations but free-standing compositions. They are not essentially the same, but articulately differentiated. They are not lacking all viewpoint, serving a single undifferentiated task of collecting and arranging whatever was at hand. Quite to the contrary, these documents emerge as sharply differentiated from one another and clearly defined, each through its distinctive viewpoint and particular polemic, on the one side, and formal and aesthetic qualities, on the other.

Sifra presents a proposition distinctive to its authorship, solving a problem identified by that authorship as urgent. Does the document form part of a system and contribute to the development of a system? Criteria for answering that question derive from the established analytical classification. How shall we know whether, and how, Sifra (or any other document) participates in a systemic statement that transcends the limits of its authorship's proposition? We revert to our familiar categories of rhetoric, logic, and topic, following a revised order for a simple reason, which the reader will identify presently.

1. *Rhetoric*: In our judgment we cannot find much use for shared formal traits, sufficiently similar so that, despite differences, we may impute to all canonical writings certain indicative qualities in common. The reason is that some canonical writings appeal for structure to Scripture, others to the Mishnah. That consideration all by itself suffices to dismiss the possibility that common rhetorical preferences form a diverse species or genus based on polythetic classification.

3. *Topic inclusive of proposition:* As to shared doctrinal conceptions, e.g., topics and propositions, such as many have claimed to discern, if the documents we have reviewed are indicative, then what is in common also is trivial, on the one side, or systemically inert, on the other. A simple example makes the point. Trivial is the fact that all documents appeal to scripture, that is, to Sinai; or all participants to the canon believe in one God; and similar genuinely uninteresting matters. Systemically inert are important shared convictions, e.g., concerning covenant, history and salvation, law and sanctification, that surely animate all authorships but play an active role in the systems put forth by no authorship. Relationships to scripture seem to us a hopelessly general indicator.

Then what? We should anticipate that it is in the deep structure of logic, which is to say, in the processes of thought, that we may constructively search out traits of mind, modes of thought, both common to all our documents and also uncommon to all noncanonical writings in the Judaic framework.

2. *Logic, broadly construed:* We do conceive the modes of intelligible thought and cogent discourse characteristic of these writings and, in the Judaic context, of no others, to form and define the "Judaism out there" that holds the whole together and makes of diverse writings a canon—and that distinguishes all these writings, as a group, from the writings identified as canonical by any other Judaism. Why do we think that it is in the shared modes of thought—logics or modes of cogent and intelligible discourse—that we shall find what holds together all writings of this classification and also distinguishes them from all writings of other Judaisms?

To account for the shared and public, common character of the logic of intelligible discourse as the basis for polythetic classification of documents, we appeal to the very basic trait of religion: its public and shared character. Religion begins with the possibility of intelligible discourse and cogent, comprehensible thought. That accounts for its capacity to hold together and to express the world view, the way of life, the social entity, that all together constitute the definition of the social group. Where cogent discourse (in context) takes place, there we find the social entity of which a religion speaks, the way of life and world view of which a religion sets forth and explains. Where cogent discourse ceases, there we find some other world, heretical or simply different. The modes of cogent and intelligible discourse then form the intellectual statement of the social reality that the religious group, the social entity, constitutes— and that by definition. The reason is that, as people generally recognize, an ongoing social entity inculcates in age succeeding age modes of thought that, shared by all, impart self-evidence and enduring sense to transient propositions. Minds may change on this and that. But *mind* does not, mind meaning modes of patterned thought on ephemera. In such a context, the role and uses of scripture prove far more pervasive and profound in the formation of intellect that has heretofore been appreciated. For when people write with scripture, rather than merely commenting upon or quoting scripture, they think in the syntax and grammar of scripture and so see the world through scripture. People who write with scripture are transformed by scripture.

7

Not Writing with Scripture

THE CASE OF MEKHILTA
ATTRIBUTED TO R. ISHMAEL

Sages in the canonical writings of the Judaism of the dual Torah appealed to scripture not merely for proof texts as part of an apologia but for a far more original and sustained mode of discourse. In constant interchange with scripture, they found ways of delivering their own message, in their own idiom, and in diverse ways. Verses of scripture therefore served not merely to prove but to instruct. Israelite scripture constituted not merely a source of validation but a powerful instrument of profound inquiry. And the propositions that could be proposed, the statements that could be made, prove diverse. Scripture served as a kind of syntax, limiting the arrangement of words but making possible an infinity of statements. The upshot is that the received scripture formed an instrumentality for the expression of an authorship responsible for a writing bearings its own integrity and cogency, an authorship appealing to its own conventions of intelligibility and, above all, making its own points. The compilers of Midrash-compilations, as we recognize, did not write *about* Scripture, creating, e.g., a literature of commentary and exegesis essentially within the program of scripture. Rather, they wrote *with* scripture. And that they did in many ways.

Let us at the outset specify the questions that define the point of differentiation, for a Midrash-compilation, between writing with scripture and not writing with scripture.

1. Does the document at hand deliver a particular message and viewpoint or does it merely serve as a repository for diverse, received materials?
2. Does the authorship deliver its message, its choices as to form and meaning, or merely transmit someone else's?

An authorship that writes with scripture delivers a particular message and viewpoint by appeal to the rules of thought and syntax of reflection defined by scripture. Such an authorship selects rhetoric and logic that serve its purpose. An authorship that does not write with scripture composes a repository for diverse materials of scripture, and such an authorship has no need to select rhetoric and logic to serve its documentary program.

In order to broaden the issue of this part of the argument of the book, let us further unpack secondary questions. First, do we have a cogent statement or a mere scrapbook? Comparing one compilation with another yields the correct way of finding the answer. A document may serve solely as a convenient repository of prior sayings and stories, available materials that will have served equally well (or poorly) wherever they took up their final location. A composition may exhibit a viewpoint, a purpose of authorship distinctive to its framers or collectors and arrangers. Such a characteristic literary purpose would be so powerfully particular to one authorship that nearly everything at hand can be shown to have been (re)shaped for the ultimate purpose of the authorship at hand. These then are collectors and arrangers who demand the title of authors. Context and circumstance then form the prior condition of inquiry, the result, in exegetical terms, the contingent one. Now to the case at hand.

What has been said sets the stage for our encounter with Mekhilta Attributed to R. Ishmael, for here we find a compilation of Midrashim the authorship of which did not write with scripture but encountered and utilized scripture in a very different way. To define the document at the outset, Mekhilta Attributed to R. Ishmael forms a sustained address to the Book of Exodus, covering Exod. 12:1—23:19; Exod. 31:12-13, and Exod. 35:1-3. It comprises nine tractates, Pisha (Exod. 12:1—13:16), Beshallah (Exod. 13—17, 14—31), Shirata (Exod. 15:1-21), Vayassa (Exod. 17:7—22), Amalek (Exod. 17:8—18:27), Bahodesh (Exod. 19:1—20:26), Neziqin (Exod. 21:1—22:23), Kaspa (Exod. 22:24—23:19), and Shabbata (Exod. 31:12-17 and 35:1-3). There are eighty-two sections, subdivided into paragraphs. The division of the Book of Exodus has no bearing on the lections read in the synagogue as we now know them. Moshe D. Heer maintains that the work was "probably compiled and redacted in Erez Israel not earlier than the end of the fourth century."[1]

---

1. M.D. Heer, "Mekhilta of R. Ishmael," *Encyclopaedia Judaica* (Jerusalem: Keter, 1971) 11:1269.

Mekhilta Attributed to R. Ishmael presents us with a fine case of a piece of writing that does not write with scripture at all. Whereas, as we recognize, for documents such as Sifra and Leviticus Rabbah, scripture supplies the grammar and syntax that permits an authorship to make whatever statement it wishes on whatever topic it chooses, for the authorship of Mekhilta Attributed to R. Ishmael, scripture is inert. That is to say, it is a source of information, texts that prove propositions. It also is the foundation of the organization of discourse. But when people wish to say things, they say them *about* scripture, not through scripture or with scripture. What we have in Mekhilta Attributed to R. Ishmael falls into a different category altogether, for the document comprises the first scriptural encyclopedia of Judaism. A scriptural encyclopedia joins together expositions of topics, disquisitions on propositions, in general precipitated by the themes of scriptural narrative or the dictates of biblical law, and collects and arranges in accord with scripture's order and program the exegeses—paraphrases or brief explanations—of clauses of biblical verses. Although it is generally thought that that is precisely what Midrash-compilations are meant to accomplish, as we now recognize from the other documents' address to scripture, the fact is contrary.

Out of antiquity, it is only Mekhilta Attributed to R. Ishmael that conforms to the characterization of such writings just now set forth. All others write with scripture and in no way find accurate description as mere collections and arrangements of episodic observations on the sense or implications of scripture. Quite to the contrary, the other principal Midrash-compilations of late antiquity, Sifré to Numbers, Sifré to Deuteronomy, Sifra, Genesis Rabbah, Leviticus Rabbah, Pesiqta deRab Kahana, Pesiqta Rabbati, and The Fathers According to Rabbi Nathan (which is not precisely a Midrash-compilation in any event), make use of the grammar and syntax of scripture, as we said for the composition of their message. In the framing of that message scripture forms an integral part of speech. That is why other Midrash-compilations do not exhibit the traits of a scriptural encyclopedia but conform to those of quite other sorts of writing entirely.

Mekhilta Attributed to R. Ishmael forms the exception that proves the rule. The rule is that, for the canonical writings of the Judaism of the dual Torah in late antiquity, a Midrash-compilation *always* addresses an urgent question and, seen whole, sets forth a cogent and compelling response to that question. The upshot, then, is that a Midrash-compilation in the context of the canonical writings of the Judaism of the dual Torah normally is *not* a scriptural encyclopedia but a piece of writing that utilizes scripture in some way as a medium of speech and expression. True, Midrash-compilations later on, through medieval and into modern times, fall into the mode of either encyclopedias, in the model of the document before us, or of mere commentaries, collections and arrangements of paraphrasitc materials pertinent to successive verses of scripture. Accordingly, in the context of late antiquity Mekhilta Attributed to R. Ishmael is abnormal, but the document adumbrates how matters would be carried forward for the centuries beyond. Compared with the other writings in its classification, Midrash-compilations of late antiquity, it is exceptional, and its differentiating traits show us that it forms a species unto itself, within the common genus, Midrash-compilation.

Let us spell out the abnormal character of the document under study here. Although they are connected, each of the other Midrash-compilations of antiquity constitutes an essentially autonomous statement of its own, making use of a distinctive rhetoric and logic to set forth a proposition particular to itself. The other Midrash-compilations intersect at a few places but not over the greater part of their territory. For, unlike Mekhilta Attributed to R. Ishmael, they are not mainly or merely compilations but free-standing compositions. They are not all essentially the same, but they are all articulately differentiated. They are not lacking all viewpoint, serving a single undifferentiated task of collecting and arranging whatever was at hand. Quite to the contrary, these other documents, unlike Mekhilta Attributed to R. Ishmael, emerge as sharply differentiated from one another and clearly defined, each through its distinctive viewpoint and particular polemic, on the one side, and formal and aesthetic qualities, on the other.

By contrast, in assembling conventions and banalities of the faith, the authorship of Mekhilta Attributed to R. Ishmael has made a canonical statement, one with which, we take for granted, all the faithful will have adhered, and therefore that none will have identified as a distinctive and particular program at all. In this context, "encyclopedia" forms a metaphorical synonym for "canon," and Mekhilta Attributed to R. Ishmael emerges as a document that, *in itself*, bears canonical traits of theology and law. For a canon comprises separate books that all together make a single statement. In terms of the Judaism of the dual Torah, the canon is what takes scripture of various kinds and diverse points of origin and turns scriptures into Torah, and commentaries on those scriptures into Torah as well, making them all into the one whole Torah—of Moses, our rabbi. We may say as a matter of hypothesis that the category "canon" stands over against the conception of "writing with scripture."

But a separate set of studies on the problem of "canon" is required to test that hypothesis.

Mekhilta Attributed to R. Ishmael seen whole and in the aggregate presents a composite of three kinds of materials. The first is a set of ad hoc and episodic exegeses of some passages of scripture. The second is a group of propositional and argumentative essays in exegetical form, in which theological principles are set forth and demonstrated. The third is a set of topical articles, some of them sustained, many of them well crafted, about important subjects of the Judaism of the dual Torah. Providing this encyclopedia of information concerning theology and normative behavior, however, for the authorship of Mekhilta Attributed to R. Ishmael has not required a sustained demonstration of a position, whether whole or even in part, distinctive to that authorship and distinct from positions set forth by other authorships.

This is indicated in two ways. First of all, our authorship has not composed an argument, prevailing through large tracts of the document, that is cogent in all details and accomplishes a main and overriding purpose. Nor, second, has that authorship set forth a statement of important propositions through most of the information, whether topical or exegetical, that it lays out. That is not to suggest, however, that here we have a mere conglomerate of unrelated facts. Quite to the contrary, there is no understanding the facts before us without ample access to a complete system, which is to say, the system of the Judaism of the dual Torah of the canon of which our writing forms a principal part. Accordingly, the document before us participates in a system, but its authorship in no way proposes to shape or contribute to the setting forth of the system, other than by rehearsing a corpus of inert facts.

Two considerations make us certain that we deal not with a systemically active and generative statement but only with a document that has been generated by a system. The first is that when facts—even set forth as well-composed essays of information—remain inert and contribute to the making of no point beyond themselves, we deal, not with a philosophy, but with what we call, by way of metaphor, an encyclopedia. And a document that collects and rehearses facts but does not shape them in the service of important propositions serves a purpose all its own. It is to lay out and impart information needed for a system, but it is not to lay out the system. So far as a document presents an argument of its own, reshaping information to its purposes, we may characterize it as systemic, which is to say, argumentative and propositional. When a document serves the purpose of preserving and laying out received information, taking for granted the sense and meaning of that information but in no way reshaping that information for purposes of propositional argument, we may call such a document traditional. The second consideration that when we compare Mekhilta Attributed to R. Ishmael with two documents that do constitute, whole and complete, systemically active and generative statements of well-composed propositions, we find that our document does not exhibit the traits, as to rhetoric, logic, or propositional and topical cogency, of those documents. The comparison of Sifra and Sifré to Deuteronomy with Mekhilta Attributed to R. Ishmael yields only one result: This document is very different from those affines.

Lacking all interest in cogent and sustained argumentation and demonstration of propositions set forth for argument, the authorship of our document scarcely aspires to make a full and important, well-composed and proportioned statement of its own. The nine tractates of Mekhilta Attributed to R. Ishmael, moreover, prove discrete. We have to take account of a document behind which, even at the end product, stand nine authorships, not one single authorship whose hand is evident throughout. For in formal and logical traits, all the more so in topical program, the nine tractates are scarcely cogent when seen whole and complete. They make no one point over and over again. They undertake no sustained, methodical analysis that joins bits and pieces of exegesis into a large-scale composition, bearing meaning. They do not pursue a single range of problems in such a way as through discrete results to demonstrate in many ways a single cogent position.

Keenly interested in setting forth what there is to know about a variety of topics, the sages who stand behind Mekhilta Attributed to R. Ishmael preserve and transmit information necessary for the reader to participate in an ongoing tradition, that is to say, a system well beyond the nascent and formative stage. For framers such as these, important questions have been settled or prove null. For it is a system that is perceived to be whole, complete, fully in place, that the information collected and set forth by our authorship attests. When people present writing in which scripture supplies information and propositions, but not grammar and syntax of thought, scripture plays a dominant role at the surface, but none in the substrate of the writing. That is shown here. For when facts serve not for arguing in favor of a proposition but principally for informing a readership of things it must know, then we confront not a systemic exercise expressed through sustained writing by the medium of scripture but a traditional rite in which scripture plays a formal role. That is to say, we find merely the repeating of the received facts so as to restate and reenforce the structure served by said facts. That accounts for our characterizing the document, assuming a provenance in late antiquity, as the first encyclopedia of Judaism, and our seeing the document as a prime example, for late antiquity, of how people did not write with scripture but used scripture in other ways altogether.

To take up the concrete evidence of the document, we review a single chapter to survey formal and rhetorical traits of the document, and then we shall set forth the results of a survey of the entire document.

15
Pisha Chapter 1

XV:I

1. A. "And the Lord said to Moses and Aaron, 'This is the ordinance of the passover:'"
   B. There are pericopes in scripture in which an encompassing principle is stated first of all, then the details are given at the end, and there are pericopes in which the details are given at the outset, with the encompassing principle at the end.
   C. "You shall be to us a kingdom of priests and a holy nation" (Exod. 19:6) for example constitutes an example of the presentation of details.
   D. "These are the words that you shall speak to the people of Israel" (Exod. 19:6) forms an instance of an encompassing principle.
   E. "This is the statute of the Torah" (Num. 19:2) forms an encompassing principle.
   F. "That they bring to you a red cow, without blemish" (Num. 19:2) is a detail.
   G. "This is the ordinance of the passover" forms the encompassing principle.
   H. "No foreigner shall eat of it" is a detail.
   we. When you have an encompassing principle followed by a detail, then the encompassing principle covers only what is specified by the detail.

We have a proposition B, followed by examples, and concluding with a restatement of the generalization, we.

2. A. "This is the ordinance of the passover:"
   B. "It is both concerning the passover celebrated in Egypt and the passover celebrated in coming generations that scripture speaks," the words of R. Josiah.
   C. R. Jonathan says, "Scripture speaks only of the passover that was celebrated in Egypt.
   D. "Accordingly, we have in hand only the rule covering the passover that was celebrated in Egypt. How do we know the rule for the passover celebrated in coming generations?

E.   "Scripture says, 'According to all the statutes concerning it and according to all the ordinances concerning it you shall observe it' (Num. 9:3)."

F.   R. Josiah remarked to him, "Scripture speaks all the same in this passage, which concerns the passover celebrated in Egypt and the passover celebrated in coming generations as well.

G.   "What is the point of scripture's statement, 'According to all the statutes concerning it and according to all the ordinances concerning it you shall observe it' (Num. 9:3)?

H.   "Scripture's intent is to indicate that rules that are left out [at Exod. 12:43–49] in fact apply there [to the passover celebrated in Egypt, that is, the rules given at Num. 9:2–3 and at Exod. 12:3–6, 8–10; all these rules apply to all passovers]."

I.   R. Issi b. Aqiba says, "The 'ordinance' stated with regard to the passover speaks only to the [Lauterbach:] body of the paschal lamb."

This is the familiar dispute form, which dominates in the Mishnah, consisting of the statement of a question or problem, followed by opinions of two or more authorities addressed to answering that question or solving the problem.

3.   A.   "no foreigner shall eat of it:"

B.   All the same are an Israelite apostate and a gentile.

C.   Both are covered here, for it is said, "Thus says the Lord God, 'No alien, uncircumcised in heart and uncircumcised in flesh shall enter into our sanctuary, even any alien that is among the children of Israel'" (Ezek. 44:9).

This is commentary form: a clause of the base verse followed by a paraphrase and amplification thereof. Commentary form may bear considerable complexity, e.g., secondary expansion, proof texts (as here), and the like, but for our purpose it serves no useful result to distinguish simple from complex commentary form.

4.   A.   "but every slave belonging to a man, that is bought for money:"

B.   we know only that a slave belonging to a man is covered by the rule.

C.   How do we know that a slave belonging to a woman or a minor is covered by the rule?

D.   Scripture says, "that is bought for money," meaning, under all circumstances of ownership.

This is a fixed rhetorical pattern, of which the indicators are at B, C: we know only . . . how about . . .? We call this "exclusionary/inclusionary form," since the intent is to generalize on the basis of a case, either so as to encompass other cases, as in the present instant, so to include, or to exclude other cases, so as to exclude.

5. A.   "[but every slave that is bought for money] may eat of it after you have circumcised him:"

    B.   "This indicates that circumcising one's slaves keeps the owner from eating the passover offering. [It is an indispensable action, and if it is not performed, the owner may not celebrate the rite.]

    C.   "We know that that is the rule in respect to circumcising one's slaves. How about circumcising males [for which one bears responsibility, though they are not slaves, e.g., new born male babies]?

    D.   "Lo, you may reason in this way:

    E.   "Here we find reference to 'then' and we find reference to 'then' [at Exod. 12:48].

    F.   "Just as the latter reference refers to circumcising free males, so the reference here refers to circumcising free males, and just as the reference here is to circumcising slaves, so the reference there encompasses circumcising slaves, [with the result that the same rule applies to both categories, and so long as one bears responsibility for a circumcision and has not carried it out, one cannot eat the passover offering]," the words of R. Eliezer.

    G.   R. Ishmael says, "The circumcision of slaves does not keep the owner from eating the passover offering.

    H.   "Why then does Scripture say, 'after you have circumcised him'?

    I.   "Lo, if one had in hand a number of uncircumcised slaves. How do you know that if one wanted to circumcise them and to feed them meat of the passover offering, one has the right to do so?

    J.   "Scripture says, 'after you have circumcised him.'

    K.   "but do we find that one may keep uncircumcised slaves at all?

    L.   "Scripture states, 'And the son of your handmaid and the stranger may be refreshed' (Exod. 23:12)."

    M.   R. Eliezer says, "One has not got the right to keep uncircumcised slaves, for it is said, 'and you shall circumcise him.'

    N.   "If so, what is the sense of Scripture: 'And the son of your handmaid and the stranger may be refreshed' (Exod. 23:12)?

    O.   "Lo, if the slave's master bought him on the eve of the Sabbath at dusk and did not have a chance to circumcise him before it got dark, on that account it is said, 'And the son of your handmaid and the stranger may be refreshed' (Exod. 23:12)."

This seems to us a variation on the foregoing exclusionary/inclusionary form.

6. A.   Another interpretation of the verse, "but every slave that is bought for money may eat of it after you have circumcised him:"

    B.   Why is this said?

    C.   It is to encompass under the law one on whom the religious duty of circumcision has been performed even transiently,

D. so that such a one, though the flesh has grown back and covered the corona of the penis, is nonetheless not restricted as to eating the passover offering or priestly rations that have been assigned to his master.

E. In this matter our masters in Lud voted and ruled that the regrown skin also does not interpose in an immersion pool, so invalidating the immersion on account of uncleanness [by intervening between the flesh and the water].

This is a variation on the commentary form, in that in place of verse + phrase, we have the slightly more elaborated connector language at B.

7. A. "No sojourner or hired servant may eat of it:"
   B. "Sojourner" refers to a proselyte [Lauterbach: resident alien, a heathen who has foresworn idolatry; he may be a potential proselyte but is as yet not a proselyte].
   C. "Hired servant" refers to a gentile.

This is simple commentary form.

8. A. R. Eliezer says, "Why does scripture say, 'No sojourner or hired servant may eat of it'?
   B. "It is to provide taxic indicators supplied by the rule covering the passover offering to encompass food in the classification of priestly rations, specifically so as to invalidate an uncircumcised person from eating such food.
   C. "For [the argument not constructed on the foundation of scripture's classification but only on the basis of hierarchical classification goes as follows:] even though scripture had not made this point, we might have reasoned as follows:
   D. "If in the case of the passover sacrifice, which is less weighty, the law has invalidated the uncircumcised person from eating the meat, food in the status of priestly rations, which is the more weighty matter, surely should be prohibited for an uncircumcised person!
   E. "No, if you have stated the rule in connection with the eating of the passover sacrifice, in which case scripture has limited the time available for eating the meat for those who eat it, and therefore scripture has invalidated the uncircumcised person from eating it, will you say the same in the case of food in the status of priestly rations, in which case scripture has placed no limitation on the time that those who eat it may eat it, and since scripture has set no limit on the time that it may be eaten, it is reasonable that we should also not invalidate an uncircumcised person from eating it! [That is, the hierarchical classification of D is incorrect, and so the argument fails.]
   F. "Accordingly, scripture has made reference to 'sojourner or hired servant' with reference to the passover offering and also to 'sojourner or hired servant' with reference to priestly rations.

> G. "Just as 'sojourner or hired servant' with reference to the passover offering indicates that an uncircumcised male may not eat of it, so 'sojourner or hired servant' with reference to food in the status of priestly rations indicates that an uncircumcised male may not eat of it."

This exercise, expressed in rigorously formal language, demonstrates the limits of reason in the presentation of the argument of hierarchical classification ("argument a fortiori," "qol vehomer"). The formal indicators are commonly such as we see at C: "I might have reasoned as follows," with the argument a fortiori resting on a prior act of classification, then E., "No, if in this case . . . not in that case . . . , differentiated in the following trait," and finally F with G as a restatement of the initial proposition.

9. A. R. Isaac says, "Why does Scripture say, 'No sojourner or hired servant may eat of it'?
    B. "Is it not stated, 'No alien shall eat of it'?
    C. "But if there was a circumcised Arab or a circumcised gentile, we might infer that such a one might be valid for eating the passover offering.
    D. "Scripture accordingly states, 'No sojourner or hired servant may eat of it.'"

A recurrent exercise, resorting to a single formal program, relates two or more verses on the same topic to one another. In this case we begin with "why is this said?" We then proceed to introduce a pertinent statement in some other passage, and that yields a secondary harmony of the whole. The formal clue lies in "why is this passage stated?" and similar language.

10. A. "In one house shall it be eaten:"
    B. This means that scripture means in one association formed for that purpose.
    C. You maintain that it means in one association formed for that purpose. But perhaps the sense is only in accord with the literal meaning, that is, "in one house"?
    D. When scripture says, "on the houses in which you shall eat it" (Exod. 12:7), we derive the fact that the passover may be eaten in a great many houses.
    E. Then what is the point of scripture's stating, "In one house shall it be eaten"?
    F. This means that scripture means in one association formed for that purpose.
    G. Then how shall we interpret the statement, "on the houses in which you shall eat it"?

H. In this connection sages have said:

I. "The passover offering may be eaten in two places, but it may not be eaten by two associations," the words of R. Simeon b. Yohai.

J. What is the sense of "in two places"?

K. If the people were in the house and a beam broke over them, they may go out into the courtyard.

L. If they were in the courtyard and it rained on them, they may go into the house.

M. So it turns out that the passover offering may be eaten in two places.

Here the proposition is tested and proved in a rhetorically different manner from what we called the redactional-harmonistic form, but the upshot is the same. The testing of the proposition followed by "You say, but how about . . ." certainly represents a distinctive form, designated as "proposition tested and proved."

11. A. "you shall not carry forth any of the flesh outside the house:"

B. The sense is, outside of the association formed for the purpose of preparing and eating the offering.

C. You maintain that the sense is, outside of the association formed for the purpose of preparing and eating the offering. But perhaps the sense is only in accord with the literal meaning, that is, "in outside of that house"?

D. When scripture says, "outside," which can only mean, outside of the place where it is eaten.

E. Lo, if one takes it outside, he violates the religious requirement of the rite.

F. Might we infer that the rite is nonetheless valid?

G. Logic proposes the following:

H. Peace offerings fall into the category of Lesser Holy Things, and the passover offering falls into the category of Lesser Holy Things.

I. If you have the rule for peace offerings that if one has taken them outside the temple courtyard, he has invalidated them, so the passover, if taken outside, likewise is invalidated.

What has just now been said applies here as well.

12. A. "you shall not carry forth any of the flesh outside the house:"

B. Scripture speaks of the meat in particular.

C. You maintain that scripture speaks of the meat in particular. Or perhaps all the same are the meat and the bone?

D. Scripture says, "you shall not carry forth any of the flesh outside the house"—

E. Lo, scripture speaks of the meat in particular.

Once more, a proposition is tested and proved.

13. A. "and you shall not break a bone of it:"
    B. Why is this stated? Is it not stated in any event, "and they shall eat the flesh in that night" (Exod. 12:8), which is to say, the flesh that is around the bone?
    C. You maintain that it is the flesh that is around the bone, but perhaps the sense is the flesh that is inside of the bone?
    D. Then how shall we explain the statement, "and you shall not break a bone of it"?
    E. It is the bone that contains no flesh.
    F. But what about a bone that does have meat inside?
    G. Scripture says, "you shall not break a bone in it,"
    H. whether there is meat in it or whether there is not meat in it.

The form is now a familiar one.

14. A. "[and you shall not break a bone] of it [in particular]:"
    B. But not in connection with any other Holy Things.
    C. One might have reasoned in this way:
    D. If in the case of a passover offering, which is of lesser weight, lo, one is subject to the violation of the rule of not breaking a bone,
    E. Holy Things, which are of greater weight, surely should be subject to the rule of not breaking a bone.
    F. Scripture says, "[and you shall not break a bone] of it"—
    G. ["of it" in particular], but not in connection with any other Holy Things.

The form is now a familiar one.

15. A. "All the congregation of Israel shall keep it:"
    B. Why is this stated?
    C. Since it says, "Select and purchase your lambs according to your families" (Exod. 12:21),
    D. one might have thought that just as the passover offering prepared in Egypt is valid only when prepared by a family, so the passover offering in generations to come may be valid only when prepared by a family.
    E. Scripture says, "All the congregation of Israel shall keep it,"
    F. indicating that the passover offering prepared in generations to come may be prepared by unrelated persons.

The form in now a familiar one.

XV:II

1. A. "And when a stranger shall sojourn with you and would keep the passover of the Lord:"
    B. Might we infer that, once one has converted to Judaism, he may prepare the passover offering immediately?
    C. Scripture says, "he shall be as a native of the land"

D.   meaning, just as a native of the land celebrates passover on the fourteenth of Nisan, so the proselyte celebrates passover only on the fourteenth of Nisan.

E.   R. Simeon b. Eleazar says, "Lo if one converted between the two passover rites [the one on the fifteenth of Nisan, the other on the fifteenth of Iyyar, which follows], might we infer that he should celebrate the passover on the occasion of the celebration of the second passover?

F.   "Scripture states, 'he shall be as a native of the land,'

G.   "meaning, just as a native of the land who did not carry out the rite on the occasion of the first Passover does so on the second, so in the case of a proselyte: whoever did not prepare the offering on the first passover, should do so on the second."

Whereas we see this as a variation on the pattern that tests and proves a proposition, here the inference is tested and rejected; the upshot is another variation on inclusionary/exclusionary discourse.

2.   A.   "'let all his males be circumcised; then he may come near and keep it:'

B.   "This indicates that failure to carry out the obligation of circumcising males [for whom one bears responsibility] keeps one from eating the meat of the passover offering.

C.   "we know only that that rule applies to failure to carry out the obligation of circumcising males [for whom one bears responsibility]. How do we know that the same rule applies to failure to carry out the obligation of circumcising one's recently purchased slaves?

D.   "Lo, you may construct the following analogy:

E.   "Here we find reference to 'then' and we find reference to 'then' [at Exod. 12:44].

F.   "Just as the latter reference refers to circumcising enslaved males, so the reference here refers to circumcising enslaved males, and just as the reference here is to circumcising free males, so the reference there encompasses circumcising free males, [with the result that the same rule applies to both categories, and so long as one bears responsibility for a circumcision and has not carried it out, one cannot eat the passover offering]," the words of R. Eliezer.

G.   R. Ishmael says, "The circumcision of males for whom one bears responsibility does not keep the owner from eating the passover offering.

H.   "Why then does scripture say, 'let all his males be circumcised; then he may come near and keep it'?

I.   "Lo, if one bore responsibility for two religious duties, the religious duty of preparing the passover offering and the religious duty of circumcision, we do not know which of them takes precedence.

J.   "When scripture states, 'let all his males be circumcised; then he may come near and keep it,' we find that carrying out the religious duty of circumcision takes precedence over the religious duty of preparing the passover offering."

Here too we have a variation of inclusionary/exclusionary form.

3. A. R. Nathan says, "The purpose of scripture's stating, 'let all his males be circumcised; [then he may come near and keep it],' is only to encompass the case of a slave who immersed before his master and on that account became a free man."

   B. There is the case of Beluria, some of whose slave girls immersed before her, and some of whose slave girls immersed after her.

   C. The case came before sages, who ruled, "Those who immersed before her are free women, while those who immersed after her remain enslaved."

   D. Nonetheless, the former continued to serve her until the day of her death.

This is a variation on the propositional form, in which the proposition, A, is joined with a case rather than proof texts, B–D.

4. A. "But no uncircumcised person shall eat of it:"

   B. What need is there to say this? Has not scripture already said, "No alien shall eat of it" (Exod. 12:43)?

   C. The point is, might we infer that if a person was an uncircumcised Israelite, he might be valid to eat of the passover offering?

   D. Scripture is explicit: "But no uncircumcised person shall eat of it."

The upshot is redactional-harmonistic, showing that two verses on the same subject make two distinct points. This requires a citation, then "what need . . . ?" and finally, a proposition that corrects the false impression of repetition.

5. A. "There shall be one law for the native and for the stranger who sojourns among you:"

   B. Why is this stated? Has not scripture already said, "he shall be as a native of the land"? Why then specify, "There shall be one law for the native and for the stranger who sojourns among you"?

   C. Since scripture says, "And when a stranger shall sojourn with you and would keep the passover to the Lord," we know only that, as to the passover the proselyte is equivalent to a native-born person. But how do we know that that is the case for all of the other religious duties that are listed in the Torah?

   D. Scripture states, "There shall be one law for the native and for the stranger who sojourns among you,"

   E. so treating the proselyte as equivalent to the home born with regard to all of the other religious duties that are listed in the Torah.

The form is the same as before.

We therefore identify the following formal repertoire:

1. Propositional form: a proposition followed by examples, e.g., of verses or of cases.
2. Proposition tested and proved: variation on the foregoing, in which a proposition is set forth and demonstrated by a sequence of factual statements.
3. Commentary form: clause of a verse + amplificatory phrase, with or without secondary expansion.
4. Dispute-form.
5. Inclusionary/exclusionary form, using fixed phrases throughout to find out whether a given classification is encompassed by the statement at hand or excluded from its rule.
6. Redactional-harmonistic form: Why is this passage needed? followed by another verse or treatment of the same subject, ending with a proposition that distinguishes one case from the other and shows that the Torah had to cover both.
7. The limitations of logic: Protracted, dialectic argument that reason by itself will not suffice to yield a proposed proposition so that appeal to a proof text alone suffices. This is not a narrowly syntactical form but involves a rigid organization of intellectual initiatives as much as grammatical and syntactical formations.
8. Citation-form: One form not yet evidenced is Mishnah-citation-form, which joins to a base verse or proposition (e.g., commentary form) with the word "mikan," translated, "in this connection [sages have said]," a verbatim citation of Mishnah or Tosefta or related types of statements.

Now we ask which forms predominate, and what overall documentary purpose is indicated thereby. The question at hand is this: Does a prevailing, miscellaneous rhetorical repertoire circulate more or less promiscuously among the authorships of diverse documents? In that case, the formal plan of our document is random and not indicative of a formal intent and program. Or can we show that our authorship has made choices? In that case, the formal plan of our document also bespeaks deliberation. The variation among the tractates presents an opportunity to answer the question with compelling data. We see that utilizing forms that serve to convey propositions, not merely ad hoc and episodic observations on this and that, our authorship sets forth propositions, either of a general character ("propositional form," "proposition tested and proved") or of a particular order, e.g., propositions of a determinate character ("limitations of reason"). Where we have a significant interest in making a general point through a plethora of specific examples ("inclusionary/exclusionary form" yielding rules out of cases, "reactional-harmonistic form" producing the proposition that scripture does not idly repeat itself, and "limitations of logic" showing the paramount position of scripture's taxic repertoire), the same conclusion follows. So, seen all together and over all, the rhetorical patterns, however various, characteristic of all nine tractates of Mekhilta Attributed to R. Ishmael aim to set forth first and foremost propositions of one kind or another, second, in significantly smaller proportion, commentary to passages of Exodus.

But do we have mainly a composition of propositions, or mainly a composite of comments? If we now compare the proportion of representation of the commentary form with the proportion of propositional rhetorical patterns and forms, we see that fact in a striking way. What we now take up are forms Nos. 1, 2, 5, 6, 7, compared with form No. 3, and omitting all reference to forms Nos. 4 and 8.

Propositional Forms (1, 2, 5, 6, 7)

	Number	*Proportion of the Tractate*
1. PISHA	136	136/210=64%
2. BESHALLAH	26	26/55=47%
3. SHIRATA	18	18/25=72%
4. VAYASSA	19	19/43=44%
5. AMALEK	12	12/29=41%
6. BAHODESH	46	46/73=63%
7. NEZIQIN	90	90/131=69%
8. KASPA	40	40/57=70%
9. SHABBATA	7	7/8=88%

The authorships of these tractates clearly proposed to set forth a series of propositions, either of a determinate order or principles characteristic of a variety of cases: Pisha, Shirata, Behodesh, Neziqin, Kaspa, and Shabbata. The authorships of Beshallah, Vayassa, and Amalek set forth something other than essentially propositional compositions.

Commentary Form (3)

	Number	*Proportion of the Whole*
1. PISHA	32	32/210=15%
2. BESHALLAH	18	18/55=33%
3. SHIRATA	5	5/25=20%
4. VAYASSA	10	10/43=23%
5. AMALEK	9	9/29=31%
6. BAHODESH	13	13/73=18%
7. NEZIQIN	16	16/131=12%
8. KASPA	8	8/57=14%
9. SHABBATA	1	1/8=13%

The correlation is clear. The authorships of Beshallah, Vayassa, and Amalek provide sizable proportions of phrase-by-phrase commentaries to the selected passages of the Book of Exodus. Yet even here, we must conclude, the paramount mode of discourse yielded by the rhetorical repertoire remains propositional. When we propose, as an overall characterization of Mekhilta Attributed to R. Ishmael, the metaphor of an encyclopedia, we may adduce in evidence the formal preferences of all nine authorships represented in the final document.

One may well challenge that conclusion by asking whether or not other documents exhibit pretty much the same rhetorical or formal characteristics. If that is the fact, then these results conform to a general and canonical, and not a particular and documentary, convention, and we may not appeal to formal and rhetorical indicators for evidence concerning the correct characterization of documents. We may even have to conclude that individual documents from the present viewpoint cannot be characterized ("described") at all, since all of them exhibit a random sample of formal or rhetorical traits that circulate in general but do not divide in such a way as to permit the differentiation of one document from another.

As a matter of fact, these results, which point toward the description of our document as an encyclopedia of essentially propositional, but secondarily exegetical, rhetorical formations, do differentiate this document from others. For various documents' authorships have made choices as to form and even as to the ordering of forms and the cogency of their sustained units of thought. Let us summarize the range of variation. The authorships of documents assuredly choose one set of forms in preference to another set. Within that principle, moreover, some documents' authorships resort to a fixed repertoire of forms but make no effort at ordering the forms in a fixed sequence of types. Other authorships not only utilize a limited repertoire of forms but they order those forms in a fixed way. Other authorships do not do so.

Are we able to differentiate groups of documents by appeal to the simple indicators just now noted? Indeed so. Among the authorships that have chosen a limited repertoire of forms and ordered types of forms with great care so as to establish a single, encompassing proposition (not merely so as to discuss from various viewpoints a shared theme) are those of Leviticus Rabbah and Pesiqta deRab Kahana. The authorship of Sifré to Deuteronomy chose a set of forms that differ, in part if not entirely, from the choices made by the authorships of Leviticus Rabbah and Pesiqta deRab Kahana, and that authorship has also taken no interest in the order of the types of forms that they have chosen. The compositors of

Sifré to Deuteronomy, furthermore, have had no large-scale propositional program in mind in the composition of sustained units of thought,
which, in scale, are substantially smaller than those in Leviticus Rabbah
and Pesiqta deRab Kahana. One may both group Sifra and the two Sifrés
in accord with indicative traits, differentiating all three from Genesis
Rabbah, Leviticus Rabbah, and Pesiqta deRab Kahana, and, moreover,
differentiate Sifra and the two Sifrés from one another. But to do so
would carry us far afield and is not required for the important, but
simple, proposition at hand.

The several canonical documents exhibit important differences of
rhetoric, the ordering of rhetorical patterns, and the sustained cogency
of a given large-scale composition. Some documents' authorships do not
take an interest in the order of rhetorical patterns; other authorships
exhibit keen concern for that matter. Some documents' authorships join
a large number of individual units of thought to establish a single
proposition, and that sustained mode of argumentation and demonstration characterizes every single principal division of those documents.
Other authorships are quite content to make one point after another,
with no interest in establishing out of many things one thing. These
differences entirely suffice to show us that people made choices and
carried them out, doing one thing, not another, in the formation of the
units of thought in accord with a fixed rhetorical pattern and in the
ordering of units of thought in accord with the diverse rhetorical patterns and in the composing, within a single composite, of a carefully
framed proposition to be established by these ordered patterns of a
limited sort. Some people did things that way; other people did things in
a different way. So the differences are systematic and point to choice. It
follows that the rhetorical choices of our document are not haphazard
but deliberate and point toward the presence of an authorship, that is, a
plan. If the writing is rhetorically distinctive, what about the propositions of the document? Here we find ourselves in a different situation
altogether. The authorship of Mekhilta Attributed to R. Ishmael does
not deliver a particular message, and its theological positions can hardly
be shown particular to its authorship. This writing presents information,
but no singular message: an encyclopedia, not an argument.

We now come back to the basic problem of this book: How to analyze
the uses of, and relationships to, scripture, exhibited by the canonical
writings of the Judaism of the dual Torah in its formative age. Just as, to
get their bearings, navigators take a sighting on the fixed stars, so for the
purpose of definition, therefore, canonical comparison and contrast, for
us scripture serves as the fixed star. For scripture defines the context of

all Judaic systems, hence, also of their canonical writings of all kinds and classifications. Sages in the writings of the Judaism of the dual Torah appealed to scripture not merely for proof texts as part of an apologia but for a far more original and sustained mode of discourse. In the Midrash-compilations, it was in constant interchange with scripture that sages found ways of delivering their own message, in their own idiom, and in diverse ways. Verses of scripture therefore served not merely to prove but also to instruct. Israelite scripture constituted not merely a source of validation but also a powerful instrument of profound inquiry, whether, as in Leviticus Rabbah, into the rules of society, or as in Sifra, into the modes of correct logical analysis and argument, or as in Mekhilta Attributed to R. Ishmael, into theological and normative rules on diverse subjects. Propositions that could be proposed, the statements that could be made, indeed prove diverse. Scripture served as a kind of grammar and syntax, limiting the arrangement of words but making possible an infinity of statements.

The upshot is that the received scriptures formed an instrumentality for the expression of an authorship responsible for a writing bearing its own integrity and cogency, an authorship appealing to its own conventions of intelligibility and, above all, making its own points. Some authorships did not write *about* scripture, creating, e.g., a literature of commentary and exegesis essentially within the program of scripture. Rather, as we have already noted earlier, they wrote *with* Scripture. All authorships worked out for their documents a relationship with scripture. Each turned to scripture not for proof texts, let alone for pretexts, to say whatever they wanted, anyhow, to say. They used scripture as an artist uses the colors on the palette, expressing ideas through and with scripture as the artist paints with those colors and no others. Sages appealed to scripture not merely for proof texts, as part of an apologia, but for a far more original and sustained mode of discourse.

Verses of scripture served not merely to prove but also to instruct. Israelite scripture constituted not merely a source of validation but a powerful instrument of profound inquiry. The framers of the various Midrash-compilations set forth propositions of their own, yet in dialogue with scripture. Scripture raised questions, set forth premises of discourse and argument, supplied facts, constituted that faithful record of the facts, rules, and meaning of humanity's, and Israel's, history that, for natural philosophy, derived from the facts of physics or astronomy. Whether or not their statement accorded with the position of scripture on a given point, merely said the simple and obvious sense of scripture, found ample support in proof texts—none of these considerations bears material consequence. These authorships made use of scripture, but they did so by making selections, shaping a distinctive idiom of discourse in so doing. True, verses of scripture provided facts; they supplied proofs of propositions much as data of natural science proved propositions of natural philosophy. Writing with scripture meant appealing to the facts that scripture provided to prove propositions that the authorships at hand wished to prove, forming with scripture the systems these writers proposed to construct.

Classifications of relationships to scripture are three. The first taxonomic system, one that is visible to the naked eye, instructs us to look for evidence that a verse of the Israelite scriptures illustrates theme, that is to say, provides *information* on a given subject. In the context of the statement of a document, that information is systemically inert. That is markedly characteristic of Mekhilta Attributed to R. Ishmael. The first mode of relationship, therefore, is to develop an anthology on a theme. One way of forming a comprehensible statement is to draw together information on a single theme. The theme then imposes cogency on facts, which are deemed to illuminate aspects of that theme. Such a statement constitutes a topical anthology. The materials in the anthology do not, all together, add up to a statement that transcends detail. For example, they do not point toward a conclusion beyond themselves. They rather comprise a series of facts, e.g., fact 1, fact 2, fact 3. But put together, these three facts do not yield yet another one, nor do they point toward a proposition beyond themselves. They generate no generalization, prove no point, propose no proposition. We believe that that relationship to scripture is most common in our document, least in the others under discussion. Yet even here, the number of topical anthologies in Mekhilta Attributed to R. Ishmael is not formidable.

A second mode of relationship will tell us that a verse of the Israelite scriptures defines a *problem* on its own, in its own determinate limits and terms. In the setting of a document, the problem will be identified and addressed because it is systemically active. That is not at all common in Mekhilta Attributed to R. Ishmael, whereas Sifra for its part takes a keen interest in verses and their meanings. Yet in doing so, its authorship weaves a filigree of holy words over a polished surface of very hard wood: a wood of its own hewing and shaping and polishing. Our sense is that the recurrent allusion to verses of scripture forms an aesthetic surface rather than a philosophical foundation for our book.

Yet a third points toward the utilization of Israelite scriptures in the formation and expression of *an independent proposition*, one autonomous of the theme or even the facts contained within—proved by—those scriptures. That is not the relationship established between scripture and the fundamental program of our document. It does characterize the relationship between scripture and Sifra, which is not extrascriptural but metascriptural. Scripture in this function is systemically essential yet monumentally irrelevant. Sifra in that way addresses and disposes of scripture by rewriting it in ways of Sifra's authorship's design. That is the wonder of this marvelous writing: its courage, its brilliance, its originality, above all, its stubbornness. But that is never the case in Mekhilta Attributed to R. Ishmael.

The fourth and, in the present instance, routine relationship to scripture is indicated when the focus of interest is on the exegesis of scripture. In Mekhilta Attributed to R. Ishmael, as well as in Sifra and Sifré to Deuteronomy, we have composites of materials that find cogency solely in the words of a given verse of scripture but in no other way. These materials string together, upon the necklace of words or phrases of a verse, diverse comments; the comments do not fit together or point to any broader conclusion; they do not address a single theme or form an anthology. Cogency derives from the (external) verse that is cited; intelligibility begins—and ends—in that verse and is accomplished by the amplification of the verse's contents. Without the verse before us, the words that follow form gibberish. But reading the words as amplifications of a sense contained within the cited verse, we can make good sense of them.

The upshot is simple. Where, to take up the first classification, a given theme requires illustration, the ancient scriptures provide a useful fact. That is assuredly the case not only for Mekhilta Attributed to R. Ishmael but—by definition—for all other Midrash-compilations as well. Indeed, those scriptures may well form the single important treasury of facts. But the amplification of the verses of scripture will take second place to the display of the facts important to the topic at hand; the purpose of composition is the creation of a scrapbook of materials relevant to a given theme. The verse of received scripture will serve not to validate a proposition but only to illustrate a theme.

Where, second, the sense or meaning or implications of a given verse of scripture defines the center of discourse, then the verse takes over and dictates the entire character of the resulting composition, and that composition we may call exegetical (substituting "eisegetical" is a mere conceit). This, we now recognize, is the principal relationship to scripture characteristic of our compilation.

And when, third, an authorship proposes to make a strong case for a given proposition, appealing to a variety of materials, there Israelite scriptures take a subordinate position within discourse determined by a logic all its own. When we consider the principal points of Mekhilta Attributed to R. Ishmael, we realize that that relationship to scripture does not characterize the document as a whole. Although dominant in other Midrash-compilations, this relationship to scripture is rare in Mekhilta Attributed to R. Ishmael. The upshot is that in the aggregate Mekhilta Attributed to R. Ishmael relates to scripture in ways that do not characterize the relationships to, or utilizations of, scripture paramount in Sifra and Sifré to Numbers. It appeals to scripture for information and relies on scripture to organize that information. That is to say, it is a scriptural encyclopedia: a presentation of information deriving from scripture in the order and program dictated by scripture. That is precisely what happens when people are not writing with scripture at all.

The nine authorships of Mekhilta Attributed to R. Ishmael treat as a given, that is to say, a corpus of facts or, more aptly, a body of tradition, what the other authorships set forth as components of a system that requires defense and demands apologetic exposition. For our authorship, the facts compose a corpus of information, to which people require ready access. By setting forth an important component of information, that is, the data of revealed truths of the Judaism of the dual Torah, that authorship provides such access. What is needed, then, is an encyclopedia of things one should know on themes scripture dictates, and the sequence of topics and propositions, in the order demanded by scripture, results. Each document in the corpus of the rabbinic writings of late antiquity bears points in common with others. In their ultimate condition, they came to form a tradition, understood in that sense of tradition as a fixed and unchanging essence deriving from an indeterminate past, a truth bearing its own stigmata of authority, e.g., from God at Sinai. Mekhilta Attributed to R. Ishmael constitutes a partial statement of that complete tradition. It is the first encyclopedia in the canon of the Judaism of the dual Torah that emerged from late antiquity, because it is the first full traditional, utterly nonsystemic, statement to emerge.

The comparison of Mekhilta Attributed to R. Ishmael with the Bavli, that is, a traditional as against a systemic presentation, will show precisely what this means. The Bavli provides a striking contrast with Mekhilta Attributed to R. Ishmael, for, whereas our document forms a corpus of received truth, the Bavli's authorship reshapes and re-presents truth in a highly propositional manner. How so? The appeal of the authorship of the Bavli is to the ineluctable verity of well-applied logic, practical reason tested and retested against the facts, whether deriving from prior authorities or emerging from examples and decisions of leading contemporary authorities. True enough, the Bavli contains ample selections from available writings. The authorship of the Bavli leaves no doubt that it makes extensive use of extant materials, received sayings and stories. The Bavli's authorship further takes as its task the elucidation of the received code, the Mishnah. More to the point, frequent citations of materials now found in the Tosefta as well as allusions to sayings framed in Tannaite Hebrew and attributed to Tannaite authority—marked, for instance, by TN'—time and again alert us to extensive reference, by our authorship, to a prior corpus of materials.

Not only so, but contemporary scholarship has closely read both brief sayings and also extended discourses in light of two or three or more versions and come to the conclusion that a later generation has taken up and made use of available materials. Most strikingly of all, our authorship claims in virtually every line to come at the end of a chain of tradition, since the bulk of the generative sayings—those that form the foundation for sustained inquiry and dialectical discourse—is assigned to named authorities clearly understood to stand prior to the work of the ultimate redactors. In all these ways, the authorship of the Bavli assuredly stands in a line of tradition, taking over and reworking received materials, restating viewpoints that originate in prior ages. And that fact makes all the more striking the fundamental autonomy of discourse displayed by the document at the end. And the contrast between the character of that independent discourse, the Bavli's, and the quality of presentation, not re-presentation, of paraphrase and summary paramount in Mekhilta Attributed to R. Ishmael, shows us how a systemic statement differs from a traditional one, the Bavli from Mekhilta Attributed to R. Ishmael.

In the Bavli, therefore, we deal with an authorship of amazingly independent mind, working independently and in an essentially original way on materials on which others have handed on quite persuasive and cogent statements of their own. Tosefta on the one side, scripture and a heritage of conventional reading thereof on the other—neither has defined the program of the Bavli or determined the terms in which it would make its statement, although both, in a subordinated position and in a paltry, limited measure, are given some sort of a say. The Bavli is connected to a variety of prior writings but continuous with none of them. And the opposite traits characterize Mekhilta Attributed to R. Ishmael. The Book of Exodus has defined the program of Mekhilta Attributed to R. Ishmael and determined the topics and the propositions that the document's authorship would expound.

The Bavli is an autonomous statement of a system of its own, and Mekhilta Attributed to R. Ishmael is a contingent statement of a received tradition. The Bavli's system does not recapitulate its texts. The Mekhilta's statement, in its profoundly unsystematic character, is set forth as precisely that: a recapitulation of scripture. In the Bavli, the system—the final and complete statement—does not recapitulate the extant texts. The antecedent texts—when used at all—are so read as to recapitulate the system. The system comes before the texts and defines the canon as the Bavli represents it. But with Mekhilta Attributed to R. Ishmael, all we have are the antecedent texts, the system of which—so the authorship represents matters—is simply restated in conventional amplification and loyal paraphrase.

The Bavli's statement has given us such tradition as the Bavli's penultimate and ultimate authorship has itself chosen and has itself worked out. This statement of an autonomous, systemic character we now receive according to the choices dictated by that authorship's sense of order and proportion, priority and importance, and it is generated by the problematic found by that authorship to be acute and urgent and compelling. When confronting the exegesis of the Mishnah, which is its indicative trait and definitive task, the authorship of the Bavli does not continue and complete the work of antecedents. Quite to the contrary, that authorship made its statement essentially independent of its counterpart and earlier document. Therefore, for the Bavli, the system comes first. In the present context, that means that the logic and principle of orderly inquiry take precedence over the preservation and repetition of received materials, however holy. The mode of thought defined, the work of applied reason and practical rationality may get underway. The contrast with Mekhilta Attributed to R. Ishmael is self-evident.

In its rhetorical choices, in its logic of coherent discourse, and in its topical and propositional program, Mekhilta Attributed to R. Ishmael is not autonomous but contingent, not systemic but disparate and allusive, not formed out of a generative problematic, not characterized by vigorous presentation of an urgent and compelling program of thought. When confronting the exegesis of scripture, which forms the definitive task of our authorship, the discourse is so set forth as to represent a mere continuation and completion of the written Torah. The authorship of Mekhilta Attributed to R. Ishmael makes a statement that, by its own word, is essentially a completion and fulfillment of its scriptural counterpart. Therefore, for Mekhilta Attributed to R. Ishmael, tradition comes first, and tradition is all there is.

For the Bavli, first in place is the system that the Bavli as a whole expresses and serves in stupefying detail to define. Only then comes that selection, out of the received materials of the past, of topics and even concrete judgments, facts that serve the Bavli's authorship in the articulation of its system. Nothing out of the past can be shown to have dictated the Bavli's program, which is essentially the work of its authorship. In this context, the Mishnah forms no exception, for the work of the Bavli's authorship began with the selection of tractates to study and designation of those to ignore. For the authorship of Mekhilta Attributed to R. Ishmael's nine tractates, first in place is scripture, in which, for the passages of Exodus that are treated, no one makes choices. Nearly the whole of the scriptural passages at hand are treated, and the treatment is so lacking in distinctive traits that we cannot imagine a reason for omitting the chapters of Exodus that are not covered. People who could speak in so routine a manner about this will not have run out of commonplaces for the amplification of that. The insistence of our authorship, expressed in its laconic discourse, its reference to received materials, its haphazard and unsystematic arrangement of its ideas in mere commentary form, always in response to the received text (scripture here, the counterpart of Mishnah for Bavli)—all point toward the same trait of mind: that of the traditionalist, intent on presenting truth, not on reshaping, let alone proving propositions of truth.

In the example of the Judaism of the dual Torah come to full expression in the Bavli, such tradition as the authorship at hand has received ends when the system that receives that tradition begins. So we conclude that where reason reigns, its inexorable logic and order, proportion and syllogistic reasoning govern supreme and alone, revising the received materials and restating into a compelling statement, in reason's own encompassing, powerful, and rigorous logic, the entirety of the prior heritage of information and thought. That restatement is the Bavli. And the opposite is to be said of Mekhilta Attributed to R. Ishmael. So far as our authorship proposes to set forth a system of its own, the system proves not only congruent with the received statement ("tradition," scripture) but also indistinguishable from it. Where tradition reigns, its dictates, its sense of argument through citation and demonstration through display of proof texts, its requirements of exegetical, not propositional presentation and fixed associative logic of coherent discourse— all these characteristic traits will predominate. Just as the Bavli is a systemic, and not a traditional, statement and document, so Mekhilta Attributed to R. Ishmael is a traditional, not a systemic one.

In the model of the Bavli we have claimed that the canonical documents of formative Judaism constitute, each on its own, statements at the end of a sustained process of rigorous thought and logical inquiry, applied logic and practical reason. The only way to read a reasoned and systematic statement of a system is defined by the rules of general intelligibility, the laws of reasoned and syllogistic discourse about rules and principles. In that context we point to Mekhilta Attributed to R. Ishmael as the opposite, a statement at the end of a well-protected process of tradition, of not inquiry but repetition, of not applied logic and practical reason but faithful sifting and testing of received and established truth. The way to read a traditional and sedimentary document such as ours lies through the ad hoc and episodic display of instances and examples, layers of meaning and eccentricities of confluence, intersection, and congruence.

Can tradition and system share a single crown? Surely not. The traits of mind and aesthetic of the one contradict those required for the successful formulation of the other. Yet, if the formative document of the Judaism of the dual Torah, the Bavli, demonstrates that Judaism constitutes not a traditional but a systemic religious statement, with a hermeneutics of its own, with an order, proportion, above all, reasoned context, particular to its system, then not many other authorships followed the example of the Bavli. From then to now, system builders were few, fewer still those who framed their views in a hermeneutics, an order, proportion, and context of self-evidence, wholly dictated by the system's larger foci. Only two major systems came to full intellectual and literary expression and precipitated a labor of secondary amplification and exegesis such as the Bavli brought about, and these were Maimonides's philosophical, and Moses de Leon's metaphysical, systems. Viewed as intellectual constructs, these alone compare with the Bavli— and then not favorably. The Bavli stood (and stands) in splendor, towering, governing, defining. But it stood alone.

By contrast, Mekhilta Attributed to R. Ishmael, for its part, attracted many imitators and continuators. The conception of collecting information and holding it together upon the frame of scripture attracted many, so that a vast literature of Midrash-compilation much like this compilation came into being in succeeding centuries. Not one but dozens, ultimately hundreds, of Midrash-compilations, interesting, traditional, and of course, pointless and merely informative, would fill the shelves of the library that emerged from the canon of the Judaism of the dual Torah. Accordingly, Mekhilta Attributed to R. Ishmael stood at the beginning of centuries of work carried on in the pattern set by that authorship. There would be only one Bavli, but many, many Midrash-compilations: Mekhiltas, Yalquts, Midrash-this and Midrash-that, and, in due course, a secondary development would call into being commentaries to scripture (as to the Bavli) as well. So Mekhilta Attributed to R. Ishmael formed not only a scriptural encyclopedia of Judaism but, as it turned out, the first of many, many such compilations of revealed, received truth, set forth in the framework of the written Torah.

Late antiquity produced two Talmuds, one of which made all the difference, but neither of which attracted imitators and continuators. Late antiquity produced perhaps a dozen Midrash-compilations in the model of Sifra and the two Sifrés—systemic, argumentative, original. These too found no succession in later authorships. But from then to our own day, an endless sequence of collections and arrangements of received truth have addressed the written Torah, scripture, within the intellectual framework evidenced here. The Judaism of the dual Torah began among system builders. But it endured in the hands of traditionalists. And, we suppose, that is how things were meant to be, and it is probably how things had to be. For no system can well serve a social world already well served by system builders, and every system to endure must transform itself into tradition. But fortunate are those who thrive in the age of system building, and dull is the life of those who inherit and preserve what others made up for themselves and handed on, only now not as discovered and imagined, but as merely revealed truth.

APPENDIX
DATING MEKHILTA ATTRIBUTED TO R. ISHMAEL

The prevailing scholarly consensus assigns to the present document a place within the "halakhic Midrashim," or the "Tannaitic Midrashim," that is to say, compilations of exegeses of verses of scripture that pertain to normative behavior, on the one side, and to the period of the authorities who produced the Mishnah, that is, the first and second centuries of the Common Era, on the other. The two current discussions are as follows: Ben Zion Wacholder, "The Date of the Mekilta de-Rabbi Ishmael," *Hebrew Union College Annual* 39:117–44, 1968, who rejects the received date and proposes one in medieval times; Günther Stemberger, "Die Datierung der Mekhilta," *Kairos* 31:81–118, 1979, who systematically proposes to refute Wacholder's position. In Wacholder's behalf, however, we have to note that if Mekhilta Attributed to R. Ishmael belongs to the classification of Tannaitic Midrashim and of halakhic Midrashim, as we shall see, it is quite different from the other books in those categories, Sifra and the two Sifrés, in the indicative traits of rhetoric, logic, and topical expression.

Yet that fact is not decisive standing by itself. For whereas the document at hand differs in fundamental ways from others of its species and genus, a single authorship or era in the formation of the canon can have produced writings of more than a single type.

The results of our inductive description yield a quite different possibility for the analysis of these writings, one with no bearing on dating documents. Within Mekhilta Attributed to R. Ishmael, diverse genres of scriptural writing require or precipitate use of diverse rhetorical and logical conventions. Specifically, to take one striking instance, we can demonstrate that Mekhilta-tractate Neziqin, which focuses upon legal passages, exhibits precisely the indicative traits that characterize Sifré to Deuteronomy when it treats legal passages. What this means to us is that framers of documents and perhaps also writers of individual units of thought appealed to a fixed repertoire of conventions when they dealt with one type of scriptural material, with the corollary that, when they dealt with another type of scriptural material, they responded to a different repertoire of literary and intellectual conventions altogether. That fact, on its own, would argue for a date for our document within the period in which the conventions exhibited by Sifré to Deuteronomy in its discourses on the laws of the written Torah proved vital and compelling, although we cannot dismiss the possibility of a later authorship's imitating the style of an earlier one. In any event the issue of dating Midrash-compilations has yet to be worked out with rigor, and the theoretical problems have not been addressed at all. Entirely inductive and phenomenological, the work we do here has no probative evidence to contribute, therefore, no bearing upon that problem and—mutatis mutandis—the question of dating a document furthermore yields no implications relevant to our results in this book.

8

Is Judaism a "Biblical Religion"?

DEFINING A "BIBLICAL RELIGION"

Although the framers of Judaism as we know it received as divinely revealed ancient Israel's literary heritage, they picked and chose as they wished what would serve the purposes of the larger system they undertook to build. Since the Judaism at hand first reached literary expression in the Mishnah, a document in which scripture plays a subordinate role, the founders of that Judaism clearly made no pretense at tying up to scriptural proof texts or at expressing in the form of scriptural commentary the main ideas they wished to set out. Accordingly, Judaism rests only asymmetrically upon the foundations of the Hebrew scriptures, and Judaism is not alone or mainly "the religion of the Old Testament." Since Judaism is not "the religion of the Old Testament," we cannot take for granted or treat as predictable or predetermined the entry of the Hebrew scriptures into the system of Judaism at hand. That is why we must ask exactly how the scriptures did enter the framework of Judaism. In what way, when, and where, in the unfolding of the canon of Judaism, were they absorbed and recast, and how did they find the distinctive role they were to play from late antiquity onward? That question points toward the larger issue implicit in the concern of this book, namely, the place and use of scripture in the Judaism of the dual Torah. For once we realize that "scripture" in the Judaism of the dual Torah formed (merely) one component of the Torah, everything changes. Scripture loses its autonomous standing and its paramount authority and becomes one more medium for God's revealing the Torah to Israel. And other writings enter the status of that same revelation. When that shift takes place—as it does for Judaism as well as for Christianity, each within its own logic—then what of the written Torah/Old Testament? That is what is at stake in the recognition that authorships of ancient Judaism wrote with scripture and proposed the result to form part of the Torah.

166

When the Judaism of the dual Torah had defined its matrix of myth and rite—a system of world view and way of life focused on a particular social group—then that Judaism attained its independent voice, its inner structure and logic. At that moment—but only then—scripture for its part also would assume its position as source of truth and proof for all (autonomously framed, independently reached) propositions. In the nature of things, as we have seen, scripture could form a focus of discourse only when discourse itself had expressed determinants autonomous of both the Mishnah and also scripture—determinants, or propositions prior to all else. To revert to the operative myth, it is only when the Torah had reached full expression as an autonomous entity of logic that the (mere) components of Torah—scripture, the Mishnah and associated writings alike—found their proper place and proportion.

To understand these propositions, let us return to Leviticus Rabbah. In Leviticus Rabbah we see how statements become intelligible not contingently, that is, on the strength of an established text, but a priori, that is, on the basis of a deeper logic of meaning, an independent principle of rhetorical intelligibility. The reason we say so is simple. Leviticus Rabbah is topical, not exegetical. Each of its 37 *parashiyyot* pursues its given topic and develops points relevant to that topic. It is logical, in that (to repeat) discourse appeals to an underlying principle of composition and intelligibility and that logic inheres in what is said. Logic is what joins one sentence to the next and forms the whole into paragraphs of meaning, intelligible propositions, each with its place and sense in a still larger, accessible system. Because of logic one mind connects to another, public discourse becomes possible, debate on issues of general intelligibility takes place, and an anthology of statements about a single subject becomes a composition of theorems about that subject. Accordingly, with Leviticus Rabbah rabbis take up the problem of saying what they wish to say not in an exegetical, but in a syllogistic and freely discursive logic and rhetoric.

To appreciate what was new, let us rapidly review the prior pattern of how people wrote both with and without scripture. To seek, through biblical exegesis, to link the Mishnah to scripture, detail by detail, represented a well-trodden and firmly packed path. Sifra, an exegetical study of Leviticus as rabbis read the document, shows what could be done. The exegetes there cite a passage of the Mishnah verbatim and show that only through scriptural exegesis, not through the processes of reason, can we reach the correct law. Scripture exegesis by rabbis also was a commonplace, as Genesis Rabbah indicates. Leviticus Rabbah was the first major rabbinic composition to propose to make topical and

discursive statements, not episodically, as we saw in Sifré in Deuteronomy, but systematically and in a disciplined framework. Not merely a
phrase-by-phrase or verse-by-verse exegesis of a document, whether the
Mishnah or a book of scripture itself, Leviticus Rabbah takes a new road.
The framers of that composition undertook to offer propositions, declarative sentences (so to speak), in which, not through the exegesis of verses
of scripture in the order of scripture but through an order dictated by
their own sense of the logic of syllogistic composition, they would say
what they had in mind. To begin with, they laid down their own topical
program, related to, but essentially autonomous of, that of the Book of
Leviticus. Second, in expressing their ideas on these topics, they never
undertook simply to cite a verse of scripture and then to claim that that
verse states precisely what they had in mind to begin with. Accordingly,
through rather distinctive modes of expression, the framers said what
they wished to say in their own way—just as had the authors of the
Mishnah itself. True, in so doing, the composers of Leviticus Rabbah
treated scripture as had their predecessors. That is to say, to them as to
those who had gone before, scripture provided a rich treasury of facts.

WRITING WITH SCRIPTURE
IN A BIBLICAL RELIGION

How, very concretely, do the framers of Leviticus Rabbah accomplish
that "writing with scripture" of which we have spoken? The paramount
and dominant exegetical construction in Leviticus Rabbah is the base
verse/intersecting verse exegesis. In this construction, a verse of Leviticus is cited (hence, base verse), and another verse, from such books as
Job, Proverbs, Qohelet, or Psalms, is then cited (hence, intersecting
verse). The latter, not the former, is subjected to detailed and systematic
exegesis. But the exegetical exercise ends up by leading the intersecting
verse back to the base verse and reading the latter in terms of the former.
In such an exercise, what in fact do we do? We read one thing in terms of
something else. To begin with, it is the base verse in terms of the
intersecting verse. But it also is the intersecting verse in other terms as
well—a multiple-layered construction of analogy and parable. The intersecting verse's elements always turn out to stand for, to signify, to speak
of, something other than that to which they openly refer. If water stands
for Torah, the skin disease for evil speech, the reference to something for
some other thing entirely, then the mode of thought at hand is simple.
One thing symbolizes another, speaks not of itself but of some other
thing entirely.

How shall we describe this mode of thought? It seems to me we may call it an as-if way of seeing things. That is to say, it is as if a common object or symbol really represented an uncommon one. Nothing says what it means. Everything important speaks metonymically, elliptically, parabolically, symbolically. All statements carry deeper meaning, which inheres in other statements altogether. The profound sense, then, of the base verse emerges only through restatement within and through the intersecting verse—as if the base verse spoke of things that, on the surface, we do not see at all. Accordingly, if we ask the single prevalent literary construction to testify to the prevailing frame of mind, its message is that things are never what they seem. All things demand interpretation. Interpretation begins in the search for analogy, for that to which the thing is likened, hence the deep sense in which all exegesis at hand is parabolic. It is a quest for that for which the thing in its deepest structure stands.

Exegesis as we know it in Leviticus Rabbah (and not only there) consists in an exercise in analogical thinking—something is like something else, stands for, evokes, or symbolizes that which is quite outside itself. It may be the opposite of something else, in which case it conforms to the exact opposite of the rules that govern that something else. The reasoning is analogical or it is contrastive, and the fundamental logic is taxonomic. The taxonomy rests on those comparisons and contrasts we should call, as we said, metonymic and parabolic. In that case what lies on the surface misleads. What lies beneath or beyond the surface—there is the true reality, the world of truth and meaning. To revert to the issue of taxonomy, the tracts that allow classification serve only for that purpose. They signify nothing more than that something more.

How shall we characterize people who see things this way? They constitute the opposite of ones who call a thing as it is. Self-evidently, they have become accustomed to perceiving more—or less—than is at hand. Perhaps that is a natural mode of thought for the Jews of this period (and not then alone), so long used to calling themselves God's first love, yet now seeing others with greater worldly reason claiming that same advantaged relationship. Not in mind only, but still more, in the politics of the world, the people that remembered its origins along with the very creation of the world and founding of humanity, that recalled how it alone served, and serves, the one and only God, for more than 300 years had confronted a quite different existence. The radical disjuncture between the way things were and the way scripture said things were supposed to be—and in actuality would some day become—surely imposed an unbearable tension. It was one thing for the slave born to slavery to endure. It was another for the free man sold into slavery to accept that same condition. The vanquished people, the nation that had lost its city and its temple, that had, moreover, produced another nation from its midst to take over its scripture and much else, could not bear too much reality. That defeated people will then have found refuge in a mode of thought that trained vision to see other things otherwise than as the eyes perceived them. Among the diverse ways by which the weak and subordinated accommodate to their circumstance, the one of iron-willed pretense in life is most likely to yield the mode of thought at hand: Things never are, because they cannot be, what they seem.

THE ROLE OF SCRIPTURE:
PARADIGM OF RENEWAL AND RECONSTRUCTION

Everyone has always known that Jews read scripture. Every system of Judaism has done so. But why did they do so? What place did scripture take in the larger systems of reality presented by various Judaisms? Why one part of scripture rather than some other, and why read it in one way rather than another? These questions do not find ready answers in the mere observation that Jews read scripture and construct Judaisms out of it. Nor is that observation one of a predictable and necessary pattern, since some of the documents of the rabbinic canon did not focus upon scripture or even find it necessary to quote scripture a great deal. The Mishnah, Tosefta, and important units of discourse of both Talmuds, for example, did not express their ideas in the way in which people who "read scripture" ought to. They make use of scripture sparingly, only with restraint adducing proofs for propositions even when these are based upon scriptural statements. So the paramount and dominant place accorded to scripture in Leviticus Rabbah and documents like it cannot pass without comment and explanation.

Exactly what can we say for the position of scripture in this composition in particular, and what did scripture contribute? We ask first about the use of scripture in the mode of thought at hand: Where, why, and how did scripture find its central place in the minds of people who thought in the way in which the framers of our document did? The answer is that scripture contributed that other world that underlay this one. From scripture came that other set of realities to be discovered in the ordinary affairs of the day. Scripture defined the inner being, the mythic life, that sustained Israel. The world is to be confronted as if things are not as they seem, because it is scripture that tells us how things always are—not one time, in the past only, not one time, in the future only, but now and always. So the key to the system is what happens to, and through, scripture. The lock that is opened is the deciphering of the code by which people were guided in their denial of one thing and recognition and affirmation of the presence of some other. It was not general, therefore mere lunacy, but specific, therefore culture.

To spell this out: The mode of thought pertained to a particular set of ideas. People did not engage ubiquitously and individually in an ongoing pretense that things always had to be other than they seemed. Had they done so, the Jewish nation would have disintegrated into a collectivity of pure insanity. The insistence on the as-if character of reality collectively focused upon one, and only one, alternative existence. All parties (so far as we know) entered into and shared that same and single interior universe. It was the one framed by scripture. What happens in Leviticus Rabbah (and, self-evidently, in other documents of the same sort)? Reading one thing in terms of something else, the builders of the document systematically adopted for themselves the reality of the scripture, its history and doctrines. They transformed that history from a sequence of one-time events, leading from one place to some other, into an ever-present mythic world. No longer was there one Moses, one David, one set of happenings of a distinctive and never-to-be-repeated character. Now whatever happens, of which the thinkers propose to take account, must enter and be absorbed into that established and ubiquitous pattern and structure founded in scripture. It is not that biblical history repeats itself. Rather, biblical history no longer constitutes history as a story of things that happened once, long ago, and pointed to some one moment in the future. Rather it becomes an account of things that happen every day—hence, an ever-present mythic world, as we said.

A rapid glance at the work of the authorships of Leviticus Rabbah or Sifré to Deuteronomy (or any of their fellows) tells us that scripture supplies the document with its structure, its content, its facts, its everything. But a deeper analysis also demonstrates that scripture never provides the document with that structure, contents, and facts that it now exhibits. Everything is reshaped and reframed. Whence the paradox? Scripture as a whole does not dictate the order of discourse, let alone its character. Just as the Talmudic authors destroyed the wholeness of the Mishnah and chose to take up its bits and pieces, so the exegetical writers did the same to scripture. In our document they chose in Leviticus itself a verse here, a phrase there. These then presented the pretext for propositional discourse commonly quite out of phase with the cited passage. Verses that are quoted ordinarily shift from the meanings they convey to the implications they contain, speaking—as we have made clear—about something, anything, other than what they seem to be saying. So the as-if frame of mind brought to scripture brings renewal to scripture, seeing everything with fresh eyes. And the result of the new vision was a reimagining of the social world envisioned by the document at hand, we mean, the everyday world of Israel in its Land in that difficult time. For what the sages now proposed was a reconstruction of existence along the lines of the ancient design of scripture as they read it. What that meant was that, from a sequence of one-time and linear events, everything that happened was turned into a repetition of known and already experienced paradigms, hence, once more, a mythic being. The source and core of the myth, of course, derive from scripture— scripture reread, renewed, reconstructed along with the society that revered scripture.

So, to summarize, the mode of thought that dictated the issues and the logic of the document, telling the thinkers to see one thing in terms of something else, addressed scripture in particular and collectively. And thinking as they did, the framers of the document saw scripture in a new way, just as they saw their own circumstance afresh, rejecting their world in favor of scripture's, reliving scripture's world in their own terms. That, incidentally, is why they did not write history, an account of what was happening and what it meant. It was not that they did not recognize or appreciate important changes and trends reshaping their nation's life. They could not deny that reality. In their apocalyptic reading of the dietary and leprosy laws, they made explicit their close encounter with the history of the world as they knew it. But they had another mode of responding to history. It was to treat history as if it were already known and readily understood. Whatever happened had already happened. How so? Scripture dictated the contents of history, laying forth the structures of time, the rules that prevailed and were made known in events. Self-evidently, these same thinkers projected into scripture's day the realities of their own, turning Moses and David into rabbis, for example. But that is how people think in that mythic, enchanted world in which, to begin with, reality blends with dream, and hope projects onto future and past alike how people want things to be.

The upshot is that the mode of thought revealed by the literary construction under discussion constitutes a rather specific expression of a far more general and prevailing way of seeing things. The literary form in concrete ways says that the entirety of the biblical narrative speaks to each circumstance, that the system of scripture as a whole not only governs, but comes prior to, any concrete circumstance of that same scripture. Everything in scripture is relevant everywhere else in scripture. It must follow, the Torah (to use the mythic language of the system at hand) defines reality under all specific circumstances. Obviously we did not have to come to the specific literary traits of the document at hand to discover those prevailing characteristics of contemporary and later documents of the rabbinic canon. True, every exercise in referring one biblical passage to another expands the range of discourse to encompass much beyond the original referent. But that is a commonplace in the exegesis of scripture, familiar whatever midrash-exegesis was undertaken, in no way particular to rabbinic writings.

THE RESULT OF WRITING WITH SCRIPTURE:
A JUDAIC SYSTEM

The message of Leviticus Rabbah comes to us from the ultimate framers. It is delivered through their selection of materials already available as well as through their composition of new ones. What we now require is a clear statement of the major propositions expressed in Leviticus Rabbah both through writing with scripture and also through writing without scripture but with other materials entirely. That will emerge through classification of the statements, with the notion that the principal themes, and the messages on those themes, should coalesce into a few clear statements.

The recurrent message may be stated in a single paragraph. God loves Israel, so gave them the Torah, which defines their life and governs their welfare. Israel is alone in its category (sui generis), as in Parashah 1, so what is a virtue to Israel is a vice to the nation, life-giving to Israel, poison to the gentiles. True, Israel sins, but God forgives that sin, having punished the nation on account of it. Such a process has yet to come to an end, but it will culminate in Israel's complete regeneration. Meanwhile, Israel's assurance of God's love lies in the many expressions of special concern, for even the humblest and most ordinary aspects of the national life: the food the nation eats, the sexual practices by which it procreates. These life-sustaining, life-transmitting activities draw God's special interest, as a mark of God's general love for Israel. Israel then is supposed to achieve its life in conformity with the marks of God's love. These indications, moreover, signify also the character of Israel's difficulty, namely, subordination to the nations in general, but to the fourth kingdom, Rome, in particular. Both food laws and skin diseases stand for the nations. There is yet another category of sin, also collective and generative of collective punishment, and that is social. The moral character of Israel's life, the treatment of people by one another, the practice of gossip and small-scale thuggery—these too draw down divine penalty. The nation's fate therefore corresponds to its moral condition. The moral condition, however, emerges not only from the current generation. Israel's richest hope lies in the merit of the ancestors, thus in the scriptural record of the merits attained by the founders of the nation, those who originally brought it into being and gave it life.

The world to come upon the nation is so portrayed as to restate these same propositions. Merit overcomes sin, and doing religious duties or supererogatory acts of kindness will win merit for the nation that does them. Israel will be saved at the end of time, and the age, or world, to follow will be exactly the opposite of this one. Much that we find in the account of Israel's national life, worked out through the definition of the liminal relationships, recurs in slightly altered form in the picture of the world to come.

If we now ask about further recurring themes or topics, there is one so commonplace that we should have to list the majority of paragraphs of discourse in order to provide a complete list. It is the list of events in Israel's history, meaning, in this context, Israel's history solely in scriptural times, down through the return to Zion. The one-time events of the generation of the flood, Sodom and Gomorrah, the patriarchs and the sojourn in Egypt, the exodus, the revelation of the Torah at Sinai, the golden calf, the Davidic monarchy and the building of the Temple, Sennacherib, Hezekiah, and the destruction of northern Israel, Nebuchadnezzar and the destruction of the Temple in 586, the life of Israel in Babylonian captivity, Daniel and his associates, Mordecai and Haman— these events occur over and over again. They turn out to serve as paradigms of sin and atonement, steadfastness and divine intervention, and equivalent lessons. We find, in fact, a fairly standard repertoire of scriptural heroes or villains, on the one side, and conventional lists of Israel's enemies and their actions and downfall, on the other. The boastful, for instance, include (**VII:VI**) the generation of the flood, Sodom and Gomorrah, Pharaoh, Sisera, Sennacherib, Nebuchadnezzar, the wicked empire (Rome)—contrasted to Israel, "despised and humble in this world." The four kingdoms recur again and again, always ending, of course, with Rome, with the repeated message that after Rome will come Israel. But Israel has to make this happen through its faith and submission to God's will. Lists of enemies ring the changes on Cain, the Sodomites, Pharaoh, Sennacherib, Nebuchadnezzar, Haman.

Accordingly, the mode of thought brought to bear upon the theme of history remains exactly the same as before: list-making, with data exhibiting similar taxonomic traits drawn together into lists based on common monothetic traits or definitions. These lists then through the power of repetition make a single enormous point or prove a social law of history. The catalogues of exemplary heroes and historical events serve a further purpose. They provide a model of how contemporary events are to be absorbed into the biblical paradigm. Since biblical events exemplify recurrent happenings, sin and redemption, forgiveness and atonement, they lose their one-time character. At the same time and in the same way, current events find a place within the ancient, but eternally present, paradigmatic scheme. So no new historical events, other than exemplary episodes in lives of heroes, demand narration because, through what is said about the past, what was happening in the times of the framers of Leviticus Rabbah would also come under consideration. This mode of dealing with biblical history and contemporary events produces two reciprocal effects. The first is the mythicization of biblical stories, their removal from the framework of ongoing, unique patterns of history and sequences of events and their transformation into accounts of things that happen all the time. The second is that contemporary events too lose all their specificity and enter the paradigmatic framework of established mythic existence. So (1) the scripture's myth happens every day, and (2) every day produces reenactment of the scripture's myth.

In seeking the substance of the mythic being invoked by the exegetes at hand, who read the text as if it spoke about something else and the world as if it lived out the text, we uncover a simple fact. At the center of the pretense, that is, the as-if mentality of Leviticus Rabbah and its framers, we find a simple proposition. Israel is God's special love. That love is shown in a simple way. Israel's present condition of subordination derives from its own deeds. It follows that God cares, so Israel may look forward to redemption on God's part in response to Israel's own regeneration through repentance.

WRITING WITH SCRIPTURE
AND REWRITING SCRIPTURE

The message of Leviticus Rabbah attaches itself to the Book of Leviticus, as if that book had come from prophecy and addressed the issue of salvation. But it came from the priesthood and spoke of sanctification. The paradoxical syllogism—the as-if reading, the opposite of how things seem—of the composers of Leviticus Rabbah therefore reaches simple formulation. In the very setting of sanctification we find the promise of salvation. In the topics of the cult and the priesthood we uncover the national and social issues of the moral life and redemptive hope of Israel. The repeated comparison and contrast of priesthood and prophecy, sanctification and salvation, turn out to produce a complement, which comes to most perfect union in the text at hand.

The basic mode of thought—denial of what is at hand in favor of a deeper reality—proves remarkably apt. The substance of thought confronts the crisis too.

Are we lost for good to the fourth empire, now-Christian Rome? No, we may yet be saved.

Has God rejected us forever? No, aided by the merit of the patriarchs and matriarchs and of the Torah and religious duties, we gain God's love.

What must we do to be saved? We must do nothing, we must be something: sanctified.

That status we gain through keeping the rules that make Israel holy. So salvation is through sanctification, all embodied in Leviticus read as rules for the holy people.

The Messiah will come not because of what a pagan emperor does, nor, indeed, because of Jewish action either, but because of Israel's own moral condition. When Israel enters the right relationship with God, then God will respond to Israel's condition by restoring things to their proper balance. Israel cannot, but need not, so act as to force the coming of the Messiah. Israel can so attain the condition of sanctification, by forming a moral and holy community, that God's response will follow the established prophecy of Moses and the prophets. So the basic doctrine of Leviticus Rabbah is the metamorphosis of Leviticus. Instead of holy caste, we deal with holy people. Instead of holy place, we deal with holy community, in its holy Land. The deepest exchange between reality and inner vision, therefore, comes at the very surface: The rereading of Leviticus in terms of a different set of realities from those to which the book, on the surface, relates. No other biblical book would have served so well; it had to be Leviticus. Only through what the framers did on that particular book could they deliver their astonishing message and vision.

The complementary points of stress in Leviticus Rabbah—the age to come will come, but Israel must reform itself beforehand—address that context defined by Julian, on the one side, and by the new anti-Judaic Christian policy of the later fourth and fifth centuries, on the other. The repeated reference to Esau and Edom and how they mark the last monarchy before God's through Israel underlines the same point. These truly form the worst of the four kingdoms. But they also come at the end. If only we shape up, so will history. As we said, that same message will hardly have surprised earlier generations and it would be repeated afresh later on. But it is the message of our document, and it does address this context in particular. We therefore grasp an astonishing correspondence between how people are thinking, what they wish to say, and the literary context—rereading a particular book of scripture in terms of a set of values different from those expressed in that book—in which they deliver their message. Given the mode of thought, the crisis that demanded reflection, the message found congruent to the crisis, we must find entirely logical the choice of Leviticus and the treatment accorded to it. So the logic and the doctrine—the logos and topos of our opening discussion—prove remarkably to accord with the society and politics that produced and received Leviticus Rabbah.

Scripture proves paramount on the surface, but subordinated in the deep structure of the logic of Leviticus Rabbah. Why so? Because scripture enjoys no autonomous standing, e.g., as the sole source of facts. It does not dictate the order of discussion. It does not (by itself) determine the topics to be taken up, since its verses, cited one by one in sequence, do not tell us how matters will proceed. Scripture, moreover, does not allow us to predict what proposition a given set of verses will yield. On the contrary, because of the insistence that one verse be read in light of another, one theme in light of another, augmentative one, Leviticus Rabbah prohibits us from predicting at the outset, merely by reading a given verse of scripture, the way in which a given theme will be worked out or the way in which a given proposition will impart a message through said theme.

What does it mean, then, to write with scripture? The order of scripture does not govern the sequence of discourse, the themes of scripture do not tell us what themes will be taken up, the propositions of scripture about its stated themes, what scripture says, in its context, about a given topic, do not define the propositions of Leviticus Rabbah about that topic. The upshot is simple. Scripture contributes everything and nothing. It provides the decoration, the facts, much language. But whence the heart and soul and spirit? Where the matrix, where source? The editors, doing the work of selection, making their points through juxtaposition of things not otherwise brought into contact with one another—they are the ones who speak throughout. True, the voice is the voice of scripture. But the hand is the hand of the collectivity of the sages, who are authors speaking through scripture. If, moreover, scripture contributes facts, so too do the ones who state those ineluctable truths that are expressed in parables, and so too do the ones who tell stories, also exemplifying truths, about great heroes and villains. No less, of course, but, in standing, also no more than these, scripture makes its contribution along with other sources of social truth.

Greek science focused upon physics. Then the laws of Israel's salvation serve as the physics of the sages. But Greek science derived facts and built theorems on the basis of other sources besides physics; the philosophers also, after all, studied ethnography, ethics, politics, and history. For the sages at hand, along these same lines, parables, exemplary tales, and completed paragraphs of thought deriving from other sources (not to exclude the Mishnah, Tosefta, Sifra, Genesis Rabbah, and such literary compositions that had been made ready for the Talmud of the Land of Israel)—these too make their contribution of data subject to analysis. All these sources of truth, all together, were directed toward the discovery of philosophical laws for the understanding of Israel's life, now and in the age to come.

Standing paramount and dominant, scripture contributed everything but the main point. That point comes to us from the framers of Leviticus Rabbah—from them alone. So far as Leviticus Rabbah transcends the Book of Leviticus—and that means, in the whole of its being—the document speaks for the framers, conveys their message, pursues their discourse, makes the points they wished to make. For they are the ones who made of Leviticus, the book, Leviticus Rabbah, that greater Leviticus, the document that spoke of sanctification but, in its augmented version at hand, meant salvation. As closely related to the Book of Leviticus as the New Testament is to the Old, Leviticus Rabbah delivers the message of the philosophers of Israel's history.

We have emphasized that Leviticus Rabbah carries a message of its own, which finds a place within, and refers to, a larger system. The method of thought and mode of argument act out a denial of one reality in favor of the affirmation of another. That dual process of pretense at the exegetical level evokes the deeper pretense of the mode of thought of the larger system and, at the deepest layer, the pretense that fed Israel's soul and sustained it. Just as one thing evokes some other, so does the rabbinic system overall turn into aspects of myth and actions of deep symbolic consequence what to the untutored eye were commonplace deeds and neutral transactions. So too the wretched nation really enjoyed God's special love. So, as we stated at the outset, what is important in the place and function accorded to scripture derives significance from the host and recipient of scripture, that is to say, the rabbinic system itself.

But so far as Leviticus Rabbah stands for and points toward the larger system, what are the commonplace traits of scripture in this other, new context altogether?

1. Scripture, for one thing, forms a timeless present, with the affairs of the present day read back into the past and the past into the present, with singular events absorbed into scripture's paradigms.
2. Scripture is read whole and atomistically. Everything speaks to everything else, but only one thing speaks at a time.
3. Scripture is read as an account of a seamless world, encompassing present and past alike, and scripture is read atemporally and ahistorically.

All these things surprise no one; they have been recognized for a very long time. What is new here is the claim to explain why these things are so, we mean, the logic of the composition that prevails, also, when scripture comes to hand.

1. Scripture is read whole, because the framers pursue issues of thought that demand all data pertain to all times and all contexts. The authors are philosophers, looking for rules and their verification. Scripture tells stories, to be sure. But these exemplify facts of social life and national destiny: the laws of Israel's life.
2. Scripture is read atomistically, because each of its components constitutes a social fact, ever relevant to the society of which it forms a part, with that society everywhere uniform.
3. Scripture is read as a source of facts pertinent to historical and contemporary issues alike, because the issues at hand when worked out will indicate the prevailing laws, the rules that apply everywhere, all the time, to everyone of Israel.

Accordingly, there is no way for scripture to be read except as a source of facts about that ongoing reality that forms the focus and the center of discourse, the life of the unique social entity, Israel. But, as we have seen, the simple logic conveyed by the parable also contributes its offering of facts. The simple truth conveyed by the tale of the great man, the exemplary event of the rabbinic sage, the memorable miracle—these too serve as well as facts of scripture. The several truths therefore stand alongside and at the same level as the truths of scripture, which is not the sole source of rules or cases. The facts of scripture stand no higher than those of the parable, on the one side, or of the tale of the sage, on the other. Why not? Because to philosophers and scientists, facts are facts, whatever their origin or point of application.

What we have in Leviticus Rabbah, therefore, is the result of the mode of thought not of prophets or historians, but of philosophers and scientists. The framers propose not to lay down, but to discover, rules governing Israel's life. We state with necessary emphasis: As we find the rules of nature by identifying and classifying facts of natural life, so we

find rules of society by identifying and classifying the facts of Israel's
social life. In both modes of inquiry we make sense of things by bringing
together like specimens and finding out whether they form a species,
then bringing together like species and finding out whether they form a
genus—in all, classifying data and identifying the rules that make possible the classification. That sort of thinking lies at the deepest level of
list-making, which is, as I said, work of offering a proposition and facts
(for social rules) as much as a genus and its species (for rules of nature).
Once discovered, the social rules of Israel's national life of course yield
explicit statements, such as that God hates the arrogant and loves the
humble. The readily assembled syllogism follows: If one is arrogant,
God will hate her or him, and if she or he is humble, God will love her or
him. The logical status of these statements, in context, is as secure and
unassailable as the logical status of statements about physics, ethics, or
politics, as these emerge in philosophical thought. What differentiates
the statements is not their logical status—as sound, scientific philosophy—but only their subject matter, on the one side, and distinctive
rhetoric, on the other.

So Leviticus Rabbah is anything but an exegetical exercise. We err if
we are taken in by the powerful rhetoric of our document, which resorts
so ubiquitously to the citation of biblical verses and, more important, to
the construction, out of diverse verses, of a point transcendent of the
cited verses. At hand is not an exegetical composition at all, nor even
verses of scripture read as a corpus of proof texts. We have, rather, a
statement that stands by itself, separate from scripture, and that makes its
points only secondarily, along the way, by evoking verses of scripture to
express and exemplify those same points. We miss the main point if we
posit that scripture plays a definitive or even central role in providing the
program and agenda for the framers of Leviticus Rabbah. Their program
is wholly their own. But of course scripture then serves their purposes
very well indeed.

So too their style is their own. Scripture merely contributes to an
aesthetic that is at once pleasing and powerful for people who know
scripture pretty much by heart. But in context the aesthetic too is
original. The constant invocation of scriptural verses compares with the
place of the classics in the speech and writing of gentlefolk of an earlier
age, in which the mark of elegance was perpetual allusion to classical
writers. No Christian author of the age would have found alien the
aesthetic at hand. So whereas the constant introduction of verses of
scripture provides the wherewithal of speech, these verses serve only as
do the colors of the painter. The painter cannot paint without the oils.

But the colors do not make the painting. The painter does. As original and astonishing as is the aesthetic of the Mishnah, the theory of persuasive rhetoric governing Leviticus Rabbah produces a still more amazing result.

A FAREWELL TO THE NOTION OF SCRIPTURE
AS SOURCE OF (MERE) PROOF TEXTS

We may say that Leviticus Rabbah provides an exegesis of the Book of Leviticus just as much as the school of Matthew provides an exegesis of passages cited in the Book of Isaiah. Yet, we must reiterate at the end, Leviticus serves as something other than a source of proof texts. It is not that at all. And that is the important fact we mean to prove. What is new in Leviticus Rabbah's encounter with scripture emerges—and that document stands for others in the canon of the Judaism of the dual Torah—when we realize that, for former Israelite writers, scriptures do serve principally as a source of proof texts. That certainly is the case for the school of Matthew, for one thing, and also for the Essene writers whose library survived at Qumran, for another. The task of scripture for the authors of the Tosefta, Sifra, Genesis Rabbah, and the Talmud of the Land of Israel emerged out of a single need. That need was to found the creations of the new age upon the authority of the old. Thus the exegetical work consequent upon the Mishnah demanded a turning to scripture. From that necessary and predictable meeting, exegetical work on scripture itself got underway, with the results so self-evident in most of the exegetical compositions on most of the Pentateuch, including Leviticus, accomplished in the third and fourth centuries. None of this in fact defined how scripture would reach its right and proper place in the Judaism of the Talmuds and exegetical compositions. It was Leviticus Rabbah that set the pattern, and its pattern would predominate for a very long time. The operative rules would be these:

1. From Leviticus Rabbah onward, scripture would conform to paradigms framed essentially independent of scripture.
2. From then onward, scripture was made to yield paradigms applicable beyond the limits of scripture.

In these two complementary statements we summarize the entire argument concerning the uses of scripture in the Torah of formative Judaism. The heart of the matter lies in laying forth the rules of life—of Israel's life and salvation. These rules derive from the facts of history, as much as the rules of the Mishnah derive from the facts of society (and, in context, the rules of philosophy derive from the facts of nature). Scripture then never stands all by itself. Its exalted position at the center of all discourse proves contingent, never absolute. That negative result of course bears an entirely affirmative complement. Judaism is not the religion of the Old Testament because Judaism is Judaism. Scripture enters Judaism because Judaism is the religion of "the one whole Torah of Moses, our rabbi," and part of that Torah is the written part, scripture. But that whole Torah, viewed whole, is this: God's revelation of the rules of life—creation, society, history alike.

Obviously, every form of Judaism would be in some way a scriptural religion. But the sort of scriptural religion a given kind of Judaism would reveal is not to be predicted on the foundations of traits of scripture in particular. One kind of Judaism laid its distinctive emphasis upon a linear history of Israel, in a sequence of unique, one-time events, all together yielding a pattern of revealed truth, from creation, through revelation, to redemption. That kind of Judaism then would read scripture for signs of the times and turn scripture into a resource for apocalyptic speculation. A kind of Judaism interested not in one-time events of history but in all-time rules of society, governing for all time, such as the kind at hand, would read scripture philosophically and not historically. That is, scripture would yield a corpus of facts conforming to rules. Scripture would provide a source of paradigms, the opposite of one-time events.

True enough, many kinds of Judaism would found their definitive propositions in scripture and build upon them. But while all of scripture was revealed and authoritative, for each construction of a system of Judaism only some passages of scripture would prove to be relevant. Just as the framers of the Mishnah came to scripture with a program of questions and inquiries framed essentially among themselves, one which turned out to be highly selective, so did their successors who made up Leviticus Rabbah. What they brought was a mode of thought, a deeply philosophical and scientific quest, and an acute problem of history and society. In their search for the rules of Israel's life and salvation, they found answers not in the one-time events of history but in paradigmatic facts, social laws of salvation. It was in the mind and imagination of the already philosophical authors of Leviticus Rabbah that scripture came to serve, as did nature, as did everyday life and its parables, all together, to reveal laws everywhere and always valid—if people would only keep them.

Index of Names
and Subjects

Index of Biblical and Talmudic References